Catholic with Confucian Tendencies

The true story of the extreme adventures of a

Vietnamese Boat Person

Catholic with
Confucian Tendencies

The true story of the extreme adventures of a

Vietnamese Boat Person

by

VŨ KHÁNH THÀNH

with

Christina Puryear

To my dearest wife Bùi Hồng Điệp
To my daughters and their husbands,
Vũ Khánh Hồng Linh & Colin Pennington
Vũ Khánh Quỳnh Tâm & Mark Cowell
To my son Vũ Khánh Toàn
To my beloved granddaughter Mai Jennifer Pennington
and grandson Alexander Cowell-Vũ

To the future generations of Vietnamese in the UK

Note

Death and life have their determined appointments; riches and honours depend upon heaven. (Confucius)

Vũ Khánh Thành is a Catholic with Confucian tendencies. This is important as it has greatly influenced nearly every decision in his life. His religious upbringing and cultural teachings provided a moral foundation that affected his worldview, inspired his career choices, and ultimately gave him the strength to fight for his principles both in Vietnam and the UK.

As I've come to know Thành (or as I call him, Mr Vũ) over the years I helped him write his life story, I've discovered that he is the most pragmatic idealist I have ever known. He sees a problem, he'll find a practical way to address it. He learns that someone in power commits a wrong, he will work to right it. He has high standards for leaders, and doesn't excuse himself from such principles. Once he starts something, he won't let it go; his strong sense of what is right and his determined pursuit of justice won't allow him, even if it means losing a friend or risking his life.

It was an honour and a joy to be able to help Mr Vũ tell his story of family, loss, war, flight, service and the Vietnamese community in the UK.

Thank you,

Tina Puryear

CONTENTS

ACKNOWLEDGEMENTS

Thanks to my dearest wife Bùi Hồng Điệp, to my daughters and their husbands, Vũ Khánh Hồng Linh & Colin Pennington, Architects and Vũ Khánh Quỳnh Tâm & Mark Cowell, Housing Specialists. Thanks to my son Vũ Khánh Toàn, Lawyer and my beloved granddaughter Mai Jennifer Pennington and grandson Alexander Cowell-Vũ

Thank you also to Eithne Nightingale for believing in the power of the story and being an endless source of emotional support as we navigated the road to publication.

Thank you to Paul Sherreard and the 'Flight Team' of interns at *Spread the Word* for the technical and professional support in getting the book published, and to Anita Belli for showing us the way.

Finally, big thanks to Tina Puryear for her help in co-writing this auto-biography, for putting my words on paper so they could be shared with future generations of Vietnamese in the UK.

Vũ Khánh Thành MPhil – MBE
Founder An-Viet Foundation and
Former founder An-Viet Housing Association

PART ONE

Việt Nam

CHAPTER ONE

Hunger

Chem cha lu Nhat con-do
Bat nguoi cuop cua, tha ho thang tay!
Dan ta tram dang ngan cay
Thoc an chang co, trong day cho nguoi.

Blast you! Bloody Japanese hoodlums!
Is there any crime you'd refrain from?
After pillaging our treasures,
Why did you force our farmers
To grow only jute for your war efforts?

Nguyễn Ngọc Phách (p30)

My life began when many were dying. I was born into a world that was hungry. During World War Two, when the Nazis occupied France, the Vichy government and Japan signed a treaty which allowed the Japanese to occupy Vietnam. The Japanese did not allow farmers in North Vietnam to plant rice. Instead they made us plant jute for rope making and other industrial purposes to help them with the war. In addition we were unable to ship rice from the South because the Americans had bombed the road to stop the Japanese from expanding there, and the result was a huge famine. The Vietnamese now call 1945 the 'hungry year'.

Around this time, the war was between three enemies - the Japanese, the French and the Việt Minh. The fighting became more and more violent, but then the Japanese were defeated and the French took over the country again. During the 'handover', in 1945, Hồ Chí Minh took the opportunity to declare independence. No one in my village took any notice. They were too hungry to care about the political claims made by far away leaders.

I assume that my mother died of starvation. She died in 1945, the year in which the famine killed about two to three million Vietnamese. I was an infant, and don't remember my mother's face. I only had a photograph of her. All of the children wore a white band around our arms in honour of our mother's death for a year.

I also don't remember Triêm or Chuộng. I had seven brothers and sisters, but my eldest brother Triêm, and sister Chuộng – only thirteen years old – also died in 1945 of starvation. That same year, because we were so poor, my younger sister went to live with another family who could feed her.

I don't know how old I am, and I don't know my birthday. When I asked my father or auntie, they would shrug their shoulders and say: "it was before the harvest". They didn't even remember which year. The Vietnamese in the countryside were naive like that. It was very common.

Today, I put my birthday as 15th August 1944 – Assumption Day.

The central pillar of Vietnamese culture is the family. This shapes our character. The children all respected their parents and each family had an altar where they would worship family members who died going back four generations. Each altar has a *Bài vị,* or list, of the names of the deceased we should remember and the day they died. On the anniversary of their death as well as November 1st (All Soul's Day), we remember the dead by burning incense at the altar and putting out a few bowls of rice. The Vietnamese believe that our ancestors are still among us and help us. Even though I never knew my mother, I was always comforted knowing she was watching over me.

When I think of my father now, I remember what a gentle man he was. He never shouted at me or at anyone, even in his grief. I felt loved. My youth shielded me from the weight of the sorrow that my father, my elder siblings and my aunties carried with them each day and night. The more they struggled to survive, the more they appreciated each gift of life that they witnessed.

2

They encouraged my laughter, and when I'd come in from playing in the garden, all their tears would be instantly wiped away and they would shower me with affection.

They may have been able to hide their despair, but they could not hide how hard they had to work to feed us. My father was a farmer; in fact everyone in my village was a farmer. My father found that after my mother and two siblings died, he could not support the family, especially as several of us children were too young to help on the farm. I remember when he changed from being a farmer to a businessman. He purchased two big bamboo jars, attached them to a long pole so that he could carry his products on his shoulder, and travelled from market to market. When he arrived at a market, he would unroll his bamboo mat and lay out his wares for sale. He mostly sold useful household products like needles, matches, lighters, or steel wire for the garden. Each village usually had one market day each week, so my father was able to travel to a different village every day, following the market days.

Village

Bao thuong tiec canh binh minh thuc day
Vuon day chim, troi xanh ngat, mat tuoi
Gio dong hang tre va nang nhu cuoi
Ban mot dia ngo van bung beo ngay
Me change biet tu bao gio dat day!
Toi ngoi an quen mat ca cau moi
Thay ngoai san duong dung gay romp hoi
Me trong nha ru chau nho a oi…

O how I miss days when fresh out of bed
The garden is full of birds chirping,
the sky is blue and the breeze fresh
A zephyr goes through the bamboos

and the sun is like laughing
And on the table a rich plate of freshly cooked corn
That Mother left there I know not since when!
I went right into it, forgetting even to invite
My father who was working on the hay in the courtyard
While my mother was inside singing a lullaby to a baby
grandchild…

Nguyễn Chí Thiện, 1965 (p175)

My father remarried; I don't remember how many years later, but the village was thriving again, having recovered from the famine. My village, Trang Tiền in Nam Trực, Nam Định district of North Vietnam, had only about two hundred people. The village centred on our church, which had a beautiful St John the Baptist altar. Everyone in the village was Catholic. Our village was also known locally as the Village of the Seven Martyrs, because there was a shrine where seven Vietnamese Catholics who had died as martyrs were buried. To attend Mass however we had to go to our neighbouring village, Trang Hậu, which had about five hundred people, including a priest.

I'm not sure why Trang Tiền and Trang Hậu were split into two separate villages, since we acted as one. They were traditional villages enclosed within a bamboo fence, which was tall and strong – a good defence, especially with the small thorns that made it too painful to try and get through. Each night, the village gates were closed to keep us in, and strangers out.

Everything we needed was enclosed within our bamboo fence. Essentially, in order for a Vietnamese to survive, he needs rice, *nước mắm,* or fish sauce*,* and salt. All this was within easy reach of our door. The key item, naturally, was rice, and the rice plant was essential for our survival; like the English with rain, the Vietnamese have numerous words to describe rice based on the stages of growth of the plant or how it is prepared. At the beginning of the season, when the rice grains are just harvested, a pot of rice is cooked to thank heaven and earth.

We depended on rice for more than just food. The rice plant has two parts, one is the grain that you eat, and the other part can be used to burn or to make straw to roof your house. We cooked with a fire built from a part of the rice plant instead of wood; the winters were very cold and we would burn the outer shell of the rice in order to keep warm. One of my lasting memories of my father was when we would sit together as a family, sharing a meal near one of these rice fires. My father suffered asthma, which was made worse by the cold, and he would have trouble breathing and would cough a lot.

Most traditional villages were built alongside a river, or small canal. These rivers fed the small ponds that were scattered inside our village, and which we used for everything – bathing, washing our clothes, our dishes, as well as harvesting water plants to feed the pigs. But we did not have any hot water for baths, which meant we had lots of lice. Mothers and older sisters were always picking children's hair. We would boil a little water to kill the lice in our clothes. We were always de-lousing.

I have such wonderful memories of my childhood in this village. It is a hot country so our doors were always open, which means that neighbours were always visiting and we were always welcome at other people's houses. My friends and I would run around all day together after primary school, held in the common hall, which was also used as a meeting space for the village, or as a place where the priest could teach catechism. My friends and I would play jump rope or hopscotch in the main square of the village, and we'd also watch to see if anyone was staying in the guest house, wondering if the visitor would have any sweets for us or fun stories to tell us about the outside world. Our entertainment was simple, we had plenty of fun adventures around the village and surrounding farmlands.

There were always small mobs of children running around

that I could play with until it was time to eat the evening meal. Then we would all run back to our homes and join our family. Families always ate together. In Vietnam we say that even God is not allowed to interfere with mealtimes.

The Vietnamese diet emphasises eating vegetables and rice. Some of the poorest families lived solely on this and an abundant vegetable called *rau muống*. Vegetables in soup are the mainstay of every meal. Sometimes the boiled vegetable juice is used as a soup base with tomato – a perfect meal. Herbal ingredients such as spring onion, ginger, chive, basil and mint are a must in the daily meal of the Vietnamese family. We also tend to eat a lot of seafood – fish, prawn, crab, snail and so on. And using seafood, the Vietnamese cook can produce an array of nutritious sauces, the most popular being fish sauce (*nước mắm*). *Nước mắm* is a pungent liquid used to compliment many savoury foods, in much the same way as soya sauce is used in Chinese or Japanese cooking. No Vietnamese meal is complete without *nước mắm*. Meat, relatively unimportant in the Vietnamese daily diet, consists of animals of the household such as chickens, pigs, cows and dogs. We tended to eat meat more frequently in the winter when it was colder and so our bodies needed to be kept warm and in balance. And everyone used chopsticks when eating.

I lived in a traditional house typical of that region – built in a square horseshoe shape. Houses always had three rooms, an auspicious number, and the main room was where everyone came together to eat, socialise and worship our ancestors. The two additional rooms were for sleeping. Then one of the two side extensions housed our pigs, while the other side acted as a storeroom for our rice harvest. This is also where we would grind the rice. The courtyard found within the wings of the house was paved with concrete so we could dry the rice in the sun.

Each house was self-contained and provided everything we needed. We would grow herbs for medicine or tea in the sunny courtyards, which also smelled lovely. Most houses had a pond to the side of the house for water and fish. Our garden for growing vegetables and fruit trees was at the back of the house. There were, of course, always a few chickens or ducks running around, providing eggs which could be used to feed the family or sell. Our toilets were outside the house and we dumped the waste into our gardens or rice fields to nourish the plants; nothing was wasted. All of this was enclosed within a small bamboo fence. With all the trees and the branches of the bamboo shading our house, there were always lots of birds around as well, serenading us all day.

In the village there would be someone who knew about health and balance. We used food as medicine to balance the *yin* and *yang* (fire and water) energy. Illness emerges when someone is out of balance. We see some foods as 'cold', some as 'hot' and others as 'cool' or 'warming'. Often it is the way the food is prepared that determines its *yin* or *yang*. For example, fresh ginger is 'warm' while dried ginger or grilled ginger is 'hot'. Our village 'doctor' often knew how to mix the vegetables and herbs to create harmony and help someone get back into balance – both mentally and physically.

And of course food is central to our festivals and special events. The Vietnamese feast at any opportunity. We have speciality foods we prepare for specific holidays and they are usually displayed decoratively, sometimes using special colouring. For example, green rice flake cake, glutinous rice dumplings and sugar-coated lotus seeds for engagements and weddings.

Another thing I remember about village life in North Vietnam was an inherent spirit of community. The village is the second pillar of our culture. Everyone worked for the good of our neighbours: there was stability and order; we all knew our place and were happy and we knew who to trust. Everyone strived to live by the teachings of the church and everyone respected the governing aristocracy who ethically led our community.

After the harvest, or on major occasions such as a priest's ordination, or New Year, the entire village would contribute to buying and killing a buffalo for a feast. My favourite childhood memories centre on the New Year. The entire village would celebrate for around two weeks, and there would be theatre, with many of the local villagers acting our comedies, ancient myths, or religious stories. My friends and I were also allowed to fly kites: my favourite kites had a flute tied onto the end so that they made a beautiful song as they flew in the air. In some years we would also have boat races on the river, but most of the celebration involved dressing in colourful clothes and feasting. Everyone looked after each other and there were deep feelings of generosity and kindness. There was also a great deal of laughter.

I also have fond memories of the Mid-Autumn Festivals. Following the lunar calendar, and usually held in late September, all the children would parade around the village carrying lanterns and singing. Then the entire village would meet at the central hall to eat snails. Each family had prepared ahead of time by going into the fields and picking snails for the celebration. There would be several large snails for each person, but most of us filled up on the tiny ones, simply taking a needle to spear the snail then dipping in *nước mắm* to eat. There were big bowls and everyone shared.

In a Vietnamese village, everyone behaves properly, respecting the elders. The children and teenagers were also controlled well. Children who worked hard, behaved and did well at school brought great pride to their parents. But during festivals, teenagers were allowed to be free. They could play and have fun, flirt and be together secretly in the rice fields or tree bushes. After the harvest festival there were lots of weddings.

We also had a three-day festival to honour the God of the village. This was not a God from heaven, but the spirit of someone who once lived in the village and did good things or was a hero when alive. We'd feast and put on plays and there would sometimes be cockfights or bullfights to watch.

When I was a bit older, I was thrilled to be invited to participate in the procession welcoming a new priest to the village. The celebration was called a 'priest exchange'. The new priest would be laid inside a hammock, hung between two large bamboo poles and covered with a gorgeous tapestry. We couldn't see the new priest as he was processed through the village. I was asked to carry the flag of the Vatican. We marched to the church where he said his first Mass, which was followed by a huge feast. The entire village participated.

Sometimes I laugh at the simplicity of our rural parties. Other times I feel that they were truly authentic celebrations of community. When I think back on those times, I am overcome by a sense of both contained security and freedom. To some, these terms are polar opposites, but for a young child in a small village, I had one because of the other.

To me, this seems ironic because I had already experienced a brutal attack by the Việt Minh, full name *"Việt Nam Độc Lập Đồng Minh Hội"* (translated as League for the Independence of Vietnam). At that time the fighting was between the French and the 'patriotic parties', followers of Hồ Chí Minh who wanted independence. Many who followed Hồ Chí Minh at this time did not realise or care that he was promoting communist ideology. Hồ Chí Minh rallied support by saying that he was fighting for freedom, for independence from colonial rule. Hồ Chí Minh said that to follow him was our patriotic duty. But many Catholics knew that Hồ Chí Minh was promoting Communism, and sided with the French.

I was really young when they struck our village. At the time, I did not understand why the Việt Minh attacked us. All I remember is fire. I hid in the bomb shelter with some of my siblings. My father and older brothers joined the villagers who fought to defend the village. I couldn't see what was happening, but I heard screams of anger and screams of anguish. When it finally grew quiet and we emerged from our hiding places, the first thing I noticed was that several houses had burned to the ground. Then we noticed the bodies. A few of our friends and a few Việt Minh had died.

As a young child, I quickly forgot how the entire village was permeated with fear and how scared I was. I went back to playing with my friends and feeling happy and adventurous.

But I never forgot that the Việt Minh were our enemy.

Outsiders

When I was a bit older, our village life was interrupted more and more by events beyond our bamboo fence.

The Việt Minh were still campaigning to free Vietnam of foreign invaders, the French. I remember a few operations where the French army came through our village searching for Việt Minh. Each time my friends and I would run up and ask them for sweets.

The French also came through our village when they were searching for mines. All of us children grew up with the occasional sound of mines going off – landmines planted by the Việt Minh in an attempt to destroy the roads used by the French. I knew not to play on the main roads or to play in the bomb shelters that every family built near their house.

A couple of times we heard French airplanes fly nearby and bomb an area they believed hosted Việt Minh, who were planning to attack the French army stations. Most of the bombing was far away from Catholic villages, because the French knew Catholics didn't support the Việt Minh. The other children and I weren't worried by the noise, we were used to it. It was all we knew. It was normal.

The event that made me understand that things were not actually normal was the execution of my uncle. My uncle worked for the French in Hanoi (or Hà Nội as it is called in Vietnam). He was the only one in our family who learned French — it was usually only the rich in Hanoi who spoke the language of the colonists. My uncle would come to visit periodically and when he did, he would take the local bus. One time, he was late arriving and my father and older siblings were so worried: my uncle had warned them that he and others like him were in danger. We kept listening out for any sign of a problem, fearing any loud noise might be gunfire signalling another skirmish between the Việt Minh and the local self-defence groups. It was silent. Yet, my uncle never arrived and we feared the worst.

We later learned that the Việt Minh captured him on his way to our village. He was in prison for several months. My auntie and others took food, but we weren't allowed to speak to him or see him. The only news we received was the date of his execution. He was taken to the nearby market. I was praying at the church with the rest of the village when I heard the gun shot that killed him. He was executed in front of the tree that my father often went to in order to sell his wares.

By 1952-53 the Communists had gained control over the majority of North Vietnam. Only the French and Catholic strongholds, like my village, were still independent, and we were determined to stay so after hearing the stories about what the Communists did once they were in control. Initially, our resistance was to protect our village from outsiders and their violent attempts to seize power. Then the resistance turned to anger and determination to protect our Catholic faith – it was no secret that Communism was anti-religion. The church was the heart of our village and family life; our faith was part of our blood. We didn't want anyone coming in to tell us to stop worshipping.

Quickly, however, our resistance was based on fear as we learned about the other brutal changes they made in the name of equality. They immediately began implementing their land reform policies, making poor farmers even poorer, and those who were better off were called 'Capitalist' before being killed. The rich included all *địa chủ*, 'boss of land' or landowners – even if the landowner only had family members working on his land. Many were tortured or imprisoned in bleak conditions. Hundreds of thousands died brutal, painful deaths. I heard rumours that they would make the *địa chủ* dig their own shallow grave and then push them in and bury them alive – killing them by having a buffalo pull a plough over the soft dirt. The stories that were told around the village were terrible. We all grew to hate the Việt Minh more and more.

Displaced

For many years, the French controlled the major cities in the north while the Việt Minh had more widespread control of the countryside. But then the Việt Minh began to move on Hanoi. So the French ordered many of their soldiers to withdraw from their current locations across the countryside to help protect Hanoi. Without the French to stop them, the Việt Minh attacked many Catholic villages. There were huge battles between the Việt Minh and the Catholic villagers who had organised themselves into self-defence groups. This made most Catholics even more wary of living under Communism.

Then suddenly, the French suffered a humiliating defeat at Điện Biên Phủ. This brought all the forces together, including the USA and communist China, at an international conference in Geneva. They agreed a cease-fire with the Việt Minh, and a Convention was drafted. The country was temporarily divided along the 17th Parallel. Under the agreement, the French were to move to the South and then, when safe to do so, leave the country. This same agreement stated that the Việt Minh, who were by this time a national movement, were to move the North.

The Convention also stated that Hồ Chí Minh would retain control of the North and Emperor Bảo Đại would remain Head of South Vietnam until elections in 1956, when the people could vote for the leader of a newly reunited Vietnam. The Americans pressured Bảo Đại, a controversial figure, to appoint Ngô Đình Diệm as Prime Minister because he was against colonialism *and* anti-communist.

So the price of peace was a divided country. And the result was a mass migration. Over 5,000 Việt Minh troops did move North. But most of the migration was south. As agreed, the people from the North and the South had three hundred days to move if they wanted. The international community helped to ensure there was safe passage for those who wanted to relocate. For those moving to the South, people were protected from Hanoi to Hải Phòng and then went on a French or American ship to Saigon (or Sài Gòn in Vietnamese). But not all Catholics had a safe passage. The Việt Minh always tried to stop the migration, usually violently. There was a massacre in Quỳnh Lưu, a district in central Vietnam. The Communists killed those trying to move south. The Việt Minh had more weapons, and the French no longer supported the self-defence troops. Many died on the sea trying to get to Hải Phòng – some tried to escape on bamboo rafts.

At that time, many Catholics moved to the south because the Catholics did not want to live under the Communists. The Catholics of the north were very organised: each diocese, with the protection of the Catholic self-defence groups and French soldiers, moved to Hanoi to join the safe passage south. In the end, around one million people from the north, two-thirds of them Catholic, moved south in 1954.

I was one of the refugees. At that time, I had moved to Hải Phòng to join my older brother, Hãn. Hãn had moved to Hải Phòng a year earlier to work as a teacher. My brother also asked my father and the rest of the family to move as well – he was really worried about the family surviving as Catholics under Communist rule. My father said that I should go on to help Hãn and his wife, who wanted me to live with them to look after their daughter. My father said that he and the others would come after the harvest. Hãn paid a lady from our village to bring us to Hải Phòng, and I travelled with Hãn's wife and baby. I was less than 10 years old.

I stayed in Hải Phòng for three or four months, but my father never had the chance to join us because the Communists were trying to stop people from moving. My new surroundings quickly became normal and mostly, I would play with my niece in the area around the house: I was having too much fun to feel homesick or worry about the future. Then, the Americans flew groups of Catholics south on one of their giant airplanes.

I travelled with Hãn and his family and it was to be my first of many flights.

CHAPTER TWO

Resettlement

Wheresoever you go, go with all your heart

Confucius

This was the first time that I had been so far from my family, but I don't remember a great deal about how I felt at the time. I guess even then, I stayed focused on the present and looked to the future. If I was sad, I don't remember crying. If there was a hole in my heart, it was immediately filled by the glamour and excitement of the big city.

When we got off the aeroplane, we were directed through Saigon to where the refugees were temporarily housed, and the journey from the airport to the town hall was awe-inspiring. Saigon was so magnificent. The further we went into the city, the more people crowded the streets, yet despite all the people, the streets still managed to have room for hundreds of bicycles, motorbikes and cyclo-drivers, cars and coaches. The beautiful, big buildings and the markets and street vendors on every corner spoke of grand opportunities and wealth. Saigon was so civilised, and I was excited.

There were so many of us moving south that the South Vietnam government temporarily housed us in the Town Hall, in schools, and even in a race stadium. International charities donated tents and food supplies, including cheese and powdered milk. No one ate these – they are not traditional Vietnamese food – so we fed the cheese and milk to the animals. We were among those staying in the town hall for a couple months.

Once people arrived, officials interviewed them and,

depending on their profession or career, moved them somewhere for more permanent settlement. The theory was, if a man was a fisherman in North Vietnam, his family could move to the sea, farmers could move to the countryside, and so on. The areas surrounding Saigon were sparsely populated - it was mostly jungle - so there was plenty of land and little local resentment at our arrival. Each family received 700 đồng, a tent and hammers, or knives, and other basic equipment needed to transform the jungle into a home.

The entire resettlement programme was well organised and very successful. The South Vietnam government worked closely with local leaders, such as Bishops or village leaders, in organising everyone, and in the end, the internal refugees were relocated in South Vietnam at very little cost. Within a year, most of us had established villages with our own schools, hospitals and churches as well as homes.

At first my brother Hãn's family lived in a community of big houses, free of charge, in Tam Hiệp, a ward within Biên Hòa, (at that time, the area was on the outskirts of Saigon). But these houses weren't built for permanent residence so we had to fix them up. When Hãn went into the jungle to chop the tree down, I'd help to cut the smaller branches, which we used to replace the roofs made of leaves which were quickly constructed by the government. We also fortified the walls with the wood and added aluminium, given to us by the government, for more sturdy roofs. I really liked when we didn't have to sleep on the floor anymore because we had enough wood to make beds for everyone. There were no official schools for us yet, so I spent the time playing with my niece and other children my age when I wasn't helping with the house.

Looking back, I remember thinking that everything that was happening was normal. I felt safe and cared for and quickly adjusted. However, as we settled into our new lives, South Vietnam became a very unsettled place because of the power struggles. The National Liberation Front (NLF) was created in the south and campaigned, using violence, for the unification of Vietnam under the Communists. Because he did not sign the Geneva Agreement,

Diệm did not have to participate in national elections against Hồ Chí Minh: instead, he held general elections in the south only. He won these by an overwhelming majority, making him the first President of the new Republic of Vietnam and Saigon became the official capital.

Around this time, there was also a 'sect crisis' – the Hòa Hảo, Cao Đài and Bình Xuyên were all religious sects with wide political and military support. When my brother and father spoke about these sects, they told stories of leaders who ran brothels on the side or received financial support from the mafia. These religious leaders didn't sound very religious to me. These sects wanted representation in the South Vietnamese government, but Diệm refused. The majority of people in the countryside supported one of the sects, but the French and Americans supported Diệm. He also had support in Saigon, especially from those of us who had migrated from the North – Diệm was Catholic too.

Diệm recruited Vietnamese soldiers who fought for the French and had them join the Vietnam Army. My brother Hân joined this army, which meant that we moved to Sóc Trăng then Cần Thơ. Many young men joined, as it was hard to find work and many wanted to fight the Communists. With his renewed troops, Diệm fought the sects in a violent struggle. Finally, Diệm won the internal fighting and ended the sect crisis. My family was pleased that Diệm won, because we did not want to be ruled by the mafia or groups who were anti-Catholic: that was the terror we had just fled. I remember hearing some fighting and I remember my brother and his friends talking about the events. Diệm seemed to share our vision of a society based on traditional Vietnamese values.

Seminary

*Happy is the man who finds wisdom and understanding
for the gain from it is better than gain from silver and profit better
than gold.*

Proverbs 3:13,14

People sometimes comment on all the turmoil in my early life – so many moves, civil war, and separation from family — but I was very happy. I did not grow up with a mother, but instead always had many brothers and sisters, aunts and uncles and we all took care of each other; so to live with my brother and his wife seemed quite normal. The move south was a fun adventure to me.

We learned that my father's sister, Vũ Thị Liễu and her family also made it to South Vietnam as refugees so I went to spend a year with her in Trung Chánh, near Saigon: my auntie wanted me to look after my younger cousins. While there I was able to attend school again – year five, the final year of primary school. However, I was very good so they bumped me up to year six, the start of secondary school.

In late 1956, I moved back to live with my brother Hãn's family who were now living in Gò Vấp. He was still in the army. A new secondary school that was affiliated to a Catholic seminary opened in the city and the educational lessons were standard and open to everyone. Attached to the school was a 'Little Seminary' – a boarding school run by Catholic Brothers. Boys who joined the 'Little Seminary' were thinking of joining the priesthood.

I enrolled in the school and I didn't hesitate to join the Little Seminary. The initial reason I joined the Little Seminary was simply because it seemed like the normal thing to do. I was not afraid to leave my family to live in the seminary; it didn't occur to me to question my family's offer to go, and I wanted to be a priest. It was a natural choice in the same way a caterpillar naturally chooses to build a cocoon.

I was part of the first class of students in this new school. Those of us in the Little Seminary met for prayers and Mass at 5.30am and attended additional religious lessons after lunch.

After about a year at this 'Little Seminary', I was chosen to go to Bà Quẹo, Tân Bình District of Saigon, with Father Superior Vũ Khánh Tường and two of the Brothers. The Brothers seemed to like me; if I saw something that needed to be cleaned, I'd do it. I think it was because I always took care of others growing up, and no one had to tell me what needed to be done. That's why I was chosen to go to the new site. They were making plans to build a new house for our seminary, and I was the cook. I had to shop for the supplies and cook simple meals for them, and I loved it. It was another new adventure. This lasted for about four or five months, then in September 1957 the temporary house in Gò Vấp closed, and in Bà Quẹo the new school officially opened for secondary students, or high school students. I was old enough to be placed in year seven; four Brothers looked after us on a daily basis.

Our daily life was mainly the same once the secondary school opened. Every day, we would wake up at 5.00am for Mass, meditation and prayer at 5.30am. After Mass, we would attend classes which began at 7.00am and finished at 12.00 noon. This is the normal school schedule in Vietnam, which followed the French system, and like the school in Gò Vấp, the mainstream education classes were open to all children in the area, not just seminarians. After lunch, we had a one to two hour break, during which most of us took a nap, then we would get up at 2.00pm to study and read on our own, under the supervision of Brothers. We could finish at 5.30pm and have an hour of free time to have a bath or wash our clothes (by hand since we did not have a washing machine). Dinner was at 7.00pm; then we would go to church to pray, and be in bed by 9.00pm.

On Saturday mornings we would all contribute to the

communal work in the garden and house, while we had the afternoons free to go out and wander around Saigon, visit friends or play football. On Sundays of course we had Mass. After Mass, all of the seminary students had to attend group meetings for about an hour, to discuss amongst ourselves issues about the running of the seminary – is the cleaning rota sound? Is everyone contributing to the work in the garden? Then we spent an hour listening to the Father Superior talk about his views of the running of the seminary. He would notify us of anything he did not feel was right, and point out what was not in order. This was followed by Father Trần Học Hiệu's lecture on the history of the Catholic Church or about Catholic doctrine. After our lunch and rest, we would meet at 2.00pm to practice singing for the choir. At 4.00pm we had free time where we would usually play football – nothing serious or formal as we didn't have a coach. At 6.00pm we would attend a Benediction service – a service where the priest puts the holy bread in an ornately decorated cross specially made for this purpose and we would pray. We would then have a thirty minute break before dinner at 7.00pm followed by prayer and singing vespers. I loved that part of the day – so beautiful, like angels singing. Then we'd go to bed.

This routine continued for my entire time at the school. Even to this day I awake at 5.00am. The predictability of the strict timekeeping made me feel secure and safe. Each day was soothingly similar.

Nothing seemed to change, yet the school was constantly in a state of growth and expansion. Year by year more students joined the seminary. When the school opened, I was one of only twenty to thirty students. By my third year, the seminarians had increased to around fifty to sixty, and each year more classrooms were built until it looked more like a proper school instead of a building site. Before long, we even had enough space and students for a primary school as well.

My Father Superior was very good at raising funds to pay for all the new buildings and teachers. All of the outside, nonseminarian students paid school fees and to supplement this income, Father Superior would borrow money from people in the community to build the school. People were very willing to lend him money because they knew he would pay it back in monthly instalments, with interest. In Vietnam, when a priest has his own school and seminary, it is easy for him to borrow money instead of getting loans from a bank or trying to raise money through a savings account. After only five years, our Father Superior had built a school, a seminary house, and had begun work on boarding rooms for the school. It was a clever way to raise money for development.

By the time I had reached the end of year nine, I had earned the equivalent of the GCSE in the UK but my school did not have any higher classrooms for me and my friends. To continue for years 10-12 (the equivalent of A level), I had to commute into Saigon to study. I was still a seminarian, still going to Mass in the mornings before class, and having prayers in the evenings.

While I enjoyed the ritual and security of the seminary, I have to admit that I found all the time in prayer boring. My friends and I would rather be outside instead of in the church praying. One of my favourite chores was to prepare for the evening prayer and Benediction. We would be responsible for burning the incense and preparing things in the back room, so we weren't expected to sit in the pews and pray as normal. We were very happy when it was our turn on the rota.

Of course, during this time, some of my fellow seminarians chose to leave the seminary early, to no longer pursue a path towards priesthood. While some left voluntarily, a few were asked to leave. This was the only thing that frightened me at the seminary — at the end of the year, the Father Superior always met a few seminarians in private to talk to them. Then after the talk, he would tell some of them: "I'm sorry, you are not suitable for the priesthood," and send them home. I always worried that this would happen to me. I was frightened of the shock it would be to my family, and I was frightened of bringing shame.

Teaching

If you plan for a year, plant a seed. If for ten years, plant a tree. If for a hundred years, teach the people. When you sow a seed once, you will reap a single harvest. When you teach the people, you will reap a hundred harvests.

Kuan Chung

When I was in year 11, a few of us asked if we could teach at the primary school. My friends and I taught students in the first three years of primary school, age five to eight. Father Superior also invited a few teachers with proper training and a teaching certificate to teach the older primary school students, years four and five. Using seminarians to teach saved Father Superior a lot of money.

I had received no proper training for teaching, just a few weeks instruction on methodology and introduction to the curriculum. Mostly, we learned from experience. Each classroom had around 30 students, and we were given a textbook to teach from for each subject, such as maths or reading. It was very simple. We were a private school, but we followed the government curriculum for maths, simple science, writing and reading. Even for young students such as those in my class, we taught in a more formal way than in the West. For example, for the reading lessons in Vietnam, the children were expected to sit down in the classroom and repeat the sentences in Vietnamese. I would correct their intonations and explain the story in relation to the lesson.

The textbooks included stories or essays explaining Vietnamese culture and ways of life in Vietnam, such as the importance of respecting your parents. The government textbooks covered many different topics ranging from simple literature to essays on Vietnamese culture, and like in the West, the young students could read stories of our ancestors and myths and legends.

One key difference between Vietnamese lessons and those in the West however was that much of Vietnamese folklore is written as poetry or proverbs. Even when young, Vietnamese always read and recite folk poetry and proverbs. We have a long tradition of this art form that is enjoyed by everyone, regardless of age or class.

Political poetry flourished under Diệm's regime. The fighting of the war did not impact on our daily life in the south as much as the growing resentment towards Diệm. He was once referred to as the "last Confucian" because he promoted the ancient belief in the benevolent rule of enlightened elites. But by the early 1960's he had demonstrated to many that he was a repressive dictator with a corrupt and nepotistic government. The pro-communist groups in the south used this to justify violent rebellions, but what really changed the public's view of Diệm was his brutal response to the mass protests by Buddhists monks. Diệm was killed in a US-supported coup in 1963 and the Vietnamese generals who overthrew Diệm also killed his brother. Afterwards, the leaders changed frequently, and the South Vietnamese military concentrated most of their energy on their own internal struggles for position in the government.

The poetry we discussed in the classroom was appropriate for that age group – about nature and about our history. While teaching the classic poets, I was also reading more contemporary poetry about the political situation. My eyes were opened to the danger of un-challenged power and the suffering of the people when a leader pursued their own greedy ambitions instead of serving the greater good. The poets wrote things that made me sad sometimes, but more often, the truth told in the poems made me angry.

Courtship

A person is born with desires of the eyes and ears, and a liking for beautiful sights and sounds. If he gives way to them, they will lead him to immorality and lack of restriction, and any ritual principles and propriety will be abandoned.

Xun Zi

Because I became a teacher very early and because I worked in a serious position quite young, I became an adult very quickly. My life was very formal. To many, it seems strange that I never became involved with girls like most young men my age, but I took my work seriously and I didn't want to abuse my role as an authority figure. I also did not want any rumours. As a seminarian headed for Catholic priesthood, rumours would spread if anyone saw me meeting a girl in my private time.

I didn't think much about girlfriends at the time. All of us seminarians felt we had normal lives, and I never heard stories of fellow seminarians becoming involved with girls. I think, because my seminary was open, allowing us to live a more normal life and to meet girls, we didn't have the disturbed libido of those who attended closed seminaries. If any of my peers had girlfriends, they kept it very secret. Mostly, when some of the men left seminary and found a job outside, attended university or joined the military, they would come back to meet some of the girls that they were friends with during seminary, and then get married.

I was not involved with girls in high school or university or grand seminary, but I was too busy to notice. I was studying and teaching, and, as a young teacher with such a structured daily routine, it was difficult to contact girls. There were many female students in my classes, and some were very charming but because of my position, and also being under the eye of the other Brothers and Father Superior, it was not easy to get out and socialise with girls, and so I was not involved with anyone. No time, no girlfriend.

Seclusion

The unexamined life is not worth living.

Socrates

In 1963, after I received my A-levels, I went to university and studied Occidental and Oriental philosophy. Usually, seminarians did not attend university until after having been ordained into the priesthood, but my religious order was not strict. My Little Seminary was more modern, and my teachers wanted us to have an open mind, to study religion and theology part of the time and, the rest of the time, to attend secular classes. Father Hiệu and Father Superior encouraged me to attend university.

At university, we read all the great Western philosophers including Plato and Aristotle, Descartes and Kierkegaard, as well as the major Eastern philosophies – Confucianism, Buddhism and Taoism. I felt at home among all the books, discussing the new ideas with friends and listening to the insights of the professors. Poems and prayers I grew up with gained new meaning with my expanded understanding of philosophy. I cannot express how exciting this time in my life was.

When I graduated from the seminary and went to university, I continued to teach, but this time literature and history in secondary school. At that time, I taught 12 to 16 hours per week. On Sundays I got together with Father Superior and the other seminarians to discuss theology and the rest of my time, I was one of three assistant supervisors for the boarding school. The students had dedicated study time between 2.00pm and 5.00pm, and I would have to look after them during this supervised study time. They could talk quietly with a friend while they studied, but I had to make sure they did not disturb the others, stop them from fighting, and so on. On Saturdays, the students could go home for the weekend and stay with their families, returning later on Sunday afternoon. I enjoyed being a teacher: I enjoyed this time of my life: I was very happy, and felt free.

I graduated with a BA in 1966. After I finished university, with my degree, I could have found a good job, and I already had experience teaching. I had multiple options for my future, but I wanted to be a priest. I wanted to serve, to teach, support my community and make my family proud; so, I went on to Grand Seminary. Grand Seminaries were for those who wanted to continue their studies at a college level and become a priest. I was one of four from our Little Seminary's first graduating class to move on to Xuân Bích, the Grand Seminary in Vĩnh Long run by the St Sulpice Fathers.

The Society of Saint-Sulpice is a Catholic religious order based on the life and works of Saint Sulpicius, a 7th century bishop in France noted for his piety. Jean-Jacques Olier founded the order in 1642 in Paris for the purpose of educating priests. The Sulpician seminaries, found in areas around the world that were colonised by France, quickly earned a reputation for their strict moralistic teaching. It was not easy. After a week, one of my friends dropped out straightaway, and at the end of the first year two others left. Luckily five new students from my Little Seminary arrived the second year, so I still had friends and familiar faces around me.

I think people dropped out because life in the Grand Seminary was totally different from what we were used to. On the surface, things did not seem different – for example, daily life at the Grand Seminary was much the same as the Little Seminary: prayer and Mass before breakfast, followed by classes in philosophy, history, Bible studies, and Catholic doctrine; lunch and break began at 12.00 noon and then time to study.

There were subtle but important differences however. During

the study time, we'd have supervised study time in class for a couple of hours, before being allowed to study on our own in our rooms for the rest of the afternoon. At 6.30pm, we had a brief period of personal time before dinner, 8.30pm was evening prayer, then to bed. On Saturdays we had plenty of free time after our cleaning duties and we often filled the afternoons playing volleyball or football. We were only allowed to leave the seminary on Sundays after Mass, and only for a few hours to visit people in the parish. Then we had to go in pairs and report back to the Father Superior on our return. Thus, during most of our week, we were completely separated from the outside world. Seclusion was the main difference between my 'Little Seminary' and Grand Seminary.

Whenever there was any free time during our strictly scheduled routine, all the seminarians would gather in the hall to see if the post had arrived. We all wanted to see who received mail and this was our only connection with our family and friends in the outside world. Occasionally, some of us also received letters from former students, but we were not really allowed to reply to former female students – we had to be careful that correspondence did not imply getting involved with girls. Those who received mail felt very lucky.

Doubt

Doubt is a pain too lonely to know that faith is his twin brother.

Kahlil Gibran

I had a few close friends and sometimes, we were badly behaved. We would go to the roof and stay awake talking about girls, or gossiping about rumours of who in the seminary had a girlfriend.

All of us at the Grand Seminary were assigned mentors, and one of my friends, Hoàng Tấn, often talked to me about his conflict with his mentor. Some seminarians continued studying under their mentor from Little Seminary and Tan was one of many who, at Little Seminary, would spend the summer at their mentor's parish church.

Tan's mentor was a powerful priest in the Mekong Delta and held great influence with the military and civil office in the area. Sometimes the people went to the priest to ask for help if they were having difficulty complying with military service demands. For example, if a family only had one son and was therefore afraid of him joining the military service, they could bribe Tan's mentor to influence the military to allow the son to serve on the local force, and thus remain near the family.

This corruption greatly disturbed Tan, but what most upset him was that this priest was deceitful and two-faced. The real man was cold and quick-tempered. He was mean to Tan and others when he knew no one important was around to observe him. But if someone was around who he hoped would give him money, then his mentor would be friendly.

"What do you mean?" I asked.

"There are too many stories to tell, like the time when he told me to cook him some soup. He sat there quietly, and slowly took a bite. He was still. No expression on his face to tell me what he was thinking. Then suddenly he threw the bowl of soup across the room and told me to make more and to do it right this time."

"Then why did the villagers put up with him? How could anyone worship with a man like that?" I couldn't believe it.

"Thành, no one else really saw that side of him. Or if they did, they couldn't do anything since they needed him. He was very powerful. He had some of the local military officials under his thumb. That same night after throwing his soup, my mentor heard 'the signal' - usually someone kicking a duck to make it quack outside his window. This meant someone was coming to the priest to make a 'deal'. A smile would cover his face and he'd be friendly, kind and act sympathetic."

I could tell this was bothering my friend. In the early days when I heard stories like this, I would try to make him feel better by reminding him that most priests were good and kind people who wanted to help their community. I believed this; this was why I wanted to be a priest. As I would speak these words that I hoped would comfort, I would be thinking of the priest from my childhood village who was so gentle and generous. "But how do you know?" he'd ask. "To many people, my mentor seems kind, but behind their backs his true nature emerges."

Because my friend questioned the integrity and honesty of other priests, it made him question whether or not he wanted to be a priest.

Tan's story also disturbed me. I became aware of more and more stories of corruption, of men who seemed to be priests not because of a calling to serve God or their community, but because of a priest's power and position in society. I think it is important to understand the view of Catholic priests in Vietnam at that time. In Vietnam, Catholics were taught that priests were like a second Christ, or a representative of Christ on earth. It was thought that priests were on the seventh level of holiness because of seven years of seminary. Because of this prestige, becoming a priest was a way to move into upper society. Here in the West, those who entered the priesthood often moved down in society because they had to give up any previous wealth and live a poor life. But in Vietnam, it was a way to move up. You gained power and respect.

This high status extended to the family – the parents also gain more status in society if their son becomes a priest, suddenly addressed as Ông Bà Cố, meaning "uncle", or "parent of a priest". Many parents hoped that one of their sons would become a priest.

Another key motivator was the money - priests, as well as their families, also received good financial support. Priests in Vietnam were able to take the collection for themselves, and most priests were very rich. No one questioned this.

And at that time, with the war, some men joined the priesthood to avoid serving in the military. In general, those who did not have a university degree or qualification found it difficult to get a job and were often conscripted into the military. Priests, however, were exempt from serving in the military.

The more my friends and I spoke about the corruption, the more I noticed. I heard increasing stories of priests who had wives and girlfriends. Tan would laugh with the others when they had discovered one of our Father's had a wife. But then he'd go quiet. When I'd ask what was wrong, he would remind us that earlier in the week, that same Father preached about how it was very important for people of faith not to have sex. This hypocrisy bothered me as well.

Some of my peers left seminary because they wanted to get married and have children. At Grand Seminary we were locked behind closed doors. This was very difficult for many - they realised how serious the celibacy issue was. But corruption or celibacy vows are not the reasons I left the seminary.

I stayed for two years because I wanted to serve and I always saw the church as a way to do this. I thought I had strong faith. I had grown up with both the teachings of Catholicism and Confucianism: all of my life, both had fit together naturally since everyone in my village made it so. And at university, my new understanding of philosophy actually expanded my understanding of Catholic theology.

But slowly, I realised I had attached myself to a vision of what the church represented in a community and so attached myself to its teaching without question. As I grew older, a few small seeds of doubt took root inside my heart and, like a weed, wound itself into every corner of my consciousness. At first I didn't even allow myself to ask challenging questions, but once my friends voiced the concerns and doubts I avoided, I couldn't hide from them any longer. Was this because I was growing older and thus more independent, thinking for myself more? Was this because of the seclusion and enforced time to study in Grand Seminary? Or perhaps because I could no longer distract myself with busy tasks and responsibilities? I'm not sure what happened, but the more I reflected on my faith, beliefs and way of life, the more I realised that the Catholic doctrine no longer seemed to inspire me.

I often shared my conflicting views with Tan when we were sitting on the roof at night. "Our ancient philosophies are based on an assumption that nature and humans are innately good. In the Oriental way of life, there is good and bad in everyone and our main goal in life is to improve ourselves." I'd repeat this over and over.

Tan would agree, but couldn't see why this was a problem for my faith. So I'd remind him how this was different from the Catholic teaching. I'd say, "Catholic doctrine says, because of Adam and Eve - original sin - humans are imperfect sinners by their very nature. To Christians, humans have fallen from grace and the only way to get out of this state of perpetual dirtiness is by God's grace. Only God can help us."

Tan would nod slowly but then remind me that this is what it says in the bible and thus must be true. But I disagreed. "The God in Catholic doctrine is based on the Jewish bible. Judaism, Christianity, Islam are all desert religions. Life in the desert is very hard, existence is fragile and their people have been immersed in conflict from the beginning of history. I guess this is why people in that part of the world feel helpless and powerless and at the mercy of God. They must feel that there is nothing they can do except appeal to God for help and this has shaped their world view – appease God so that He won't turn on you suddenly and cast you down."

"But our life in Vietnam and in the East is also very fragile. That is no different for us. We also need God's intervention."

"No," I said, "That is opposite to Confucian philosophy, which gives us ethical guidelines that promote personal growth and harmony between people. Just as a diamond begins as a simple stone, we have the potential to be perfect. Like polishing the rock to make it become radiant, our duty in life is to work on improving ourselves daily. By working on improving ourselves daily and doing our best to follow ethical behaviour towards others we can live in harmony and lift ourselves up."

Tan would look at me with fear in his eyes. He was struggling with the hypocrisy he saw in the behaviour of priests he knew, but he still believed in the doctrine. He was worried I had lost all my faith and belief in God. "But you always had such strong faith, how can it just disappear? The philosophies might be different, but what about faith? Confucianism is about ethics, what about God?"

And he was right. He reminded me of the core message of all religions: the quest for perfection so we can be closer to God. That is why I believe that for humans, it is not enough to rely simply on ethics. To believe that we can become better men, we have to believe that something else exists.

Decision

So I remained conflicted. I knew that the Confucian and Eastern world view matched my own world view on the innate goodness of all people and in the importance of each individual to strive to better themselves. But I also had a strong tie to the church which taught of the love of God. The two doctrines by their nature would not allow for both, yet I believed both.

I spoke to my friends until late in the evening. I continued to read, not just ancient philosophers but also contemporary poets. I listened to the news on the radio when they allowed us. I went round and round and eventually, I think it was my anger and impatience that fuelled my decision. I wanted to serve, I wanted to help others. The stories of corruption related to politicians as well as priests and there was a war going on outside the seminary walls. There was violence, injustice and suffering outside and I was inside safe, only able to offer prayers and philosophy. I was missing the time in my past when I was able to do both – study philosophy and also teach and help others.

I spoke to my mentor about my feelings, about the growing part inside me that felt more comfortable with Confucius's teaching to act and live life fully, about my increasing desire to leave the seminary to return to normal life. He and I discussed the crisis I was having about the doctrine, but in the end, he told me it was my decision. He said that if it would help my decision, I could stay outside the seminary for a while and then, if I wanted, I could return. He also gave me the option of going to stay in another diocese. As I was leaving his office, my mentor kindly told me that if he were Bishop, he would ordain me straightaway. He said that I had lots of experience in life, but more importantly, he respected my deep thinking about the theories and doctrine of the Catholic Church, and also my knowledge of human nature and philosophy.

I was humbled by his praise, but it did not change my mind. I knew that I had profoundly changed and that the seminary was no longer my home. I no longer wanted to be a priest. After struggling for so long trying to reach a conclusion, I was surprised how simple it was to leave once I had made up my mind. I told my Father Superior. He agreed to let me go and supported my decision to return to my former seminary in Saigon to continue to teach and also look after the boarding school for the rest of the academic year.

Looking back, I realise now that I enjoyed my time in seminary – the routine, the discussions about philosophy — but I didn't actually like church. I went to church because it was a duty. When I was young, I didn't question if I believed or not and in a sense, if I'm honest with myself, I often felt bored. I'm very pragmatic and like to be active instead of praying. But I don't regret my time at seminary, where I received a good education. I imagine it was like the military — I trained to be more self-disciplined, and my character is suited to that life. I think it was beneficial also because, living in a small community like that, we all learned about the importance of being kind towards each other.

It was not too much of a shock to leave the quiet, secluded sanctuary of the Grand Seminary. I think my time in the Little Seminary, where I was able to spend summers with my family, as well as my time teaching, kept me grounded and confident in my ability to deal with the realities of daily existence. But things were changing. When I left the seminary, I went to stay with my brother who had moved to Saigon to join the police force. I continued to teach in some other high schools.

It was 1968 and the war was escalating.

CHAPTER THREE

War

Tren Manh Dat

Tren manh dat Dang gieo mam toi loi
Trong lanh cung phai tanh hoi
Tre con chua nui mat da tu roi
Bao luc div e rat voi!
Chet tran, chet tu, hoi oi xa hoi!
Biet bao la va goa, con coi
Ban tron roi lai ban ca mo hoi
Ma doi ret van quan cho som toi
Manh dat cho trong vas am hoi
Thuc gia tieu sau chai nuoc la dun soi

Water Drunk

In this land sown with the seeds of crime
Felony soils the purest of innocent minds.
In this Party-dominated land, even children
Soon learn the trade of violence in prison.
What a society, the one we're living in!
Where war and persecution keep engendering
More widows and orphans that it can afford!
What a society, the one we're working for!
Where women must sell their bodies and do hard labour
And still are ravaged by cold and hunger!
While the whole country is praying for redemption
Water's the only spirit with which to get drunk!

Nguyễn Chí Thiện, 1964

There was always war. I lived the first 30 years of my life in a country at war with itself. No one could pretend the fighting was not happening. The war affected everyone in some way, even if they weren't on the battlefield, yet, like most people, I continued living a normal life in spite of the war. I went to school, I worked, and I dreamed of what my future would be like. For the most part, the actual battles were fought far from me. Until the end, gun-fire and explosions were usually only experienced through the TV or radio.

Yet the war, the violence between the North and the South, the fight between the communists and the anti-communists, was an ever-present shadow that touched all aspects of life. Violent protests by the Việt Cộng in Saigon, perhaps ending in damage to a bridge or a block in the road, would disrupt our daily routine, but the inconvenience was usually short-lived.

This changed in 1965 when the US sent their first ground troops to Vietnam following an attack on two of their ships in the Gulf of Tonkin. The war between the North and South escalated terribly, and more people had family affected by the war. Tensions were high. But even after learning about atrocities in the countryside on the news and radio, people continued to do their best to lead life as normal – going to work, to school, getting married, having children. People still respected each other, especially the elders and teachers. People still generously shared food and celebrations with their neighbours, and people still helped those in need. The Vietnamese, despite the war, continued to be very honest and to treat others like close friends.

The most visible change to life in Saigon, with the escalation of the war, was the increase in the number of refugees who lived in poverty. But the most significant change to life in Saigon occurred with the arrival of the Americans in 1965. Suddenly there were people with different demands and ways of living and lots of money to spend making sure they got what they wanted. What this meant was that an entire industry developed around serving the American troops. Also, there were new things suddenly for sale on the market that originated at the PX – the shop for American soldiers – and US dollars became a new, second currency.

The most noticeable impact of this change was the increase in the cost of living for us. No matter how rich or poor to begin with, we found we had to do more in order to maintain our standard of living, but gradually this was not enough. For instance, civil servants or teachers were never rich, but they had a stable life. But after the Americans arrived, everyone, including civil servants and teachers, wanted more things, more Western conveniences and this meant they wanted more money. They wanted bigger houses, a new car, and girls wanted Western style clothes.

Suddenly, it was no longer desirable to be a teacher or civil servant when there was easy money to be made by working in a bar that served the Americans. Many restaurants and bars and hotels sprouted around the city to serve the military, and the more aid and trade that came to South Vietnam, the larger the business class became. Banks, import and export businesses, service agencies, and retail outlets emerged quickly and with it a growing wealthy class.

Even the military was affected. With the Americans pouring in so much cash, the South Vietnamese army became even more corrupt. High-ranking officers would somehow take the money intended for the war effort and open their own businesses on the side.

Then we started to notice it wasn't just the financial climate that changed. Vietnamese morals were disturbed by the arrival of the Americans and girls discovered they could make lots of money by working in a bar. As the war continued, some of these young people became addicted to drugs, usually heroin and corruption increased. The Church still held great influence, but was not able to get involved in a way that had much impact; for example, it couldn't prevent the opening of bars. Most people tried to continue to live a moral life as normal, but of course, this was difficult.

Then, early in the morning on 30 January 1968, there was a wave of attacks that broke out in cities and towns in Central Vietnam. While watching the attacks on TV, most of us in the south were putting together our final preparations for the start of *Tết* - the Vietnamese New Year, and the most important holiday of the year. My family was no different. Weeks before the start of *Tết*, my brother and his family cleaned every corner of their house: his wife bought new clothes for everyone and prepared special sweets in advance. We were all working hard to make sure everything was in order. I knew any money I lent earlier in the year would be paid back this week as no one wants to have debts carried over into the New Year. All these preparations are vital as the Vietnamese believe that the first week of *Tết* will set the precedent for how fortunate the year to come will be. By the end of the day, every newsreader on TV and radio was frantically interviewing political figures or military strategists to discover the impact of the fighting. Most came to the same conclusion: that this was a well-planned offensive and we should expect more fighting. I didn't pay too much attention; I had no idea that these first attacks were only a diversion. To me, they were just battles taking place between strangers far away.

The next morning everyone woke up extra early in anticipation of the fun celebrations that were to begin that day. But there weren't any. Instead of fireworks and parades, there were explosions and gun-fire. Saigon was under attack.

Today this is known as the *Tết Offensive*. The National Liberation Front (the Việt Cộng) and the North Vietnamese Army (NVA) launched a huge offensive and simultaneously attacked almost eighty different cities, towns and military bases, including the one in Biên Hòa, in South Vietnam. The NVA and Việt Cộng also attacked the American embassy.

We were all caught off guard. None of us saw the attack coming, not even the President or the American military. We later learned that the Communists entered southern cities in pairs or small groups, disguised as refugees or peasants. Some also disguised themselves as South Vietnam soldiers returning for holiday leave. In all, the equivalent of almost five battalions entered Saigon without any notice. Weapons were brought in on flower carts or in coffins or inside vegetable trucks. These troops and weapons joined the network that was already present in Saigon.

The Communists claimed they had 'liberated' the areas they occupied, including Huế and large areas of Saigon. Suddenly, parades of men waving guns marched through the streets praising the Revolution. I think they hoped that the people of the south would rally to the cause and support the fight against the South Vietnamese government and the Americans, but no one did.

The plan apparently was to overwhelm and stretch the South Vietnam army and the Americans, in order to deliver a humiliating defeat similar to Điện Biên Phủ. The Communists wanted to show the world, especially the Americans, that they were everywhere and couldn't be controlled or contained. The mastermind behind this plan, General Võ Nguyên Giáp, hoped that his inevitable success would cause the Americans to withdraw from the war.

Courtship – II

Hold faithfulness and sincerity as first principles

Confucius

A counter attack was immediately waged and there was open fighting in the streets all over South Vietnam, including Saigon. The Tết *Offensive* had woken everyone up – South Vietnam and the Americans fought back with fierce intensity.

Before the Tết *Offensive*, I was introduced to a girl who was a law student. She was the only member of her family still at her parents' house, and her father was a highly ranked military officer, a Lt. Colonel I believe. I would visit her at her parents' house regularly and her family were always happy when I came around. Suddenly they learned that her brother-in-law died early in the Tết *Offensive*.

During all the fighting and confusion, I did my best to help this girl's family. They wanted to hold a funeral, but the fighting was too violent to even think about planning one. No one knew when the fighting would end and her family had no idea what to do with the body. Most people stayed inside their home during the worst of the battles, and I didn't want my friend or her family to put themselves at risk. So I carefully worked my way around or through the fighting to go to her house to help her family get his body to the hospital, until things calmed down enough for a funeral. It was very strange. There would be rapid gun-fire or explosions on one block, but a few blocks away it would be calm and there would still be people going about their business as if nothing was happening. It was frightening to hear gunfire nearby – there was some fighting only one kilometre from where I lived. But the fighting never lasted very long and after waiting a few hours, I would leave the house and continue my errands for my friend's family.

I think having something important like this to focus my mind on helped me to cope with the fear. It is amazing what courage you discover within yourself when you know someone is depending on you to help. Her family was so grateful for all my help, and they said they would be proud for me to become part of the family. Because of my commitment to help her family during the *Tết* fighting, everyone assumed that she and I would get married, but it was very strange: she and I never saw each other as boyfriend and girlfriend; we only saw each other as friends.

Recaptured

Pyrrhus, when his friends congratulated him for his victory over the Romans under Fabricius, but with great slaughter of his own side, he said to them, "Yes; but if we have such another victory, we are undone."

Francis Bacon

Fighting ended in Saigon by 5th February. It was only a week of fighting, but it was so intense, there were a lot of burned out buildings, and guns everywhere. Most people stayed home, and children didn't go to school and the quiet on the street after the fighting was almost as frightening as the explosions. It wasn't natural. But, what was most unnerving was the number of dead that had to be recovered. Thousands of Communists died in the fighting and I am still haunted by the memory of turning a corner and being startled to find a bulldozer slowly pushing a huge mound of dirt into a ditch. As I moved closer, I realised it wasn't dirt, it was a pile of dead soldiers.

Like Saigon, most towns and villages across South Vietnam were easily recaptured from the Communists, but others endured harsh battles for a long time. Huế was not freed until the end of February, but when the fighting was over, thousands of people from Huế were missing. Years later, the South Vietnam government found mass graves —- the total number of bodies unearthed came to around 2,500. Many of the victims found were Catholics who had sought sanctuary in a church but had been taken out and later shot. Apparently, the Communists did not waste any time in Huế in identifying and eliminating anyone that was a perceived threat to them.

In the battle of Khe Sanh, the NVA attacked a US military base with intense bombing. The Americans retaliated. The bloody battle lasted 77 days. Eventually, in mid-April, Khe Sanh was recaptured. Official records say that the *Tết Offensive* officially ended in September.

In the end, the whole thing was a military disaster for the Communists and General Giáp. About 4,000 of the South Vietnamese and American military were killed, but around 14,000 civilians and 45,000 Việt Cộng and NVA died. Although it was a massive defeat for the Communists, we know now that the *Tết* Offensive was the beginning of the end of US involvement in Vietnam. It appeared that for many Americans who had believed that the war was being won, the intense battles showed the strength of the North, and the sight of Việt Cộng troops holding the US embassy was a symbolic turning point for many American supporters.

It was also a turning point for many of us in Saigon too. Until then, we felt safe in the city. The war was far away, only on the TV. But the *Tết* Offensive reminded us how quickly the tide can turn in war and how fragile 'safety' really is.

Courtship III

Secret forces are bringing compatible spirits together… When deep friendships exist, formalities and elaborate preparations are not necessary.

I Ching

It didn't take long before everything was back to normal in Saigon. There were a few reminders of all the fighting that took place in early 1968 – some buildings were only skeletons after being hit by explosives, some street vendors never returned to their usual corner – but on the whole, we all fell back into our routines.

In 1969, I took on a second teaching job in Biên Hòa. This meant that every day I drove from Saigon to Biên Hòa. A few months later I was offered another teaching assignment which meant that gradually, over the course of the year, I found myself spending more time in Biên Hòa than in Saigon. When in Biên Hòa, I stayed with my brother-in-law.

I suppose that is why I never really said good-bye to my friend or her family. When she tried to contact me, I wrote a simple letter to her saying: "I'm busy; if I have time I will contact you again". I bet her parents were shocked, but she and I knew we wouldn't marry because we were simply friends. I don't know where she is now, but I heard she left in 1975 so I guess she is in America.

So in all this time, I had never really had a girlfriend. When I left the Grand Seminary, I tried to contact some female friends who often came to Mass at my Little Seminary, and there was one in particular that I hoped to get to know better. At that time she studied at the Regina Pacis School, a highly respected girl's school run by French Sisters. I went to Mass a few times hoping to see her, but she wasn't there. I then went to see her family who lived next to the Little Seminary. Her mum really encouraged me to try to contact her and seemed to try to push us together, but she and I never had a chance to meet. We were both so busy. She was always studying or working and I was busy teaching and before long I forgot; I got caught up in my work and never got around to contacting her. I laugh about this now – how could I forget? Later on I heard she married a military officer who died during the war. I haven't heard anything about her or seen her since she was in school.

Before the *Tết* Offensive, I had gone to Biên Hòa to enquire about a teaching job and I met Bùi Thị Điệp, who was only sixteen years old at that time. We simply talked as friends. I enjoyed her company but did not think much about it. When I arrived in Biên Hòa to start teaching a year later, I saw Điệp again, but this time she was much more mature. I went to see her at her family home. We never went out or anything, just talked at her house. I was teaching at the time and working on my campaign, but I did see her quite often. Once I went to a public park with her for a walk. I wanted to kiss her but just then a plane flew overhead and Điệp said 'No - the pilot can see us!'

It was a while before I was able to finally kiss her – I was so busy working. But I knew I wanted to marry her. I knew she would be a good wife – I knew she would look after her husband and children, and I knew she was morally a good person. After about six months, in June 1969, we married. It was very simple.

My wife Điệp is a very good, devout Catholic. Her family is also originally from the North and it is common for those who moved south to be very strict Catholics. My Catholic faith is very open, but the pragmatist in me decided she could carry on with her religious way of life and I could with mine.

CHAPTER FOUR

Councillor

We have to be the change we want in the world.

Mahatma Gandhi

Politics and religion. Both are designed to unite people, but when you talk about religion or politics, it often divides. Yet I still see the good in both systems – if you do the right thing in these posts, you can be a great influence for the people. Confucius lived during a time of great disorder when people lived immorally and in his wisdom, he knew that if people returned to the principles and beliefs of the ancients then there would be stability again. One of his rules said:

> "If you govern your province well and treat your people kindly, your kingdom shall not lose any war. If you govern selfishly to your people, your kingdom will not only lose a war, but your people will break away from your kingdom."

I believed this to be true. I was teaching at the time, but then grew increasingly frustrated at the older councillors who only said 'yes' to whatever was asked by the local authority. They were the same as the priests who used their position to gain wealth, and just wanted to use their political power to improve their family's standing. They did not get involved in helping people or trying to do anything to improve life for their constituents, such as building new roads or improving the schools, and no one seemed to question the work they did. If something had been commissioned by the local authority, no one monitored to check whether the taxpayers received a quality service. In other words, those in power were not ruling wisely.

I couldn't just complain about it. I've learned, if I'm angry, I need to do something about it. In 1970, I stood for election in Biên Hòa province. I didn't have to think about it, I just knew that I had to act. I did some planning and I chose Biên Hòa because the majority of people were Catholic: as an ex-seminarian, I hoped most of the priests would support me. When I was elected at twenty-six years old, I was the youngest councillor in Vietnam. While a councillor, I continued teaching.

Fights

To see what is right, and not to do it, is want of courage or of principle.

Confucius

The changes to life in Saigon meant that there was an increase in poverty for some fleeing the war while others became extremely rich from the profits of the war, and I couldn't help but feel disappointed in the changes to the character of the Vietnamese. What angered me the most was the corruption, especially by people who were abusing their power. The political and military leaders had a responsibility to the people and instead they only looked after themselves. I was raised in a traditional village with traditional values. Although I knew that I couldn't return Vietnam to how it was before the war, I could try to do my best to be the kind of leader that I would want myself and to use my new position and influence for the good of the people as taught by Confucius.

I'm not sure why, but I began my tenure by challenging the General. That may have been the stupidest or the bravest fight I've ever started. Lieutenant General Đỗ Cao Trí was the most powerful General in South Vietnam. It was the early 1970s and Vietnam was still at war. He was a very talented leader and had the respect of everyone in the military, even President Nguyễn Văn

Thiệu. On the other hand, General Trí was also corrupt. He abused his power, and knew everyone was so afraid of him that he could do anything he wanted without being challenged. General Trí led the Vietnamese invasion of Kampuchea, against the wishes of the US military. Rumours also spread that General Trí stole gold and US dollars while in Kampuchea, but I never learned if this was true or not. But he did pillage and plunder while there. He made no secret of this fact — when he was in Kampuchea he even stole herds of cows and goats. Everyone could see them – he let them freely wander around the local parks in Biên Hòa, destroying everything. They even destroyed the grounds of the town hall, but no one complained to the General. When some goats wandered into local offices, no one would dare kick them out for fear of upsetting the General.

But that was not the only complaint against him. My constituents were disappointed because General Trí did not do anything to benefit the people of the area, even though he was born in Biên Hòa. He supported building the highway from Saigon to the seaside resort, Vũng Tàu, via the largest military base in Saigon, Long Binh, instead of Biên Hòa. I know in the West, most people are thrilled when major roads do *not* go through their village – Westerners prefer the quiet and privacy. Not in Vietnam. Vietnamese know that highways bring economic development, and the residents of Biên Hòa wanted the road to go through their town to help it grow.

The list of offences by the General was long and no one dared to challenge him, but for some of us, when the General approached the council about the Mayor's house, that was the last straw. Since the war, the Generals in the South Vietnam army had used the Mayor's house as their residence, and General Trí was pressuring the council to transfer the Mayor's house to the military so that he could officially live there permanently. The house in dispute was a gorgeous place within a lovely park by the river, next to the town hall. I gave a speech at the council where I said that we should not agree to transfer the house to the military because the military, and therefore the General, already had barracks and property for military officers. I then got caught up in the moment and spoke bluntly about General Trí and his desire to use Biên Hòa without any regard for the needs of the citizens. As a leader I said, he should set a moral example of good ethics and keep the good of the people, not himself, as his top priority.

The newspapers and press reported my speech everywhere. Word spread like wildfire that I dared to publicly say bad things about the General. The mayor of Biên Hòa, Colonel Lâm Quang Chính, was really shaken. Remember, this was all occurring during the war. Colonel Chính's appointment as Mayor had to be approved by General Trí so he did not want the General upset. He shared his concern with the chairman of the council, who was my friend.

"Thành, Colonel Chính is in a panic. He doesn't understand why you willingly provoked such frenzy. Why did you publicly denounce the General? Are you crazy?"

I replied casually: "It needed to be done. He was abusing his power and the people were angry. I didn't say anything they didn't already know or feel".

"I can't believe how calm you are. Listen, you are in great danger. Stop shaking your head and listen to me. Apparently the General phoned the Mayor and threatened to find you when he returns from Kampuchea."

I wasn't worried. "The Colonel is just saying that because I've captured the attention of the people."

"No," my friend chided, "The Colonel is also worried for his life. The General threatened him directly as well. Thành, you need to get out of here."

"What do you mean?"

"You need to hide somewhere, otherwise you'll be killed. You know how powerful that man is. He has over 25,000 soldiers at his disposal. We're at war, Thành. It would be easy for General Trí to have you 'accidentally' shot."

I could see my friend was serious. My calm was shattered. What could I do? Where could I hide? No matter where I went in South Vietnam, General Trí and his military could find me. But I didn't need to flee. Three days after the conversation with my friend, General Trí died; his helicopter blew up. No one knows what happened.

I could breathe again because General Trí was dead. The people in Biên Hòa were really taken aback when they learned of the General's death. Apparently, after my speech, a huge tree in front of his house suddenly fell down in a storm, and the people now believe that the fallen tree was a sign that things were going to change. But at first, things did not really change for me. There was too much corruption and injustice going on.

I received several complaints from people in my ward about the local police chief who had a bad reputation. He was always drunk and he did not carry out his job well, or in a professional manner. But this was not what people complained about. Many came to me with stories of how the local police chief intentionally made life difficult for them. The only way to prevent him from issuing a ticket for a non-existent offence, for example, was to pay him a bribe. When I investigated I found enough evidence to bring the issue to the council. But I knew a further investigation by the council would not be enough to stop this local police chief. All he would have to do is bribe the chief of police for our zone and he would be able to stay in post. This often happened at high-ranking levels.

After the incident with the General, I learned the way to really make an impact was to make sure the media learned about our council meeting. The media attended and published the complaints about the local police chief, and the central police force was then under great pressure to take action.

Our local police chief was, not surprisingly, very angry with me, and he brought me to Court. Because of the accusation of corruption, the chief of police of our zone – the third region – had to get involved. The irony was that we all knew that the chief of police routinely appointed local chief officers who were loyal to him in order to secure his position. These handpicked local chiefs, like our drunken chief, proved their loyalty through bribery.

In Court, I stood across from the chief of police. The courtroom was full of his supporting police officers who knew that if he fell, they all did. This powerful chief of police said I had no evidence about the behaviour of his staff. Then it was my turn to speak. I could feel the hatred coming from the eyes of all the police as I walked to the stand, but rather than make me nervous, it made me more determined to speak. My defence was simple.

"State your name." "Vũ Khánh Thành"

"You are charged with making false accusations against the local police chief. What do you have to say?"

"I am an elected councillor. Many people from my ward complained to me about the local police chief. As is my duty, I brought these complaints to the council to discuss. These meetings are public. Anyone can attend the meetings, including the media. What the media wrote about the local police chief was discussed openly in the meeting. The stories published by the media did not come from a private interview with me, but from the public meeting."

The police lawyer was pacing across the courtroom as I spoke. When I finished he asked what evidence I had to prove my accusations. He had a small smirk on his face as if he thought he was already victorious.

"As I said, I am a councillor. I am a teacher; I am not a detective. It is my job to take issues that my constituents bring to my attention to the council for discussion. If there is a complaint against a public official, it is not my job to provide the evidence. All I can do is raise the concern."

Before the lawyer could change the subject, I continued. "It is the job of the chief of police to investigate the behaviour of his staff."

Except for a few of the villagers who supported me, no one in the Courtroom seemed pleased with my testimony. In the end, it was a hung jury and they could not reach a verdict. So I received three months' probation. But that did not slow me down. I put in an appeal, and in the meantime, I continued investigations of complaints against the police. Every year I made the police angry. There were many police officers who abused their power and exploited people in my ward. This kind of corruption existed in South Vietnam, but it was very minor compared to the Communist regime now. This is because we had a free press at that time and as in the West, the parliament and justice system were separate.

I disdain corruption, especially by people in positions of power. Confucian doctrine teaches that people in every position of life should live up to the proper responsibilities of their office, beginning with the ruler. Only then will the people be inspired to do the same and live virtuously. So when I received complaints of a parish priest who was blatantly corrupt, I wanted to take action. Priests should set a good example help others, not steal from their parish. This priest had a road built into the jungle and he charged any vehicle that entered the jungle a fee. Many local farmers needed to go to the jungle to cut trees for wood. This priest felt he was powerful enough to be exempt from the laws that stated one must have planning permission to build a road, and tolls collected should be paid to the state. Instead, this priest kept the money for himself. The priest got away with it because he had so much power, not because of the prestige of priesthood, but because he had a good connection with the provincial military officers and politicians. No one dared touch him.

Although the priest had power, he did not have the respect of the common people. The people in his parish told me that he was a very proud and arrogant man who looked down on everyone. They also told me that he had a secret wife somewhere. So, I worked together with the village officer to try to learn the truth and gather evidence. I used a camera to photograph lorries entering the jungle, and I took photos of someone collecting money from the drivers.

I then went to find the priest's wife. I heard she had just had a baby, and my investigations revealed the priest named as the child's father on the birth certificate which was very serious evidence against a 'celibate' priest. I had all the evidence I needed. I approached the inspector – the same one who helped me in the investigation against the district chief – and we discussed what to do. The inspector was also Catholic and an ex-seminarian. We decided to go to the Bishop first and try to persuade him to take action to discipline the corrupt priest. If the Bishop agreed, we would vow to keep the matter secret from the public, but if the Bishop ignored our case, we planned to take the story to the media. With all the evidence against the priest, the Bishop did not need much persuasion and he moved the priest to a parish far from the city to another district, a place where he had less power and influence.

I also remember the time I fought with the district chief – the equivalent of a mayor in the UK. In Vietnam, during the war, the district chief was always a military officer, usually a Lt Colonel. I received complaints about this district chief accepting bribes from people who did not want to serve as a soldier so I found one family who were particularly upset and asked them to testify. I gathered other evidence and took it all to the local inspector. Luckily, he was a very honest inspector and he agreed to investigate the case. In the end, the council agreed to dismiss the district chief from his post and go to trial. He was sent to prison. However, after two years, South Vietnam was 'liberated' so he was released from prison and was exempt from imprisonment in a Communist re-education camp because any criminal of the South Vietnam government was a friend of the Communists.

Election

Toi Van Mo Hoai

Toi van mo hoai mot giac mo
Giac mo khong biet tu bao gio
Co khi tu thuo long cay dang
Som biet doi tan bong doi cho...

Mot chieu nhu chieu trong tho
Giua khi khong tuong cunh khong ngo
Co ban tay nho day thuong men
Tet lai doi toi xac tua vo

Bien song lenh denh mot cham mo
Noi chim, vo tan noi bo vo
Buom tan, cheo gay, cho xo vo
Toi van mo hoai mot giac mo...

A Dream I Have

A dream I have for a long time now
One that I don't even remember when it started
Possibly it was since I knew bitterness
And early came to know the fading of hope...

It was one of those dream evenings, as in poetry
When I least expected it nor hoped for
A soft and tiny hand full of tenderness
Rewove my life, which was hardly alive then.

Now a dim point in the middle of the vast ocean
Dipping and bobbing, lost in the immensity
With sails torn and oars broken, waiting for catastrophe
A dream I still have since long, long ago...

Nguyễn Chí Thiện *1960*

In between the fights and investigations of corruption, I used my position as councillor to set up four new local high schools. I also worked closely with the *Bình Định Phát Triển Fund* to build new classrooms, to repair and asphalt the local roads, and to run electricity for the first time to the surrounding rural area. I enjoyed the work, and liked knowing that I was helping people. I intended to run again in the next election.

In the meantime, President Thiệu formed a new party called the Democratic Party. It was created in order to show the public and the Americans that South Vietnam did have more than one party. President Thiệu's supporters were part of the Democratic Party, symbolised by a picture of a bicycle on all their campaign posters and adverts for the 1974 election. The Democratic Party was the government party, and the catchy slogan they used was "simply take your bike to the polling box", meaning vote for those with a bicycle next to their name. I became part of the opposition and my name did not have a bicycle next to it on the polling form. I received lots of votes. When I first ran for office, I only had 20,000 votes and came in fifth out of seven elected in my province. In the 1974 election, I received 43,000 votes making me the top candidate.

Yet somehow I lost the election. The reason the government gave for this discrepancy was that, because of the war, many polling boxes from the countryside were delayed. Somehow, when all the votes from the countryside came in, none of the opposition candidates had enough votes to be elected in our province. When the results were announced, we all knew the election was rigged. I organised a demonstration in every Catholic parish along Highway 1 – the main road linking Saigon, Đà Lạt (or Dalat) and Biên Hòa. The people were furious at the corruption, and some burned tyres for three days and three nights to stop all the vehicles. The opposition party MP came to talk to the people during demonstration. Finally, the chief of the province lost his post, but the opposition candidates were not reinstated.

At the time I was extremely upset. I found my job as

councillor very fulfilling and I was looking forward to serving my community for four more years. But now, looking back, it was good I was not re-elected.

CHAPTER FIVE

Fall

Three Poems

War

A woman shrieking
in the city
in the night
in the dust
in the hospital
now a strand of hair hanging at bayonet point

Softly

The land still grows
but men are drained of passion
why is poetry today
so sad
like a prayer?

Testimony

On the deserted rockland
above the layer of prehistoric soil
bleached-white bones
facing time
cause in those coming after
a twinge of sorrow.

Đặng Thiêm
(War and Exile: A Vietnamese Anthology, 1989 p 156)

I can still see it as if it happened yesterday. I can't imagine it was forty years ago. It all happened so fast. I remember such sad things — still there, in front of me.

The Fall of Saigon.

War in Vietnam actually began in 1945 after the Japanese surrendered at the end of World War II. As European powers agreed to let Vietnam, Cambodia and Laos return to France as a colony, Hồ Chí Minh declared the People's Democratic Republic an independent nation. However, his was only a resistance movement at that time. The skirmishes between the Việt Minh and the French gradually escalated into a full war, but officially the war between the North and South did not begin until 1954 when the French withdrew from Điện Biên Phủ, and Vietnam was divided between North and South along the 17th Parallel.

During this phase of the war, there were minor victories on both sides, but they were followed by setbacks. No one was really optimistic when the Vietnamese Communists entered into agreement in 1969 with the United States, the then Republic of Vietnam (South Vietnam) and the Communist-run National Liberation Front of South Vietnam (NLF). These agreements culminated in the 'Paris Agreement' in 1973 where the United States agreed to stop all military activities against North Vietnam, not to intervene in the military or internal affairs of South Vietnam, and to withdraw from South Vietnam. The Paris Agreement also mentioned, a bit more indirectly, that North Vietnam would stay out of South Vietnam. But after the signing, Vietnam was still divided and communist soldiers were still in the south.

The Paris Agreement was signed at a time when both the North and the South were weakened, but that did not stop either side from fighting. At first the battles were mild and short lived so the United States did not respond.

Then there was the fall of Bình Long Province on 14th January 1974. This wasn't a standard skirmish between two tired enemies. It was a terrible battle: very gruesome, with a great deal of death and injury on both sides. Through the news and television, I could see that both sides fought very hard to win that battle. I think the South assumed the US would intervene once it was obvious the North violated the treaty, but in the end, after many died, Bình Long province was under Communist control and the US did nothing.

Less than a year later, North Vietnam again violated the Paris Agreement and attacked Phước Long Province in South Vietnam. The United States protested only diplomatically, and made no military effort to enforce the treaty. This should have been a clue that the war had changed.

But it was the battle at Ban Mê Thuột, a province in central Vietnam, that foreshadowed the coming death of South Vietnam. It was a brutal battle between the North and the South and the endless explosions shown on our television screens appeared too appalling to be real. On 11 March 1975, South Vietnam's army totally failed and the Communists now controlled that area. Ban Mê Thuột was a strategic city. The French recognised this long ago when they said 'whoever controls Ban Mê Thuột controls all of Vietnam'. This meant that after 30 years of war, the wind was changing.

The President of South Vietnam appealed to the Americans. President Thiệu knew that without the Americans, the Communists would win. The United States did nothing. Instead, there were rumours that the Americans were packing up to leave.

So President Thiệu ordered a withdrawal of troops from the central highlands. To this day, I'm still not clear why. I assume that the order to withdraw came as a surprise to the military too, as they didn't seem to have a plan. That must be why everyone in that area seemed to panic. Massive numbers of soldiers, as well as civilians, ran. Everyone tried to flee the central highlands at once and by any means possible – military jeeps, motorcycles, even carts congested the main roads. Entire families were hanging onto the tops and sides of the buses and trucks. Only those on foot could move. They were on the road for almost two weeks, with no access to food and water. It was a death trap. The North Vietnamese army fired artillery and dropped bombs on those fleeing to Saigon. It was carnage. People now refer to that journey as the 'convoy of tears'. An estimated 40,000 people died.

The whole of South Vietnam was shaken; we all felt that the US totally ignored us and didn't rescue South Vietnam. Everyone was listening to the BBC and Voice of America which fed us all details of what was happening on the battlefield. We all knew it would end very soon.

They attacked city after city moving south: Quảng Trị, Tam Kỳ, Huế, but there was still no help from the US. Then on the 30th March, Đà Nẵng fell – I heard that General Ngo Quang Truong was kidnapped and held on a US ship. This meant that the South Vietnam troops fighting in Đà Nẵng had no leader. The result was confusion on a huge scale, and without a leader, the troops lost the spirit to fight. The result was a mass surrender of 100,000 South Vietnamese soldiers. The soldiers for the South abandoned their posts and stopped fighting. Instead, military personnel used the army's equipment to evacuate their own family. It was 'every man for himself'.

The North Vietnamese, fuelled by their easy success, pushed toward Saigon.

As the North Vietnamese neared Saigon, there were a couple of weeks when the South Vietnam army restored its strength and conviction and gave a good fight. But that must have been the last of everyone's strength. It felt as if all of South Vietnam had given up. Even then, I saw with my own eyes many soldiers returning back to my village. They looked horrible. The soldiers returned by foot instead of in army vehicles and were dirty, and had abandoned their guns and equipment. They were tired and could not speak because they were so frightened. What struck me the most was how vulnerable they looked, but worse still were their looks of disbelief. They had lost all hope.

I was still in Biên Hòa, but after I heard about the fall of Long Khánh in mid-April, I knew there was no hope at all. I put my wife and three children on my motorbike and drove to Saigon, where we stayed with relatives. Saigon was overflowing with refugees, people who had fled the invading troops that were marching down the country. We were one family among thousands.

Luckily, I had family in Saigon so we had a place to stay and were not as vulnerable as those from the provinces entering the city from the ports. Locals mobbed them and took valuables they had carried all the way. I heard that vendors exploited the desperate refugees by charging inflated prices for food and water. Even some South Vietnamese soldiers apparently joined in the looting.

Every day all of us watched the news, read the paper and met with friends – especially those with a connection to the government. We all wanted to know what was happening. We all wondered where we would be safest; should we stay or leave? The uncertainty was exhausting.

On 20th April, President Nguyễn Văn Thiệu resigned and left Vietnam for Taiwan a couple days later. Vice-President Trần Văn Hương replaced him as President and, newly instated, tried to rally everyone – civilians and soldiers - to organise defence of the "4th military region" – the Delta River area. But it was too late.

In looking back, it is odd to me that Saigon, during daylight hours, was the one place that seemed untouched by the war at that time. Saigon looked different, the city was overcrowded with refugees as the people in Biên Hòa and Long Khánh fled to Saigon or to Cần Thơ – another big city in the delta area. This meant that there were now even more refugees in Saigon, many of whom had to sleep on the street and beg for food. Many of the refugees were gathered around the American embassy. Although Saigon sounded different because we could often hear gunfire in the distance and more frequent planes flying low over the city, it did not feel different. Everyone seemed to walk down the crowded streets as if everything was normal. Most people still went to work. Vendors kept selling and restaurants were still open. Everyone seemed calm as if they had no idea there was a war.

Nights were different though. Rockets began landing in Saigon. Like the *Tết* Offensive in 1968, the bombs were sporadic and only killed where they landed and we were lucky that none fell near us. But the noise and the trembling ground terrified my children. When we heard the rockets, my wife and I would grab the children and run to the innermost part of our house and crouch against the wall in a huddle. The children would cry, then the bombs would stop and we'd try to sleep. But it was hard to sleep the last few days since there were explosions somewhere in the city throughout the night.

On 27th April, North Vietnamese soldiers surrounded Saigon. There were many South Vietnam soldiers in Saigon, but they did not know what to do. At this stage, there was no one really commanding the South Vietnam army effectively – no one had a plan. North Vietnam bombed the central part of the city which caused chaos. People were looting, and no one knew where they could run for safety. I could hear people running up and down the street shouting for friends or family. I stayed in my relatives' house with the family and waited, listening to the radio for any sign of hope.

On 28th April, President Hương, after only a few days of running the country, resigned and asked General Duong Van Minh to become President of South Vietnam. At the time, people thought President Minh was in the pocket of the French government, and we hoped that meant President Minh and the French had a solution to the conflict. Rumours spread that President Minh and the French had convinced the NLF to comply with the Paris Agreement. People hoped that the North and South would agree to be two independent nations and stop fighting. These rumours spread through the city like fire. We all wanted the rumours to be true. Instead, it turned out that President Minh had no allies willing to help so he called for a ceasefire, which was ignored.

The next day, President Minh ordered all foreigners still in South Vietnam to leave within twenty-four hours, and the US President ordered the evacuation of Americans. This caused everyone, not just the Vietnamese working directly with the

Americans, to panic. People mobbed the airbase trying to escape. This was senseless because the Communists had just bombed the airbase in Saigon in the hopes of grounding the modern American aircraft to keep for themselves. At the same time, hordes of people struggled to get into the US embassy, hoping they could leave with the Americans, who had helicopters ready to evacuate their own people from the city. Some of my friends – former high-ranking officers in the South Vietnamese army or government – were among those who received special messages telling them to be at the embassy at a specific time for the helicopter to collect them for evacuation. The chaos prevented a few of them from ever entering the embassy, and they were left behind. I heard that some who had an invitation were beaten back by the Americans guarding the US embassy – the crowd was so thick and frantic that the soldiers didn't dare to let anyone in for fear of starting a stampede that couldn't be stopped.

Masses of people also went to the Saigon River, in hopes of escaping with the Vietnamese Navy who still had ships there. I was among them, I took my family to the river where I saw many people trying to get on to a ship, and just as many people getting off the ship. There was such confusion. No one knew whether or not the ships would actually be able to leave and get to safety in international waters. No one knew how long they would have to wait. No one knew if there was even a captain or crew on the ship. It was too crowded. People were hysterical and it felt dangerous.

In the meantime, no one - Communist or otherwise - was doing much to stop the looting. There were small gangs of people, who seemed really poor and desperate, who took advantage of the chaos to break shop windows and steal everything.

No one could believe how quickly the war was coming to an end. My mind was in chaos, and I could not think. I was unable to stay out in the mayhem of the streets with my family for too long, so I turned away from the river and returned to the house. I tried contacting friends or other relatives, but most of the telephones were cut off, and I couldn't make connections with anyone. So I listened to the radio. Around 3.00pm, it calmed down a little, and I went back to the Saigon River. The Việt Cộng were watching people trying to get on the ships that remained at the dock, and they were watching as others tried to get off the ships. They did nothing, however, and seemed okay letting people try to escape.

For years after the fall of Saigon, I regretted my decision not to get on that ship. I was not as confident as those who boarded, including a friend of mine, that the ship would reach safety. I had to make a quick decision and had to think about the safety of my family. But that was why the decision was so difficult. How could I be certain that fleeing would be safer than staying? As I stared at the ship, I had so many things running through my mind. I left the river and went back to my relatives' house so I could think. Away from the hyper-desperation and panic of the docks, I was able to think about the long term. With all the panic, I naturally wanted to flee, yet I truly believed Vietnam was the best place in the world to live. This was my home. My ancestors were here, and the soul of the land was interlaced with my soul, so I chose not to leave. On that day 6,000 Vietnamese were evacuated. That night, the city was overflowing with residents and refugees frightened of what was going to happen next.

On the 30th of April, I awoke early because, not very far from the place I was staying, there was heavy gunfire. When I looked out, I saw the disaster. There were groups of soldiers running, dropping their guns and removing their army uniforms and helmets. I could see many others had done the same because there were guns and helmets scattered all over the place. Then, in front of my eyes, I saw a military vehicle with North Vietnamese soldiers approach a group of soldiers and start fighting. At this point, there was no longer any organised fighting – the skirmishes between individuals who were still highly strung and over-zealous, shooting at anyone who appeared threatening.

It was obvious the South Vietnamese army was in disorder. They surrendered instantly, yet the North Vietnamese did not know what to do so they walked around the city. Some occupied military bases, others just sat around, while others continued fighting in anger. I don't think they had planned for such a quick success. The North Vietnamese soldiers were apparently told not to fight unless they met resistance, but some individual soldiers were frustrated and continued fighting.

I later heard about many suicides during this frenzy – high ranking officials who had spent most of their career fighting the Communists suddenly couldn't face the shame of losing. Or perhaps they couldn't face a life not being a soldier.

I ran back into the house to be with my family, and we stayed inside for a while, but as quickly as the fighting started, it stopped. It became very quiet. It was 11am; on the television, I saw the red and blue Việt Cộng flag flying from the presidential palace. President Minh put out a broadcast message of unconditional surrender.

Eventually we tried to get out, fearing the worst and thinking we might need to escape. So once again I took my family on the motorbike and went to the Saigon River. Along the main road to central Saigon, the situation was the same as the day before. There was a lot of military equipment, including guns, dropped along the streets, which were full of families pushing their way to the river. I could see ahead of me that some of the naval ships had already left the port but there were still some there. As we crossed onto the main road, an army jeep exploded right in front of us and went up in flames and I saw two South Vietnamese soldiers die violently right in front of me. I stopped instantly as if I had hit a wall. I couldn't breathe. If we had arrived one second earlier my entire family would have died.

I am not sure what kept me moving, but I got to the dock on the river. I saw again that just as many people were trying to get off the boat as trying to get on. I was still uncertain about what to do. It felt too dangerous to get on the ship. It felt dangerous to stay.

Then, I saw, up close, the North Vietnamese soldiers. I was shocked by how very young the soldiers were. They were only fourteen or fifteen years old, and looked very innocent. They were walking around central Saigon in amazement, gasping at the tall buildings. They seemed so naïve, like they were as surprised as we were that they were in Saigon. I asked myself how it was possible for young, innocent soldiers like these to beat the South Vietnamese and the Americans.

I turned away from the ships and headed home.

I was very close to my brothers and sisters – we all love each other and look after each other. Especially my older brother Hãn – I remember him the most because never in my life did I hear him raise his voice. If one of us children did something he did not like, he would quietly say: "Don't do that", and we would obey. Both he and my sister were not very well educated, but they were very wise. They taught us all about the importance of tradition and living in harmony with each other. They taught us the importance of family.

Hãn's wife worked for American Airlines, and in 1975 they offered to take his family to America. When his wife told him the news, Hãn said no. For Hãn, family came first and since he couldn't bring our sister or me to America he wanted to stay in Vietnam with his family.

Re-education

Wave after wave of barbaric red tide
Submerged the past and the future
Blood, tears, sweat, dribble:
Everyone transformed, unrecognisable!
Terrified, stopped dead, paralyzed!
History is suddenly wildly rolled back
To become an open season for tigers, leopards, snakes and millipedes
Thousands of denunciation stages are set up on broad daylight
And just when earth-sky paled in dread
The tricky murderers
Raised their cups to victory and celebrated

Against an immense background of hunger and cold music
Interwoven with a refrain of death and separation
The prisons started their infamous business
Collecting
From the cities and country, mountains and seas!
The mangroves and reed and jungle
Are nourished by corpses

Nguyễn Chí Thiện, Excerpt from *The Swamps*
(War and Exile: A Vietnamese Anthology, 1989 p170)

I left Saigon the next day, to return to Biên Hòa. On the way home, I saw that thousands of people were travelling toward Saigon while masses were leaving the city. Lots of buildings had been burned and there were clothes, weapons, and even military cars along the road. I saw bodies as well, soldiers from both sides dead; bodies abandoned on the road; all evidence that fierce fighting carried on to the last day.

Even after all this time, I have trouble describing what it was like. I felt as if I had blown up — I felt as if my mind and heart were in the air, not in my body. Deep surprise. Anxiety. Yet I somehow got my wife and children back to Biên Hòa. My body kept moving forward while my mind seemed to be somewhere else.

Arriving home returned me to my body. It was about lunchtime, and we went straightaway to shop for basic supplies like rice and fish sauce. Everyone else had the same idea, and the streets were packed full of families trying to buy basic food, but it was very difficult. The shops didn't want to sell, as they didn't know what the future held, and did not want to take Vietnamese money.

That same evening, a former student of mine came to see me. I was taken aback. I thought back to the last time I saw this student. It had been about this time last year, when he and his friend were arrested right before their final exams. I had gone to the police station and asked what charge was made against my students. There had been a minor incident but the policeman recited that it was a Việt Cộng plot. I asked what this had to do with my students. The policeman shrugged and said their fathers were known Việt Cộng suspected in the incident and so they arrested the sons as well. I reminded them that if they had no evidence that the sons were also involved it would be a breach of their rights to hold them. I then asked that they were released so they could take their exams. I guess the police listened to me because the two boys were able to graduate.

But why was he at my door tonight of all nights? I could tell he was so excited, he couldn't stand still.

"What a victory!" he exclaimed. Before I could think of a way to gently let him know I did not share his feelings, he boasted

"'I have never forgotten how you helped us. We were Communist all along. We were involved in the incident and I had no idea if we would ever get out of jail. But you got us out so quickly and easily...'"

He went on and on recounting that event until I interrupted him to ask, "Why are you telling me all this tonight?"

"Like I said, I never have forgotten how you helped us and now we are in a position to show our gratitude." He then asked me to come with him, he wanted to take me to what would be translated as the 'revolution's secret meeting place' — the Communist's underground hiding place.

"Why?" I asked.

"I want to introduce you to the Party's Secretary for the ward. I know he has an important job for you in the new regime," he said, almost leaping from his chair. He was so excited and seemed to assume this was something I wanted.

I shook my head. I didn't want to be rude, so I simply said "I'm a teacher. I was simply doing my job." The student's face fell.

"What do you mean? But you helped us knowing we were Việt Cộng. You supported the revolution."

"No," I replied. "Whether you were guilty or innocent,

without evidence, they had no right to hold you in jail. I was your teacher and did not want to see all your hard work in school go to waste because you missed your final exams."

"But you were always fighting the government. You wouldn't have done that if you weren't Communist," he said with a voice of disbelief.

"I always want to work to make society better. My conscious makes me. But I don't want to be a Communist or a nationalist. I don't want to pick sides. I simply want a fair, just society," I replied as I walked him to the door. I had no interest in joining him at their former hiding place. I had no interest in joining the Communists. I had no idea how my refusal would be interpreted by the new leaders, but I could only hope they would recognise that I wasn't a threat.

I kept my head low. I refused to be any part of the May Day celebrations that next day even though it was an event to celebrate their victory, so the Communists expected everyone in the town to attend. The news of the event, and the command for all to attend, was announced over the loudspeakers, the radio, and on posters around the town. There were also many 'opportunistic' people who were running around rallying support – individuals who wanted to prove they supported the new regime in the hope that they would be dealt with kindly. The people in general were very frightened of the Communists, and they knew that every order must be obeyed. No one resisted, which I thought was ridiculous. I stayed at home with my family and closed the door.

After the May Day celebration of the Communist Party victory, the loudspeakers started calling former army officers, police, and local government officials to 'register' for re-education or study. They were told to come forward and, if a high officer, to bring enough food for one month, while others only had to bring enough for one week. At that time, no one knew of the horrors some men would face or the years they would spend starving in a cage whilst being 're-educated'.

They told teachers to register at the local education

department. Within a few days of the announcement, over a hundred of us sat together in a big school to learn about the victory of the Communist party and their army, communist doctrine, and the crimes of America and other capitalist countries around the world. After the lecture, they divided us into groups of thirty per classroom to 'discuss'. After the discussion, each of us had to write a summary of what we had learned from the lectures and discussions. Each of us had to attend these sessions every day, all day, for two months.

The Communists also made each teacher write out information about his or her personal life again and again. It was a bit like handwriting our CV over and over again. They wanted to know the names of all our family members, especially our father's name, our religion, all the work we'd done and so on. You would turn it in and then a few months later, they'd insist that you do it again. It was one of their ways of finding out if you were hiding something.

My experience was tedious, but not traumatic like it was for those shipped off to re-education camps – usually men who were once military officers or government officials for the South. The re-education camps were often artillery bases or military camps during the war. The camps often had large open spaces in the centre of some small huts, the entire camp encircled by barbed wire. The prisoners had to sleep on the dirt floor in small, crowded huts. The huts were often damaged and would leak during the rains. Food was rationed and most of the prisoners remained hungry and, over the years, many good men died from malnutrition or disease. I'm not sure if that is how my wife Điệp's brother died in a re-education camp. It was very difficult to know what to say to my children when they asked about their uncle.

In speaking to men who were eventually released from the re-education camps, they told me that the unknown was the worst part – they had no idea how long they would be detained. They were originally told they'd only be away from home for a few weeks and yet for many, years and years went by without any indication of when they would be free again. They were only told that they would be able to go home once they had showed 'good will and progress'. The camp leaders often tried to make this sound like a gift, reminding the prisoners that under the policy of the 'Revolution' their crimes deserved the death penalty, but the Revolutionary leaders were 'compassionate' enough to offer re-education as an alternative.

Apparently, in the early days, the lower ranked guards were a bit friendlier and sometimes helped a few of the sick prisoners. But, once the re-education camp system was in full swing, the staff were watched as much as the prisoners. This quickly created an environment where everyone abused their power. Prisoners were physically beaten or kept in solitary confinement for days if they committed only minor offences. The short-tempered guards took every opportunity to humiliate the prisoners.

The prisoner's day usually started with a line up, roll call, and head count. Then they'd be given their orders for the day with different 'battalions' given specific tasks – usually hard labour needed for the maintenance of the camp or production 'for the good of the people'. The 're-education' was designed to make sure everyone understood the 'extent of their offences' through labour and study. The men, like me, also had to sit through lectures and discussions about American imperialism or the history of Vietnam's struggle. In a re-education camp however, prisoners also had to study the 'crimes committed by oneself'. Almost monthly, each prisoner had to write a twenty-page report on their past crimes, beg the Communists for a pardon and promise to study hard to become a good citizen. These self-criticism reports were read over by the Communists, comparing them to past reports, and if found inconsistent, the prisoner was punished. The Communists would interrogate people repeatedly, trying to catch out deceit and lies.

But even more torturous was when each prisoner had to announce his or her 'crimes' in front of the other prisoners. They also had team discussions where each prisoner self-critiqued and self-denounced his or herself – the other team members were then encouraged to point out what they forgot to mention and denounce each other in order to look favourable to the guards. You cannot imagine what this did to everyone. They were alone; they could trust no one. To denounce another prisoner may make someone's prison time shorter, but it also meant the prisoner would be ostracised. But to not denounce another prisoner meant the men weren't progressing as good Communists and would be held longer.

This psychological pressure was not the only form of torture used by the Communists in the re-education camps. One of my former teachers was in a re-education camp for 18 years. For these eighteen years, my teacher was hungry, fed just enough rice to keep him alive, and the entire time, his leg was chained. Now his leg doesn't work, it looks like a skeleton; there is no muscle left. He told me that having his leg continually chained did not only mean he could not walk around freely. The chain affected everything – even going to the toilet. My teacher, and the others who were also chained, had to sit and sleep in their own faeces. The re-education camps were monstrous. They used pressure on the mind and spirit and would push people to the edge.

Flight

Nam-ky Khoi Nghia tieu Cong-ly
Dong Khoi len roi mat Tu-do.

When Justice Street is re-signed with abandon
Boulevard of the Great Southern Revolution,
The bells of General Insurrection
Ready toll the death of Freedom
That's how the southerner's view their 'Liberation'

Nguyễn Ngọc Phách (p55)

Escaping Vietnam became very fashionable. Once people had tasted what life under Communism really meant, they plotted to escape.

But the practical reality of organising a trip was very difficult because the police controlled everything. When you went from village to village or from town to town, you had to have permission from the State. If you had permission, you were allowed to buy a place in a car or bus, but that did not allow you to avoid the police checks of luggage and any items you brought with you. So it was very difficult for those organising an escape. First, they had to have a boat or ship, but if they did not already own one, the police would really question why you wanted to buy a boat at that time. If you had a boat or managed to buy one without too much trouble, you had to prepare it for the open sea, ensuring you had a strong enough engine and that it could hold all the people. The organiser also had to purchase enough food and supplies to last the trip. So the organiser had to purchase and move large quantities of food, water and oil from place to place and then hide it. To get around police suspicion, many tried to buy small amounts of food over time, but then it was challenging to get enough food for forty or fifty people in time.

But that challenge was minor compared to the actual day of escape. Without detection, forty to fifty people had to get out to the boat. Usually the ones trying to escape were not from the local village and if they were from the city and had paler skin and dressed in nice clothes, the police would stop them straightaway. Even if they were able to dress in such a way that they blended in with the local villagers, their accent was different and they would attract attention whenever they spoke. Where could they hide and wait until it was dark enough for them to sneak to the sea? After 1975, everyone had a duty to report to the local police any guests who stayed overnight with them.

Because of the need for secrecy, it was rare that you could knowingly speak directly with the organiser, and you would only learn about trips through the middlemen. You often did not know what the ship would be like, or how many people were going. You had to trust that the organiser was not a corrupt person after your money; and you had to trust that he was not working with the secret police. That is why thousands of stories spread about escape tricks. The organisers had many ways to take money from you, and there were so many possible ways a trip could go wrong and fail. That is why I failed five times.

Once, I tried to go to Phan Thiết - a city near the sea in central Vietnam. I went alone to Phan Thiết and stayed with my friends who lived near the area. I waited throughout the night for a safe opportunity to get out to the boats on the sea. I waited again a second night, hoping for a window when no police would block my access to the sea. But at that time the area was too heavily guarded so I returned to Saigon.

CHAPTER SIX

Communism

Originally, the leaders in Hanoi remembered how disastrous it was for the North when the Communists forced the change to socialism too quickly. So the North assumed it would make the change to communism in the South a bit more cautiously. The North wanted to allow time to reorganise the economic systems and train the workforce. For example, they allowed a free market to remain in place for a couple years while they began to centralise things like the banking system.

We know now that there were tensions between the North Vietnamese army and the National Liberation Front (NLF). They both pursued Communist ideals, but the North had their vision of what this meant and the NLF did not appreciate the North's determination to control everything. To make the unification of Vietnam whole and complete, the North Vietnamese merged Communist groups with their northern comrades and replaced anyone in a position of power, regardless of whether they were Communist or not, with a cadre from the North. Members of the NLF were upset that members of the North Vietnam Communist Party implemented all the new policies. Not long after the fall of Saigon, this rift between leaders was one of many reasons why the government had to change their original plan to integrate the North and the South slowly over five years or so, and instead move quickly. The ultimate aim of the economic reforms was to deprive people of their wealth and eliminate private commercial activity. The policies changed more than just the economic structure of the country. They changed everything, including the character of the people.

Communist doctrine claims that by altering the 'supply' side of economics, the 'demand' side would change, resulting in equality. Well, it did not really work. There were no essential 'supplies', so that was a change, and everyone was equally poor, so that was a change. But demand? That never changed. We could not obtain essential things, not even petrol. With the government unwilling or unable to supply what was needed however, people needed to find new ways to meet the demand. Many were very clever. I don't know how they did it, but some even found a way to use charcoal to fuel a bus – I saw the machine in the back of the coach. The boycott by the United States meant that we had an even harder time accessing goods. The Vietnamese therefore had to rely on re-using the old instead of buying the new, more modern technology which the rest of the world had.

Many also resorted to stealing. When working in a shop or factory, they would sometimes take a few small things in order to survive. For some, this was devastating; to become a crook in order to survive seemed necessary but went against their character and moral upbringing. Sadly, over time, these feelings of guilt disappeared.

My family was forced to sell everything we had to get some money to survive. Every family was the same. People were selling possessions such as cameras, watches – especially ones with the date as well as time - furniture, bicycles, and motorcycles. But not cars; there was no petrol of course, so cars were useless. People only wanted to buy the tyres because people used them to make sandals strong enough for the jungle or to work in. For some reason, a very popular item that sold was old clocks, the ones that chime every hour. And also sewing machines were popular. Some people sold items on the street or in a market, but often, you did not have to do anything to sell your possessions. Huge numbers of people from the North would come to your home to ask you to sell. There was such a huge demand at that time, everywhere.

This huge demand for our possessions mostly came from

people who moved to the south after the war. After 30th April, people from the North were able to come to the South, and they came *en masse*. I'm not sure how they were able to do it; whether the government organised it or not, but they brought down a huge number of lorries to move the goods from north to south. They had permission to do this, but in the South, we couldn't even move from city to city. The people from the North were ignorant of modern Western life. Some arrived barefoot. They would move into a house and not know what the toilet was and so assumed it was a nice place to put live fish. They thought ceiling fans were torture devices for beheading people. They fell in love with teacups with handles – they had never seen anything like them before. Everything was new and modern to them. The North had lived under Communism for 20 years by the time the war ended and although the people there had some paper money, there was nothing to buy. They had nothing; they were so poor and were amazed at all the wonders of the south. The North was emptied by 1975 with all the money going to the military. They thought the south was like heaven: they admired the cheerful people, that everything was so beautiful, so modern. They couldn't wait to 'liberate' us and make us as poor as they were.

The other key policy designed to 'build socialism' was the change of currency. In the autumn of 1975, the South Vietnam currency was recalled and changed to the North Vietnam currency. This in itself was not chaotic, and we could continue to use the old currency the same way as the new currency, but the old notes became more and more rare. Then suddenly in 1978, the government announced another currency reform. The announcement was made on the same day throughout the country and no one had any advance notice – the government kept it a secret until they were ready.

From that day forth, the old banknotes were invalid and could only be exchanged at designated places. The surprise, however, was that in cities, a single person could only withdraw 100 đồng, a couple could withdraw 200 đồng, and 50 đồng for each additional family member up to 500 đồng. Those in the countryside could only withdraw 50 đồng for the first two family members and 30 đồng for each additional person up to 300 đồng. Luckily, they did not ask about gold or diamonds, so many Vietnamese were able to hide some gold. Extra money was to be deposited in a bank, but only after owners had proved that they earned it 'honestly', by their own labour. The Communists tried to comfort us by saying that those who had good plans for economic development for the country would be able to withdraw their surplus money in the future. Otherwise, bank deposits were 'frozen' so they lost the money. This devastated everyone, and as in the North, it made the entire country extremely poor.

From the beginning, the Communists used the army to do everything, as well as those individuals who had secretly supported the Communists; people who suddenly appeared and began working for the government. They were often the ones who were the quickest to demonstrate their power. You could see in the glimmer in their eye and in their voice that they loved their new power.

Flight – II

"If a lamppost could walk, it would try to escape too"

(Vietnamese comedian, interviewed on BBC, early 1980s.)

All the political, economic and social changes introduced by the Communists took Vietnam back to a prehistoric age, and everyone was trying to escape.

As I went about my business trying to buy and sell used electrical equipment or sugar, I was also on the continual hunt for information about planned trips to escape, and my aim at that time was to discern which trip was authentic. There were so many frauds set up by corrupt people, who would convince others to pay a couple ounces of gold for a deposit on a guaranteed ship. Some people were making a fortune out of the desperation.

For my second escape attempt, I went to Rạch Giá - a town in South Vietnam. It was far from Saigon, near Thailand and the island Phú Quốc – home to a very large, very famous prison used by the French authorities. My friend in Biên Hòa, Cương[1], organised this trip over a year. Cương had brought his relatives from North Vietnam to come south, and two of them had become fisherman near Rạch Giá. Cương knew that, because his relatives were from North Vietnam, they would not attract the attention of local authorities and the police. It seemed to work. Because they were fishermen, they were able to contact the former officer of the South Vietnam local authority who had a big boat, without raising suspicion. Cương told me the boat was big enough to hold 100 people. I believed him and agreed to go with the whole family.

We travelled from Saigon to Rạch Giá. To do so I had to get permission from my local authority to visit relatives near to Rạch Giá. We tried to dress like poor locals. It was a long bus journey - the police stopped the bus many times in an attempt to catch middlemen trying to bring rice from one area to another. We did not reach Rạch Giá until late in the day, and I went straight to the local church where Hoàng Tấn, a friend of mine from the seminary, was parish priest. I hadn't seen my friend Tấn for many years, and we were both overwhelmed to see each other again. My family stayed with him in his parish house, and Tấn and I stayed up talking the whole night. In the morning, I brought my family to the place where we were to find the 'taxi' – a very small boat that was to bring us from the river to the coast, but because I talked through the night with Tấn, I slept too late and we missed the taxi. We missed the boat that would take us to freedom.

---

[1] Name has been changed to protect identity

I was devastated. My family and I returned to the bus station to purchase tickets back to Saigon. While there, I saw Cương. He told me the trip went really well. He said he was sorry we missed the boat. Then, before I went to leave, Cương gave me an ounce of gold because I had introduced some of my friends to him who paid him to be on his boat to escape.

After I returned home, I could not stop thinking about the boat I missed. I was so angry with myself for sleeping late, and I felt terribly unlucky to have missed my chance for freedom. I obsessed over my poor luck for about a month, but then I received a letter from Thân Toàn Dất[2] - someone who I recommended should join the escape trip. Dất told me that the boat sailed out to sea for about half an hour, then turned around and returned to land, at which point everyone on the boat was arrested and put in prison in Rạch Giá. A few who had family with enough money were able to bribe the police so they could get out after a month. Others couldn't afford to bribe the police and were in prison for up to three months. The ones who were the most vulnerable were the people who had all their gold with them on the boat – when the police capture you they take your gold and money before putting you in prison.

Dất also told me that the police were looking for me having discovered that I was supposed to be on the boat with my family. Usually those organising an escape try to ensure that key categories of people are on board the boat such as a doctor to help anyone who gets sick, and a priest to comfort the passengers. They often try to have someone on board with some power or influence, most often because of connections with the former government. People believed, regardless of whether it was true or not, that those affiliated with the former regime might have the respect of officials in places like Thailand or Hong Kong, safe neighbouring countries. It was hoped that the local government would respect former government officials and thus be more likely to allow us to stay, or

---

[2] Name has been changed to protect identity

at least contact international bodies like the UNHCR.

Organisers often wanted me on a boat therefore because I was a councillor and could speak a little English. There were also rumours or gossip that I was friendly with former President Thiệu - his brother was a teacher in the same high school I taught in. When Thiệu became President of South Vietnam, his brother became ambassador in Taiwan. When Thiệu's brother invited me to become part of his team in Taiwan, I was a councillor in Biên Hòa so I refused. That's why I was on the list and thus why the police were looking for me on the boat.

When the friends who I introduced to Cương in Rạch Giá returned home, they were very angry with me. They began telling others that I made a lot of gold by convincing people to pay for a place on a fraud escape boat. They spread rumours that I worked with the organisers to make lots of money. But I did not get any money; I only introduced them to the organiser who I truly believed was planning a legitimate escape. It was up to my friends to meet Cương and pay him directly if they wanted to join the boat. My friends condemned me for being corrupt. But this was very common; there were thousands of trips that were false and thousands of true trips that failed.

Reforms

Duoi dan ra khoi cua nha
Bat di kinh-te that la xot xa
Khong sao song duoc cho qua
Nen danh lai phai tro ra Sai-gon.
Chang ai guip do cham nom
Cung nhau vat vuong, lom khom via he.
Man suong chieu dat phu che
Sinh ra benh tat kho khe om dau.
Nhung ma co song duoc dau?
Bo-doi keo den, hang xau xuc lien.
Chung dem bo tai Tam Bien
Rung sau nui tham oan khien buoc vao

Having thrown thousands out of their homes
Police sent them to the New Economic Zones.
Unable to make a living, these poor citizens
Just returned to live precariously in Saigon.
Without any help forthcoming, however,
They're reduced to huddling in the kerb.
Sleeping in the open, exposed to the elements,
Many fell sick on the furnace-hot pavements!
That wasn't the end of their miserable life:
Soldiers soon came and tied them in a file
Then dumped the lot in the tri-border area
Deep in the forest of Laos and Cambodia.
The six thousand who were sent on this trip
All died of hunger in a matter of weeks.

Nguyễn Chí Thiện (p68)

The second big communist reform was the end of private commerce. The state decreed that it was going to confiscate all the property of the 'Capitalists'. This really frightened the people because it meant that if you owned a large house, an art collection or a factory, either small or large, the government would come and take it over for 'the people'. In industry, the staff and managers of the factory would often be allowed to continue working in the factory for six months or a year while the Communists worked beside them and learned how to run the factory. Then, they would bring in enough of their own people and sack all the original staff. The principle was that anyone who was rich would walk away empty-handed under communism.

Actually, they wouldn't walk away; they were sent away. Those who were seen to own great wealth were called to account for their wealth - their possessions were taken from them and they would be labelled as exploiters of the people. One day a man would wake up to police at his door announcing that he was middle class, that he was a Capitalist, then he'd be out. Some of those targeted felt such despair that they committed suicide. The despair was not just the loss of money and status but the fear they'd be sent to the 'new economic zones' (NEZ), which was the Communist policy of forcing the middle class or business owners to cultivate new areas for production.

There were several motivations behind the creation of the NEZ. After the Fall of Saigon, there was massive unemployment in the south because all the police and military personnel there instantly lost their jobs. Saigon was still full of refugees; and now we had a new type of refugee in the city; those whose economic welfare depended on the American soldiers such as restaurant owners, bar girls, prostitutes, or import/export businesses who were now unemployed.

At the same time, there were shortages of everything, including food. So there was a great need to cultivate more land to increase food production after decades of war, as well as a need to repair some of the infrastructure.

So in theory, the plan to move all the unemployed to uncultivated land to grow next year's harvest doesn't sound too bad. But it was the government's plan to include the 'Capitalists' in the NEZ as punishment that caused incredible misery. Having confiscated money and possessions from the 'Capitalists', The Communists would send them to the jungle empty handed so that they could labour for the people in return for their years of exploitation. They were left to their own devices to survive. These people had no experience of living in the jungle, and they had no shelter from the rain. They had to cut their own trees and make their own huts. It meant, basically, that the government was going to let the people die.

You can't imagine what life was like after the war. After years of fighting, there were also many wounded soldiers unable to work. After years of Westerners increasing the demand for drugs, there were also large number of heroin addicts. Disease is another side effect of war. Vietnam was no exception; tuberculosis and malaria were on the rise after the war, and became a growing threat with the influx of people living on the streets of Saigon. And medicine was scarce – most medical supplies were kept for the army or party members. In 1975, my second daughter Tâm had a high fever and blood came out from her skin. We call it *sốt xuất huyết* (I think you call it dengue fever). At first we thought she had a normal cold with a fever, but then she got worse, so we took her to hospital. They were able to help her, but the doctor told us that if we had arrived there an hour later, she would have died. With everything that's happened in my life, that was the most scared I've ever felt.

But what made it even harder to recover from the destruction of war was the Communists. You also can't imagine what it was like after the Communists took over. You can't imagine how people survived. There was a rise in crime and suicides, and also a rise in rumours. No one could see the reality or the whole picture. There were no independent reporters, and no one could investigate what was happening or expose injustice or abuse. The media, all the transport, everything was now controlled by the government.

All the news we heard came from people who returned from the jungle. They came back and told us: "it was horrible, we had empty hands. We could not dig in the ground to plant anything. We could not live". So they would return to the city to become beggars on the street. No one can explain what it was like. Even relationships - you could see how the relationships between members of a family changed. No one helped each other, and if you were hungry, no one could help you. Only those who had some hidden gold could find food to eat and support each other.

The Communists targeted big houses. They did not care about small ones. My family was poor so I had a small house and they didn't pay attention to me. It was the same at the schools as well. The Communists changed the boards of management and head teachers straightaway, but the normal teachers like me were still allowed to teach, at first.

It took them a year to learn about the regular teachers and replace the ones like me who had some relationship with the previous government. So after I finished teaching, I opened a small shop, and Điệp looked after it while I went around to buy stock. I bought various things from others to resell, and we also made a few things ourselves to sell, such as banana cream fruit. But we were most successful buying broken refrigerators and freezers cheaply, having someone repair them and then reselling for a profit. The most popular were the ice cream freezers. Some villages did not have a proper electrician to repair machines, so I paid someone to fix the electronics, and then sold it on for a profit. I got on quite well, and made better money than when I was teaching. The Communists did not try to take over my business because it was very small, and they couldn't control everything at once. However, I sometimes thought that they intentionally cut the power to certain regions on a regular basis to prevent any private businesses from thriving. Regardless of strict controls, the government were powerless to stop the illegal trading, and eventually they let it happen to a degree because people had to survive. I was part of the black market, and running the shop gave me time to contact people to plan my escape.

Around 1977 the Communists took action to end the free market. The larger private shops were replaced by state owned shops, and everything was distributed by the state. For instance, they would say at the shop, 'today we have sugar' so everyone would queue for hours to buy sugar. Even if you didn't need sugar, you would queue and buy some anyway and then resell. So when the government sold sugar, I would buy it from the state store for £1 then sell it later on the black market for £2 or £3. In addition, the police gave each head of household a form to register all the members of the family. This family list, with an official stamp by the police, was used as a type of ID and ration card. Each week families had to show their family list and then they were given a token, which stated how much of the weekly supplies the family was entitled to. So for instance, if the state delivered cloth to a village one week, small families with four members would only get one metre of cloth while larger families might get five metres of cloth. The same with food supplies or other essentials – some families would get five kilos of rice, others ten kilos, depending on the number of family members.

That's why everything was very expensive and people had such a difficult time buying basics. The Vietnamese basics are rice, *nước mắm* (fish sauce) and salt, the production and distribution of which were all now controlled by the government. The government set up stores and gave the people tokens to use in the store, but there was never enough; an area might have 20,000 residents for instance, but the ward would have only a few stores run by the government. And of course the staff of the stores, even staff of the local authorities, would not put the goods in the shop but would instead sell the goods on the black market. So when the people came to the shop with their tokens, the staff would say 'no more'. That was life, and it was very exhausting and frightening. You never understand Communism without living in it. The main point was that the government controlled everything, and because they controlled people's stomachs, it was easy for them to get people to do what they wanted.

It did not take long for people to adapt to this system, but it was tiresome, especially all the time spent in a queue. It became a running joke. In Vietnamese, the acronym for 'Socialist Republic of Vietnam' was 'XHCN'; and a few clever individuals quickly realised that the same initials, in Vietnamese, could stand for *"make country go down the well"* or *"make you queue all day"*. And it was true, Vietnam was going down a well, and everyone was in a queue. There were so many middlemen around, and I was one of them. Buy, sell, buy, sell – and hope for a profit. If you were clever, you would hide any gold or US dollars you had and sell them secretly for a lot of money. People who wanted to buy US dollars or gold would approach you at your home, on the street, in the market and ask if you wanted to buy or sell. There were so many ways to make money, and many different ways to survive. But at a cost.

This change to the economy turned Vietnamese culture upside down. With most people working in a co-op instead of for themselves, there was no motivation to work. At factories, even in schools, the targets were crucial but people quickly discovered that if they lied on their reports, they would be praised for their success by the government. Soon everyone was lying. The new regime didn't even bring an end to the corruption in government – it only increased. In all aspects of life, there was incredible discrimination against those not part of the Communist Party. People were afraid to talk to people associated with the South Vietnam government or army. Everyone would keep their distance, even in the same family because they were so afraid of the secret police. With my background as a councillor, I found former friends and even some family would avoid me. People stopped visiting their parish priests as well, purely because they feared the secret police. People no longer felt they could trust anyone, and Vietnamese lost the ability to trust. Everyone was frightened of being linked with the resistance. The Communists' greatest weapon was fear.

Flight – III

Suat Com Toi

Suat com toi mot hom danh do
Toi con duong dau kho nhin theo
Thi nhanh nhu moi dan heo
Bon, nam daub ac dam treo len nha
Boc an mot luc sach lau
Mieng cam, mieng dat, lau bau chui nhau!

My rice portion

One day by mishap my rice portion got overturned.
In my disappointment I was still figuring out what to do
When quick as a bunch of pigs
Four, five guys, white-haired, scrambled one on top of another
And just as quickly, made a clean job of the stuff
Grumbling, cussing, and chewing all at the same time on that mixture of
rice and dirt

Nguyễn Chí Thiện, 1966

For my third escape attempt I went to Vũng Tàu, which is 100 km from Saigon. It was a very famous area near the sea, part of Biên Hòa province. Vũng Tàu was not far from us, and I had many friends there. For this trip, I went by myself. The trip was well organised and I was confident that this one would be successful. Everyone who intended to escape had to go to a small river, and then float down the river to the coast; the night was moonless, so it was very dark. There were ten of us in the boat going down the river, and behind our boat was another group of about six. The police stopped both boats. The police took everything I had with me, all my gold and money.

I was held in prison for a month. It was not a real prison, but was actually a police station with a few small temporary rooms around it with aluminium roofs. It was very hot, and we all had to sleep on the floor – there were about twenty men in one room and ten women in another room. It was overcrowded. At first none of us were allowed to contact our relatives, and we were forced to work very hard in the jungle each day, cutting down trees, preparing soil for planting, making barbed wire fencing. Each day they only fed us one bowl of rice, and sometimes they would also give us the cobs from corn after they had eaten all the kernels off. We were all so hungry that, when we were working in the jungle we would try to catch insects or rats, anything we could find to eat in order to survive.

The luckiest prisoners were the ones who were given the task of feeding the pigs. If they were very careful, they could eat some of the food given to the pigs, which were given better food than humans. The police could eventually sell the healthy pigs and make money. Prisoners, however, were useless except for labour, and any who were caught taking rice or bananas from the pigs were beaten severely.

At the end of the day when we would collapse with exhaustion, the police would call us together and make us write out our life stories. Again and again every day, similar to what they did to those in the re-education camps. The police were trying to find out our relationship with the former government or the American CIA. They also interviewed each of us over and over again - they wanted us to name others who also were involved in the planning of the escape.

That was one of the hardest times of my life. We were treated worse than the pigs. We all felt sick from the labour and lack of food, but were expected to keep working under the brutal sun.

After a couple weeks, if we pleased the police and did not cause trouble, we could finally contact our family and relatives. I was there for a month, and was lucky because my wife was able to bribe the guards for my freedom with gold we had hidden away.

Others struggled to get bribe money and so were there for much longer.

Family

If a man withdraws his mind from the love of beauty, and applies it as sincerely to the love of the virtuous; if, in serving his parents, he can exert his utmost strength; if, in serving his prince, he can devote his life; if in his intercourse with his friends, his words are sincere – although men say that he has not learned, I will certainly say that he has.

Confucius, *Analects*

Now that the country was reunited, I hoped that I could be reunited with my family in the North, especially my father, whom I hadn't seen him since I left when I was very young, because of the war. In fact, I didn't have many memories of my father except that he never shouted at me. He was a very sweet and gentle man, and was also a devout Catholic. I wanted my three children – my daughters Linh and Tâm, and my son Toàn - to know him and respect him.

I knew my father would never move and I knew I would never live in the North again. This made it very difficult for my brother's family and mine in the south to demonstrate our loyalty to our father on a daily basis. This is central to Vietnamese culture, often referred to in the west as 'filial piety'. Confucius considered filial piety an imperative moral conduct, saying we should love our parents and be respectful, polite, helpful, dutiful and obedient. But I know our father knew we loved and respected him even if we weren't there to help him on a daily basis.

Control

The Final Freedom
I am near dying, exhausted, this morning on the hill
All around me are the sounds of pickaxes
Friends, are you digging a grave for the prisoner?
Leave him alone in the sun.

Look at him, his face totally at ease
Suntanned, he seems asleep in slumber
They had wanted to confine him, to poke fun at him
He went right into it, accepting the game

For his commitment has long since been made
He buries himself in the wind, at horizon's end.

Trần Kha
(Translated by Nguyễn Ngọc Bích; War and Exile: A
Vietnamese Anthology, 1989 p204)

The secret police, naturally called the "People's Police", was a powerful force. You never knew who was part of the secret police, you did not know who was hired by the government to follow you or report on your activities. This meant that the Communists controlled our thinking, and our relationships. They even tried to control religion.

In South Vietnam after 1975, all seminaries were closed. All the religious property had been taken over by the Communists, and only churches were allowed to stay open. I remember how they took over my own Little Seminary where I had studied. By the time

I left, it had a building for the seminary and a building for the high school as well as the boarding area for the students. It had grown very large. The Communists took over the school area straightaway, but they did not take over the seminary until a few years later, in 1978.

To take over the seminary, they created a story to arrest my Father Superior. The story began with Mr Hồ Ngọc Ánh. Mr Ánh was a handicapped soldier from South Vietnam. One day he came to Bình Triệu church. He chose to pray in front of their statue of St Mary. Suddenly, Mr Ánh was cured. I don't remember what St Mary gave to him, but he was blessed with a miracle. Mr Ánh went to see my Father Superior, Father Tường, who was parish priest there and also director of the school. Father Tường was so happy for Mr Ánh, and they prayed together gratefully. They laughed and cried about it, and to mark the occasion, Father Tường took a photograph with Mr Ánh. My Father Superior was so moved by Mr Ánh's miracle, that he spoke about it in his sermon during the following Sunday Mass. The next week, the police searched the school, the seminary as well as Father Superior's room. They found the photograph of Father Tường and Mr Ánh, and took it away with them. The Communists were determined to prevent the news of the miracle from spreading, but they were too late. People throughout the parish heard about Mr Ánh's gift from the Virgin Mary, and thousands had come to the church to learn about what had happened.

The Communists asked Father Superior to get in their car. The police told the crowd at the church that it was nothing serious, and that they simply wanted to interview him at the district office. They assured everyone that he would return shortly, but of course he never returned.

Father Superior was put into prison, firstly in Saigon for about a year, and then the Communists took him to central Vietnam. This was an overcrowded prison in a small village near the jungle. At one point, a group of people from the United Nations visited some prisoners in Vietnam, and the Communists wanted to make sure they showed the international delegates that they had very good prisons with good standards of accommodation and healthy prisoners. Of course, to do this, the prison officials made careful preparations, which included keeping only the healthy-looking prisoners in the prisons that the UN officials were scheduled to visit. They took the sickly prisoners into the jungle and kept them out of sight.

The members of the UN group were allowed to interview some prisoners, and the interviews usually took place with the help of interpreters chosen by the Communists, but the Communists did not realise that Father Tường could speak English and French very well – he had studied for his PhD in Paris. My Father Superior told the UN officials the truth and said: "If you want to see what life is actually like in the prison and the real condition of the prisoners, you should return without an appointment". The international delegates did return without any advance notice, and when they toured the prison the second time, they saw the truth. They witnessed the prisoners who were only skin and bone; very weak and frail, very hungry. They observed how overcrowded each cell was, often holding around twenty individuals in a tiny space. And they saw, smelled, and felt how filthy and unsanitary the facilities were.

Of course, when the officials from the UN left, the prison guards asked the prisoners what they had told the UN officials, and they targeted the ones who spoke foreign languages and had talked with the UN, including Father Tường. He was questioned and beaten repeatedly. A few months later, he died.

Flight – IV

Tu Buoi Dang Ve

Tu buoi Dang ve ho mac toi tham
Do thong cam chi ngoi choi choc lat
Mieng thit mieng tha bo roi dua bat
Tre gia khao khat thang nam!
Con cho con meo mat tich, mat tam
Vi dau nong noi?
Chiec keo Dang dung cat tem phan phoi
Gao ngo tung lang tung can
Da cat nho tinh than cot nhuc
Manh ao nieu com, cuoc doi rua muc

Vo chang cay chong, con chang cay cha
Me hien danh om bung tong thai ra
Gio tet noi chi chuyen nguoi trong ma!
Chao oi, buon tat ca
Mat ca roi nhung ban tinh ca
Nhung dieu ru triu men thiet tha
Can bo voi tat u hoi am bu
Tre con doi chot coi lam lu
Con dau bi, dao, khang, cu?

Tieng sao dieu voi voi chieu thu
Chi con la am huong vi vu cua thoi xa cu
Luyen tiec, than van di tu luot lu
Thieu chi rung ru hoang vu
De dat vang sao cung anh sang mua thu
Dung nhung trait u lam tru!
Oi tu buoi Dang e lam chu
Kho nhuc chat chong khong the do can!
Cu Mac oi, mia mai va qua du!

Catholic with Confucian Tendencies

Con chuot ma co dip thao than
Cung ba cang bon chan
Chay khoi cai thein duong cua cu!

Since the Party's coming

Ever since the Party's coming family visits
Are reduced to a few minutes thanks to an unwritten code
Chopsticks and bowls are dropped at the mention of meat
An item dreamed of by old and young alike year after year!
Even dogs and cats have disappeared, vanished.
Why?
The scissors used by the Party to cut ration cards
Have divided rice and corn into ounces and pounds
They have also cut up our blood ties
Our clothing and rice pots, rotting our lives
Wives no longer can trust husbands, children their parents
Virtuous mothers must agree to aborting their babies
What else is there to talk about on anniversaries
of those already in the graves?
O it is all so sad
Gone are the love songs and endearing lullabies
Which have been with us since infanthood
Our children are now cripples,
not having enough to eat or wear
Let alone playing marbles, pitching coins,
spinning tops or stick-batting
The lilting kite-flute of an autumn evening
Is now only the lingering echo of a time long past
Do no complain or lament, else you all go to jail!
For there is no lack of jungle land
Turned by the yellow-star flag and the autumn light
Into historic jail sites!
Ever since the Party's coming and ruling
Misery and hardships pile high, unaccountable!
Hey Karl Marx, my old friend, that is enough!

Vũ Khánh Thành

Since given the chance, even the rats
Would be running their tails off
Out of this Paradise of yours!

Nguyễn Chí Thiện 1996 (p222)

So many people were trying to leave Vietnam that the radio and TV, all run by the Communists, announced daily that refugees were bad people, lazy people who didn't want to work under the Communist regime. The government would say that the men who tried to escape were all criminals and the women were like prostitutes. We heard this daily, but it failed to stop a mass exodus.

By this time, I had attempted to escape from Vietnam once per year between 1976 and 1979. My next attempt to escape was from Cà Mau, a village in South Vietnam at the very bottom tip of the country, the furthest distance from Biên Hòa. Some people from Cà Mau came earlier in the year to Saigon to see my sister's husband who had been stationed in that area as a soldier a long time ago. The visitors from Cà Mau told my brother-in-law that they were organising a trip.

My brother-in-law told me about the trip and was confident it would work. I approached the visitors from Cà Mau to learn more about it. They told me that if I could get five people, each paying three ounces of gold, then my family could go for free. In the end I found ten people to go with me to Cà Mau.

It took longer to get to Cà Mau from Saigon than to Rạch Giá, since we had to change buses several times – splitting up onto different buses as well – so as not to attract the attention of the police at the many checkpoints. The police were searching everyone to catch those transporting more than they were permitted to carry. If you were found bringing anything, even rice, without the proper permission, you would be arrested.

We finally met the organisers in Cà Mau around 5 pm - they took all of us - fifteen in total - to an empty room above a coffee

96

shop so we could hide until dark. The organisers instructed us to go to the local football stadium to pay our money at 9 pm. From there we would be taken by boat taxi to the ship.

After handing over the gold, the organisers went with us to the place where the taxi was supposed to be waiting for us. To get to the canoe, we had to walk through some muddy fields, and then had to take a ferry across a small river. We then resumed our walk through the muddy fields - Cà Mau was a very new town built in the delta region of the country – all below sea level. I remember it was the last day of the month, and it was very dark. We walked for almost an hour, but hadn't gone very far because it was so dark and difficult to move quickly. Suddenly, police surrounded us and asked us to hand over our gold and anything in our pockets, saying that they were going to take us back to Cà Mau.

In a flash, I remembered what had happened to the passengers in Rạch Giá, I remembered what had happened to me in Vũng Tàu, and I couldn't face going back to prison. Without thinking, I quickly walked away into the dark fields where the police – or criminals dressed as police – had surrounded our group. I was holding my son Toàn who was only eight months old. I acted on instinct, and simply carried Toàn into the rice fields where we hid.

I waited around an hour. I couldn't hear anything, and began to worry. I came out of the fields and did not see anyone. I shouted, but no one answered. I called for my wife, but there was still no answer. I became very frightened, since I did not know where I was and did not know how to get back to Cà Mau. I looked around in panic, but then I noticed a spotlight far in the distance. I trudged along the muddy fields towards the spotlight, calling for help as I moved along, and about half an hour later I came to the edge of the river. I shouted loudly and tried to run, hugging Toàn to me. There was a boat just leaving the banks of the river, so I shouted loudly, begging it to stop.

It was my wife who replied. I saw the boat turn around, and it picked us up. My wife was crying, and couldn't stop sobbing. She was in shock. She later told me that she had asked the boat to wait for me for a long time. She explained that I had gone missing with our eight-month-old baby - without milk or a blanket to stay warm. The boat owner had agreed to wait for a while, but couldn't wait any longer. They had just pulled away from the shore when, at the last minute, I appeared. She was so shaken, so frightened and now, so relieved.

My wife told me that the police had searched every member of the group, had taken all their gold and money, and had then left them to find their own way back to Cà Mau. Luckily, I was not searched and so I had some money with me. We had just enough to buy bus tickets back to Saigon. As with the Rạch Giá trip, the ten people in my group, most of them friends and relatives, blamed me.

Morals

Dat Nay

Dat nay chang co niem vui
Ngay quet mo hoi, dem chui le uot
Trai Linh, trait u nguoi di khong ngot
Nguoi ve thua thot dam ba...
Tre con doi xanh nhu tau la
Cay bua phu nu dam dang
Chon thon trang vang bong trai lang
Giay bao tu roi day mai ra
Buon tat ca
Chi cai loa vui!

There is no joy

There is no joy in this land
Where brushing off sweat during the day

One must still dry up tears at night
Where to boot camps and jails people end up unending
Only to come home two, three out of ten...
Children are green the colour of young banana leaves
While the ploughing and harrowing is left to women
The countryside is deserted of its young men
And death notices cover the thatch roofs
O everything is so sad
Only the blaring P.A system is full of joy!

Nguyễn Chí Thiện (p195)

Communism is a kind of religion, only with guns and prison. The Communists don't teach morals the way we understand them: be kind to others, help the poor, be a good person. No, the Communists taught 'fighting morals'. This was not questioned when fighting Japan, France, the USA or China, when the existence of a common 'enemy' at least gave the Communists a reason to promote fighting morals. But there was soon no one to fight, so people began to fight with each other. They would stab each other in the back. The foundation of Vietnamese society is trust; we survived for millennia by helping each other. Now, no one helped each other anymore.

The Communists also taught 'Revolutionary Morals', which included the tenets of supporting and protecting the government and the Communist regime. It became good to report on others. In religions, people would pray and try to help each other. With Communism, people had to lie and report on their friends in order to save themselves. Communists hosted 'discussion' groups in the communities, led by a Communist officer. As in the re-education camps, the local residents were expected to condemn others as 'capitalists' or anti-communist. Neighbours and friends were forced to turn against each other instead of help each other as we'd always done. Under the 'Moral of the Revolution', you were praised if you were very active. The better you were at reporting others and controlling others in your group, the more likely you were to be promoted as leader of the group.

The Communists created groups for men, groups for women and groups for children. Each group was told to watch the other, to report anything that went against the regime. This completely went against everything at the core of Vietnamese culture – trust and respect for family. For generations, Vietnamese children respected their parents. Now the children were being used to control the parents.

The Communists had many tactical ways to organise and control, to the point that no one trusted anyone and no one told the truth. This completely changed the Vietnamese mentality. I'm convinced, as Confucius said, that if a doctor makes a mistake, he kills one person; if an army general makes a mistake, he kills a small group; but if a mistake is made in the culture or religion, then it kills an entire generation. The Communist regime has killed several generations.

Resistance

In the name of Freedom and Happiness,
fighters, let us break these chains!
In the name of Freedom and Happiness,
fighters, forward march
Wait for us, darling, by our white-haired mother
As our attack force will go after the Rising Sun march!

Phan Tấn Hải
Excerpt from 'A Fighter's Song'
(Translated by Nguyễn Văn Sơn and Nguyễn Ngọc Bích; War and Exile: A Vietnamese Anthology, 1989 p220)

Thus, with the change of the currency, the reorganisation of 'enterprise', the new economic zones, the confiscation of private property, the abolition of religion, the re-education camps, the secret police, the control of travel and movement and all freedoms, the Communists changed the country. In less than a year, the country I knew was totally destroyed. It was frightening. The Communists had shattered the resources of the country and destroyed the mentality of the people. They controlled the economy, religion and social life.

But there was some resistance. I was not formally part of it, although the Communists suspected me and I secretly admired most groups who continued to stand up to the Communists. During that first year when I was teaching under the Communist regime, I received a letter from the committee of the Executive Department of the police headquarters in Biên Hòa province. The letter called me for an interview at the prison. The prison had belonged to the South Vietnamese government, but now it belonged to the Communist regime. I was taken to a small office in the prison and told to sit in one of two chairs in the room. The room was dark, and there were no windows, but there was a small light hanging from the ceiling. The table was large for the room, so when I sat across from the officer, he seemed far away.

During the interview, they asked me many questions about the time when I was councillor. I told the officer that I had fought against corruption in the South Vietnam government, demanding justice and equality, but I hid the fact that I was still a member of a political party after leaving as a councillor. I knew that if I declared that I was a member of a political party that was not Communist, I would immediately be sent to a re-education camp. It was not a secret in South Vietnam that I was a member of the non-Communist political party, but the Communists did not yet know who all the members were. Either they did not care or they were too busy to find out until now. I assumed this is why I was called in.

Instead, they asked me about my relationship with Father Trần Học Hiệu, the Catholic priest who was my teacher in the Little Seminary and who also managed the high school where I had studied. A few years after I had left the seminary, Father Hiệu joined the army chaplaincy, and then went to Paris to study for his PhD. When he returned to Vietnam, Father Hiệu taught at the university, and over the years he gained more respect from the people because of his intelligence, kindness and experience. After the Communists took over the south, Father Hiệu and a few military officers organised resistance against the Communists in the jungles of Biên Hòa province, and because of his status in the community, his resistance movement had a lot of support in the area.

The officer questioned me the whole day about my relationship with Father Hiệu. He asked again and again about the last time I met him, what we talked about, and so on.

I told him the truth. At the time I was innocent and did not understand what they were accusing me of. I told them that I saw Father Hiệu last on 1st May 1975, one day after the 'Liberation of Saigon', when we talked about the fighting the day before and our plans, but it was a simple and friendly chat, nothing special. At the end of the day, the officer showed me a leaflet with my name and signature, declaring my support for Father Hiệu's resistance movement. I denied any tie to Father Hiệu's call to stand up against the Communists. Of course in theory I supported Father Hiệu, but he never mentioned any resistance when we met in person, and when I was invited to join his group later, I felt hopeless and could not see that there was anything we could do, so I refused. My name was there on the leaflet though, and I was a bit nervous that the Communists wouldn't believe me, but I knew the truth. Although my name was on the leaflet, I never signed it, and pointed out that my signature had been forged. I knew I was innocent, but I didn't know if the Communists would believe me.

The officer released me however and let me go home and the

other teachers, my neighbours, and my family were surprised to see me again. Before I went to the interview, friends in my parish prayed for me, everyone was worried that I would not be allowed back home. The Communists, at the end of a day of repeated questions, finally told me that they knew all along that I was not involved in Father Hiệu's resistance movement. The officer told me with a smirk on his face that if they had truly suspected that I was involved, he would not have invited me to talk but would have arrested me straight away.

Father Hiệu was arrested in late 1977. His resistance group stayed active in the jungle area where there was a large population of Vietnamese who had lived in the North but moved to the South in 1954. It was a very Catholic area and deeply anti-Communist. Writings about Vietnam after the Communist victory often say there was little resistance, but I remember two big battles between Father Hiệu's resistance movement and Communist soldiers. In both of these battles, the resistance won. The Communists had to retreat, and Father Hiệu's group arrested eleven soldiers from the North Vietnamese army and five local soldiers. The resistance released the captives when Father Hiệu intervened. For the third battle, the Communists sent very large forces to surround the area, and they arrested Father Hiệu with four other members of the group.

Father Hiệu was tried in the 'People's Court'. His trial was publicly quite important because it was one of the first Court cases involving clergy after the 'liberation' of South Vietnam. The Communists allowed most of the priests of the diocese of Xuân Lộc in Biên Hòa and Saigon members of the parish committee to attend, and they wanted to prove that they had a fair Court not just to the general public, but to the large Catholic population in the area who feared what the trial would mean for religious people everywhere.

The trial was presided over by a judge appointed by the Communists, and during the trial, the prosecutor focused on two key points. Firstly, they wanted to limit the power of religious activity in general, and secondly they wanted to remind any resistance movement that to be anti-communist was to be anti-nationalist. They asked Father Hiệu, "Were you involved in politics?"

He replied humbly, with a soft voice: "There are many ways to be involved in politics. What do you mean?" The prosecutor did not like this reply so he curtly asked again: "Were you, a religious official, a priest, involved in politics?"

Father Hiệu calmly reflected. He then gently said: "Most acts and decisions could be called political. If you believe a priest's involvement in work to bring good, to bring justice to society, to strive for equality, is political, then I am politically active. If I inspire others to also work towards justice and equality, then I am a politician. But, I am not involved in any activity to take political power."

The prosecutor challenged Father Hiệu further. Father Hiệu remained calm, but he was firm when he said: "With the communist laws that limit religious activity and the role of religion in life in general, I have no way to live under a communist regime. That is a suppression of my calling. My faith is my calling and it is all that I know to do. I have no choice but to work for the freedom of religion." As he spoke, Father Hiệu did not seem worried or scared. In fact, he seemed to be at peace.

The prosecutor used this final comment as a lead into his second accusation: that to be anti-communist is to be anti-Vietnam. Father Hiệu repeated: "I cannot support a doctrine that denies freedom of religion."

He paused only for a second before continuing: "I cannot support a regime that suppresses people and that does not govern the people well or bring peace to its people. So of course, I am anti-communist."

All the priests who were there to observe the proceedings gasped in disbelief at Father Hiệu's boldness. The Court was silent for a minute then Father Hiệu continued: "I am anti-communist, but only because I *am* such a nationalist. And like others who love their country, I fight for justice and for good governance. Because I love the motherland, I fight for a government that brings peace and prosperity to the people."

The prosecutor must have realised that he was not going to get the replies he wanted. He had expected Father Hiệu to publicly renounce his involvement in the resistance movement in exchange for a more lenient sentence. So he asked Father Hiệu about his soldiers and how many were under his management. "I was only an adviser to the group," he replied.

At the end of the trial, the judge presented Father Hiệu with a confession of his crimes. The judge announced that he would be sentenced to death, but if he signed the confession, he would be pardoned and his sentence would be reduced to life in prison. But Father Hiệu refused.

"I have done nothing wrong. If I am innocent, set me free. I have no regrets about my actions."

The Party had already decided the verdict beforehand. The role of a judge under Communism is to simply read the prepared sentence as dictated by the Party. Father Hiệu was sentenced to death.

The Archbishop of Hồ Chí Minh city tried to intervene on Father Hiệu's behalf, asking the president to reduce his sentence, but to no effect. All the priests and Catholics in the area prayed for him. Father Hiệu was kept in prison for a couple years, during which time the Communists questioned him relentlessly, but Father Hiệu never gave any information about the resistance movement. He never changed his mind or faltered in his beliefs, and he never signed a confession or did anything to have his sentence reduced.

Father Hiệu was executed in 1979.

Killed

It is hard to write about this, even after so many years. My wife was heavily pregnant with our fourth child. When she began labour, I asked the next door neighbour to come to the house to watch after the children while I took Điệp to the hospital. At the hospital, they asked Điệp how many children she had. She innocently answered that we had three children.

When our son was born, the nurses took him away and we never saw him again.

The Communists had a policy that families couldn't have more than two children and we had already exceeded that.

I don't have the words to describe how that impacted us. We have never forgotten our son, nor have we forgotten the State that so coldly killed him.

Flight – V

If you really want everything, then give up everything.

Lao Tzu

After the fourth attempt to escape, I almost lost hope. However, my desperation to flee only grew after what happened to us. I didn't expect to try a fifth time, but my cousin Thien[3] was organising an escape. He was a civil engineer, but the Communists, who wanted him to improve the irrigation system in the Trà Vinh

---

[3] Name has been changed to protect identity

province, had asked him to change and become an agricultural engineer instead. He knew Trà Vinh province really well – his mother had lived there for twenty years. Thien's mother was my father's sister, and I used to watch him when he was a baby. Later, I used to visit my auntie often, especially when I attended seminary in Vinh Long, which was very close to Trà Vinh. My family was very close to Thien's family, and I trusted him totally. Also, his timing was amazing.

By this time, the Communists had been moving down their lists of people in the south who needed to be 're-educated'. The initial targets had been all of the high-ranking officials from the South Vietnamese government, police or military as well as intellectuals. In the immediate aftermath of the fall of Saigon, the Communists ignored people like me. But now, the Communists were going through their second selection – arresting whoever had influence with the people.

I shouldn't have been surprised when the police came knocking on my door – I assumed they would figure out eventually that I was once a local councillor. Still, when I saw the uniform on the other side of the door, my heart began to race. If a Communist saw any of the local anti-Communist posters I had up discreetly around my house I'd be arrested instantly. I yelled for Linh to run and hide my posters before opening the door. When I saw who it was I relaxed a little, it was one of my former students.

"Good afternoon Thầy Thành. I cannot stay long, I have urgent news. In fact, I shouldn't even be here. If they find out, I'll lose my job. Or worse."

From the look of fear in his eyes, I knew that he meant the Communists, and my heart started racing. I had no idea what his visit could mean. "What is wrong? Do you have news about someone in my family? Is everyone okay?"

"No, nothing like that. It's about you. The provincial police have asked for your file."

I was stunned. The Communists wanted my file with the local police to be taken to the headquarters of the provincial police. It could only mean one thing.

"Thầy Thành. I had to warn you." He looked around as if checking that no one was listening. His eyes were full of fear and panic. "You will be arrested very soon."

I sat in silence letting the news wash over me. I must have sat there for a while because my student, the policeman, shook me as he said: "I have to go. I can't let them see me here. You must run. You must escape – go somewhere. You cannot stay here." And then, after making sure he wasn't being watched, he left.

I knew I did not have much time. I went to Saigon immediately, and for the moment left my family in Biên Hòa. I wanted to be in Saigon because it was a bigger city and thus would be easier to hide. I could blend in with others on the street who were victims of the Communist regime – the streets, parks, even cemeteries had many people who had been kicked out of their property, fired from their jobs, and had nowhere to go. I was too afraid to contact my sister who lived in Saigon – the police would know to go there first to find me, so I stayed with one friend one night, another friend the next night.

I eventually contacted my brother-in-law in Saigon. He had just spoken to Thien and learned that he was planning an escape trip. I contacted Thien and we agreed to meet. He told me that he needed more people to join his trip: if I helped him to find five more, I would not have to pay as much for my travel, and because I was trusted family, he said I could pay him if I succeeded in escaping and living abroad. Thien told me to hurry, as the ship was leaving the next night.

I had less than a day to decide what I wanted to do and find someone to join us. If I did decide to go with Thien, I would have to catch a bus from Saigon early the next morning to ensure that I made it to Trà Vinh in time for the group's planned departure. I had met Thien in the early afternoon and time was running out.

The first thing I needed to do was to contact my wife and tell her to get everything ready to go. I was so rushed, but I needed to be careful. I did not think it was safe for me to go to the village so I got someone to tell my wife to meet me in the market in Biên Hòa. When she arrived she had an anxious look in her eye – she and I had not been able to speak for a couple of days and she was worried. She was also anxious because she knew I must have news for her. I had no time to explain in detail so I simply stated, "Thien has organised a trip and I must go with him."

My wife shook her head. The concerned look in her eyes disappeared. I saw a glimmer of panic that was quickly replaced with pure determination. "No. No more."

Điệp was too frightened, and could not face another attempt again. "No. Not with the baby. I can't do it. Also, we don't have enough money to keep wasting on escape attempts." She had made up her mind that she was not going to put herself or the younger children through the panic of trying to escape again.

"It's Thien. I know this one is a real trip. I know this one will be successful, he'll help make sure we are safe." I said these words even though I could tell from the look in her eyes that she was not going to change her mind. She had made her decision: "No."

"But I have to go. The police are looking for me and I cannot face another visit to prison. I have no idea how long they'd keep me. Your brother died in a re-education camp. I can't let them send me there."

Điệp nodded her head. Then she suddenly said: "Take Linh with you. I'll stay here in our house with Tâm and the baby." I knew she was right. Linh was big and strong enough to handle the journey to Trà Vinh and, if we were successful, I'd have one of my children with me.

The decision was made. I had to rush again – only a few minutes to get ready before I needed to get back to Saigon. I asked my wife to get Linh and bring her to me straightaway. While waiting in the market for my wife and Linh, I met Mr Nguyễn Quốc Bao and his family. He had four or five children. I knew Mr Bao well – he was a teacher with me in Biên Hòa, and he was also an electrician – he often repaired freezers for me that I would resell.

Mr Bao was desperate to escape from Vietnam. Like me, he had tried to leave the country several times and failed, but his latest attempt had the police chasing him. Mr Bao had been planning that trip with some people he had met through work colleagues. His group decided that they needed a gun for the ship, to protect all of the passengers from Thai pirates and he was in charge of finding the gun. He brought one to the final planning meeting so that he could hand it over to the head organiser. Just as he was handing over the gun, the police barged in. They arrested most of the organisers, but Mr Bao managed to escape. When I next ran into him, he was getting his family out of Biên Hòa - the police were looking for him and considered him to be dangerous because he had been found with a gun. Mr Bao and his family all instantly agreed to come with me to Trà Vinh the next morning.

I was too rushed and too anxious to be amazed at how everything seemed to be falling into place. It was an auspicious day. My wife arrived with Linh and the other children. I'm glad we did not have long to say goodbye, because it was too painful to contemplate that I might never see them again. I think that deep in my heart I did not believe that I would actually succeed.

Linh and I met Mr Bao and his family and we all followed Thien to Trà Vinh. We travelled together, and we did not attract too much attention because Mr Bao's wife and children were with us. The police always stopped men who travelled alone together. They always feared that when three men were talking together, they were planning something against the Communists.

At Trà Vinh, we all stayed at the house of Thien's mother, my auntie. That night, Thien showed us all how to dress like the local villagers, told us how the villagers spoke when in town and so on. He wanted to make sure we did not attract attention to ourselves.

Everyone planning to escape on Thien's trip had, as usual, to find a way down the river to the coast, and by lunchtime, we were all in small boat taxis, the size of canoes, so there were only two to three in each boat. I was in a boat with Mr Bao - his wife and children were in another. Linh was with another woman and her

110

child. All our boats were scattered across the large, wide river that ran through the jungle near the beach. The women and children were taken down the river part way to a dry area where they could hide, but it was more dangerous for us men – police and officials were much harsher with men. So we floated further down river to some small tributaries and hid among the trees. All of us took detours and side tributaries to avoid the patrols. We were all in place by 3pm.

I will never forget sitting in that boat with Mr Bao. We waited for seven hours, literally hugging the trees along the river to stay hidden in our place. The trees were as thick as our arm and were the kind that could survive being almost totally submerged when the tide came in. This meant, at high tide, we were actually up in the top of a tree. Whenever someone travelled along the river – since we did not know if they were Communists or police – we had to quietly hide our boat and, clinging to the tree trunk, submerge ourselves under the water to make sure we weren't seen. Once the boat had passed, we could stand back atop the branches, clinging to the tree as the tide came in and out. When the sun went down, it was so cold standing on top of these trees with the water lapping at our feet, and we were so hungry. We had no rest the entire time.

Mr Bao and I were so well hidden that the organisers could not find us when it was time to go to the ship. They were coasting along the river with only a candle, trying to find everyone.

"Thành, where are you?" I shook my head at Mr Bao so he wouldn't respond. I wasn't sure who it was and was not going to risk being caught by the police again.

"Pssst, where are you?" they called out again. I was still too frightened to answer.

"Thành, are you still there? We want to pick you up…" Mr Bao was ready to reveal our boat, but he did not know how bad it was in prison. I wasn't ready. But whoever they were, their little boat kept trawling along the river for a long time, calling for us.

"Thành, it's me. We met this afternoon. I'm here to take you to the ship. I promise, it is I, Thien's friend. I swear it. Speak out!"

Only when he swore that he was Thien's friend did I decide he might be telling the truth. So I called out in a loud whisper: "We are here", and waved so that he could see us.

We joined the group at the edge of the jungle by the beach, and we all remained hidden. It was the end of the month so it was pitch black by midnight and very hard to see even those sitting nearby. We were waiting for the main boat to come, and when it arrived we crept out into the water and climbed into another boat. We were almost there.

We set out to sea, I assumed to rendezvous with a large ship that would take us out to international waters. But then I realised we were in that 'ship' already. It had two engines, but they were small Yamaha engines meant for canoes, not for a large ship setting out for the deep ocean. I was too anxious to be angry that Thien had lied to me when he told me it was a ship with a very powerful engine. It was too late to turn back. Doing so would surely attract the attention of any police in the area, so I decided to choose my fate on the sea instead of voluntarily going back to prison.

CHAPTER SEVEN

Sea

Au clair de la lune
Mon ami Pierrot
Flimsy is my boat
And immense is the sea

O give me some fire
And give me some love
My candle is out
And wearied is my soul...

In front lies the sea
And behind the woods
Demons all around
And tempests above
To nowhere I row
A speck on the ocean
Leaving my country
Home and family
You have a large boat
In the bright moonlight
Your sail spells Hope
Have you room for me?

Vũ Kiến
Excerpt from "In the Moonlight Bright"
(Translated by Nguyễn Ngọc Bích; War and Exile: A
Vietnamese Anthology, 1989 p216)

Our first concern was to cross the break from Trà Vinh, then continue out until we entered international waters. We used both the engines on full power to get out of sight of any police on land and to get beyond the control of any sea patrols. Everyone had to lay perfectly still to avoid detection. We travelled at the engine's top speed for a couple of hours until one of the engines broke.

The ship was only nine metres long and two metres wide, and when below deck, only the small children could straighten their legs. There was no room to really spread out. When sitting on the deck, I could easily reach out and touch the water with my hand. This was a fishing boat designed to take a few men out to sea for a couple of days, not forty-one men, women and children for two weeks.

During our first couple days at sea, we made everyone hide below deck – we wanted to look like an ordinary fishing boat with only a few men on board. At the end of the first day, we saw a large ship, but it was too far in the distance for us to tell which country it was from. So the 'captain' of the boat, Mr Hoàng Kim Bắc – a man who had been in the South Vietnam navy and had just recently been released from a re-education camp – decided we should not try to attract their attention in case it was a government patrol ship. After a few days in international waters we saw other big business ships, and we waved a white flag – actually a large white sheet – but no one stopped to rescue us.

So we floated at sea. Once we were out in international waters, everyone was allowed to come on deck and walk around. This lifted everyone's spirit. The children seemed to have fun, as if we were on an exciting adventure. I felt it too. We were headed to the unknown, but I was actually a bit excited. I had left the coast and was floating towards freedom. I think most of the others felt that way too. *"Give me liberty or give me death"* – that was our mantra, at least in the beginning.

The organisers had provided some water, petrol, rice, and other basic supplies. But we were really low on food and water by the third day so we had to ration the food to make sure the children were fed. Many of the women and children started to weaken and grow sick and weary. Everyone's hopeful anticipation changed to fear and worry. A few women began crying, shaking, but on the whole, we accepted the situation – we knew what we were getting in to. I passed the time by helping the captain try to repair the second engine, using my pants – my only spare cloth - to clean the engine parts. At this point, there was nothing anyone could do except wait.

Everyone was hungry and thirsty. I felt weak and dizzy but tried to stay alert in the hope that we would spot a ship that would rescue us. We floated, hungry, literally dying of thirst, unable to rest.

Rescue

A prayer for land
Lost in the tempests
Out on the open seas
Our small boats drift.
We seek for land
During endless days and endless nights.
We are the foam
Floating on the vast ocean.
We are the dust
Wandering in endless space.
Our cries are lost
In the howling wind.

Without food, without water
Our children lie exhausted
Until they cry no more.
We thirst for land
But are turned back from every shore.
Our distress signals rise and rise again
But the passing ships do not stop.

How many boats have perished?
How many families lie beneath the waves?
Lord Jesus, do you hear the prayer of our flesh?
Lord Buddha, do you hear our voice
Form the abyss of death?
O solid shore,
We long for you!
We pray for mankind to be present today!
We pray for land to stretch its arms to us!
We pray that hope be given us
Today, from any land.

A poem written by an unknown Vietnamese person in a refugee camp in Hong Kong
(as printed in *The Boat People: An 'Age' Investigation* 1979, p50)

We floated for nearly three or four more days.

Finally, after nine days at sea, we saw a spotlight in the distance. We tried to make our way to it. Even if the ship was Vietnamese or from another communist country, we did not care - we simply needed to be rescued. Luckily one engine was still working. We moved very slowly towards the ship, and some of us men used paddles to try to move the boat faster, but it was very frustrating because it seemed that despite our efforts we were not getting any closer. Then suddenly, like something out of a movie, we found ourselves floating alongside a huge freighter. It was like a city skyline at night; a skyscraper looming over us with all the windows lit up. Linh woke up and I remember her amazement. She didn't know what it was at first and she exclaimed, "Look at all the fairy lights!"

We reached the ship sometime after 11 pm, called out for help, and someone finally responded. It was 17th June 1979 – I don't think I had ever felt such relief. We asked them to rescue us, and after a while, the captain - I still remember him clearly, his name was Ross - agreed to send down provisions of water and food to our boat. This was my first taste of English food – they sent down crackers and English apples. I remember Linh being so excited by the apples – so much larger than Vietnamese apples.

Ross informed us that he was captain of the *Ashford*, a British ship. I was so grateful. We floated next to the *Ashford* for a couple of days. They continued to make sure we had enough food and water but wouldn't bring us on board. I'm not sure why. I know they were busy making radio contact with others, probably government officials trying to figure out what to do with us. Then a storm began to gather. Ross acknowledged it was going to be a big storm but didn't do anything. When the rain and wind began to pick up, women and children were given permission to climb on board the *Ashford*. Our small boat was rocking back and forth so hard that men from the *Ashford* came down to carry the children up. I looked up and saw Linh was safe but I could see she was terrified because by this point the wind was violently tossing our boat around in the waves. All of us men were still on deck with waves crashing over the side. When the crew from the *Ashford* realised the storm was only getting worse, they finally allowed the men on board as well. The long climb up to the ship is a blur to me now. I don't know how I made it up without falling into the dark water. The next morning when I looked down into the water, I saw only a few remains of our boat.

PART TWO

UNITED KINGDOM

CHAPTER EIGHT

Pirates

Ko Kra

In the night, straining ears hear the call
"Ko Kra! Ko Kra! — foreboding phrase —
Lights in the darkness stir action and sighs;
At corners of eyes, tears swell and spill.

"Ko Kra Island!" What name can be more horrible
For this single day of infamy?
How many more mangled bodies has Ko Kra
Than Bình Long together with An Loc and Plei Me?

Bodies of children, old men and women,
Mothers, teenage boys and girls —
This one beheaded, that other disemboweled,
One handless here, one there dismembered!

Survivors live with spirits anguished,
Life's silken threads knotted and snarled;
Young girls carry the offspring of strangers'
Wives cannot meet their husbands' eyes.

The peaceful sea writhes in sudden storm;
A vicious gang attacks at will
Looting, raping, plundering madly —
When will the blood tide ever be clean?

Ko Kra answers to no one's control;

Victims are victims still
O how can people sit watching idly
Such horrible shame and misery?

Rage at Chinh, Duan and Dong
For launching this murderous wave,
Enjoying the silver and gold of the South
By pushing people to sea by the thousands.

Over half become food for the fishes;
Another third sails to Ko Kra's doom
Their blood is still red! They still feel wounds!
Doesn't anyone else? Is all conscience gone?

Please think a moment of these innocent;
Share their agony and shame
White are their hands but black their fate!
Then rise and wipe out the pirates!
Offer, thereafter, a prayer, a tear.

Vĩnh Liêm
(Translated by R.S. Carlson and Lê Kinh Kha; War and Exile,
1989 p218-219)

On the *Ashford*, they gave us clean clothes and let us rest. Day by day we felt better and stronger. I know now how incredibly lucky we were to all make it alive: some foreign business ships rescued Vietnamese Boat People at sea, but many other refugees died from hunger or thirst, while others died at the hand of Thai pirates. 1978-1979 was the time when the world witnessed the worst and most frequent activity of Thai pirates. The increase in pirating corresponded to the increase in people fleeing Vietnam on boats carrying all their wealth with them.

After a few days resting at sea, we noticed a boat full of

refugees floating near us. When the *Ashford* got closer, I realised it was one of these 'unofficial ships' with around 800 ethnic Chinese on board. The boat was surrounded by four pirate ships. People on the boat begged the *Ashford* to rescue them, but there were too many to rescue. So while Ross radioed for back up and assistance, the crew gave each of the men from my boat a piece of wood and told us to sit on the rail of the *Ashford* and not let anybody from the 'unofficial ship' board. A few aeroplanes arrived and flew around the boat, chasing off the pirates. Then the *Ashford* said they would accompany the 'unofficial ship' to Malaysia.

Another boat saved by the *Ashford*. Without the *Ashford's* help, the pirates would have devoured the boat full of ethnic Chinese. Even outnumbered, the pirates would terrorise and pillage the refugees. The pirates, often assumed to be Thai 'fishermen', were barbaric and very brutal. They would rape and kill indiscriminately – usually tying up the men and then stealing everything on them. I heard about a man who had his finger chopped off because the pirate couldn't easily take his wedding ring. Then the pirates would rape the women, usually in front of the children. Those who protested were thrown overboard. I am a friend of a family that is still traumatised by the time their boat was stopped by pirates. The daughter and mother were raped in front of the father and others on the ship. They were still in shock when they arrived in the UK. I've also heard of families whose daughters were abducted from their ships, presumably to be sold into prostitution.

The *Ashford* remained at sea for a couple weeks before accompanying the Chinese ship to land and at the time, I didn't know why they didn't sail immediately. The *Ashford* was not a commercial ship, and the people on it seemed to be studying something under the sea. I assumed it was a secret project - maybe finding a sunken ship from WWII? But we never dared to ask. Today, I assume that the delay was because of the political tensions at the time. As I mentioned earlier, 1978-1979 was a time of great exodus from Vietnam and the neighbouring countries were turning away the refugees. Many large ships from around the world were ordered to stop rescuing Boat People and Singapore began turning boats full of refugees away from their waters.

Eventually, the *Ashford* was given permission to accompany the Chinese ship to Malaysia. For some reason, the *Ashford* didn't accompany the boat as far as Singapore, where we were taken. I remember waiting off the coast for between three and five days, while I waited desperately for paper to write letters to my family to tell them I was safe. The crew of the *Ashford* was waiting for the outcome of negotiations between Singapore and the British embassy in Singapore where the officials were still debating whether or not they should allow us to land.

Because a British ship picked us all up, we knew we would all be going to Great Britain. The UK was not really involved in the Vietnam War, and originally did not feel compelled to reach out to those of us fleeing Vietnam, but the plight of the Boat People received significant coverage in the media, raising sympathy among many in the UK. Margaret Thatcher had just been elected to power. Like her friend Ronald Reagan, she was deeply anti-communist and thus naturally loved the idea that people were fleeing communism for democratic freedom. But no official programme to assist the Vietnamese Boat People emerged until the *Ashford* and *Sibonga* headed towards Singapore or Hong Kong after picking up a large number of Boat People like me. The Singapore government told the British government the ships could not land unless the UK agreed to take the refugees to Britain.

On 3rd July, when the *Ashford* finally landed at Singapore, I met several people I knew from Biên Hòa who had been rescued by *Ill de Lumiere*, a ship from the Netherlands. I was grateful that we made it to Singapore, happy to get off the ship and know that Linh and I were safe. We stayed in a refugee camp, cramped with other families, and Linh was often off running around with friends of her age. She adapted almost instantly to our new 'home', whereas I, on the other hand, found it a bit harder. I adapted quickly to the day-to-day routine of the camp, which was easy for me. What was harder was dealing with the unknown. I wasn't sure how long Linh and I would have to stay there, and wondered when I would be reunited with my family.

Camp

I remember him when he would tear the skies, push mountains.
A man, he crossed the country in its defence.
Suddenly, he was no more than a refugee.
In the camp he stood in line for meals as if he were in a dream.

Cao Tần

Excerpt from "A Friend Asked to Return"
(Translated by James Banerian; War and Exile: A Vietnamese Anthology, 1989 p208-209)

We were all given accommodation in a refugee camp in Singapore called Hawkins Road Camp, named after the street where it was located. While there, the refugees rescued by Norway or the Netherlands were visited by representatives from those embassies. They also received language classes and were told what to expect when they arrived in their new homes. There was not much sign of the British however. Representatives from Britain only came once to do some paperwork, and then we didn't see them again until the day they flew us to London, after totally ignoring us for three months. Now that I am here and have an insight into how the government works I can laugh about it, but at the time I was so curious about what was going on. Were they going to let us go or not?

It did not really feel like a refugee camp, and was not like what you would see on television with row upon row of tents. We stayed in normal houses hired by the UNHCR on a temporary basis, with each house holding ten people. It didn't take too long to get used to that – the Vietnamese always have an 'open door', but to live 24 hours with several different families took some adjustment. But Linh played around with friends, and the children easily got on. We were free to come and go as we wanted, as long as we were back by curfew. And we could cook for ourselves. The UNHCR gave each refugee about five Singapore dollars a day so we could buy basic supplies. We also received old clothes, used pots and pans for cooking and so on, donated to us by the local people. Some even generously donated medicine as well. A local Catholic priest visited us and on Sunday and said Mass for anyone who was interested.

I volunteered as camp leader for two months, which kept me occupied, so the time flew by. I would help out with the new arrivals as needed, sometimes visiting a new ship with refugees sitting at the port. I did a lot of translating for officials as well. Then I was given the date Linh and I would go to the UK, and suddenly time seemed to stop. I guess it was because I was so excited. I knew that the day we landed in the UK would be the day when we would finally be able to start our new life in a free country.

So I quit my post as a camp leader and got a job locally doing cleaning or building work. This was what most people did. I earned about $10 a day and saved the money to buy basic things before coming to England. I bought clothes – I wanted to have a proper shirt and trousers. I also bought a few small things like a camera, shaver, and a rice cooker. I did not think there would be rice cookers in London.

After three months, Father Điểm landed in Singapore. Some people talked about him around the camp, saying he was not a real priest because they saw him get drunk after he arrived. He did not look like a typical priest, it is true. He was very slim, only skin and bones, but they did not know him like I did. I knew he got drunk because he was celebrating his escape. He had just escaped death.

Father Điệm was a few years older than me. He was a parish priest in Đà Lạt. In 1973, the North and the South of Vietnam agreed to a ceasefire, and under this agreement troops and civilians were to stay where they were. If they were in the North, in the territory of the National Front, they were supposed to stay in the North, if in the South, the territory of the Republic of Vietnam (ROVN) they were supposed to stay in the South. That is why both the North and South tried to get as much territory as possible, and both tried to expand. Father Điệm was in the area of Đà Lạt – his parish was on the border of South Vietnam and the National Front, and he cooperated with the local authority to try to expand the South Vietnam government's area of influence. When the Communists took over in 1975, Father Điệm was sentenced to death, but the officials did not know where to find him. They announced his death sentence without an arrest or trial.

As soon as the Communists 'liberated' Saigon, Father Điệm knew he would be in trouble so he immediately went into hiding. He tried to escape fourteen times and each time he failed he had to go back into hiding.

I was with Father Điệm for ten days, and then Linh and I came to the UK. In the end, I was only in Singapore for three months.

I had images of what the UK would be like in my mind, of course. When I was in high school we learned about the geography of the world, so we naturally discussed the UK. And we learned about Shakespeare and the history of Great Britain. But in the camp I wondered what it would be like to live there and to start a new life. I had an impression of the French and Americans because of their time in Vietnam, but not the British. My first interaction with the British was on the ship that picked us up at sea. Those men were friendly and helpful, and this kept me optimistic.

While waiting in the camp for my departure date, what excited me most was the freedom. We had just passed through a horrendous and unbearable time with the war and then found, after

1975, that our future was unknown. I had lived in constant fear, since the police could stop us at any time and arrest us without a court order, without a reason. This happened day after day to many of my friends and I feared it would happen to me. Now I knew that I no longer had to live in fear.

CHAPTER NINE

Arrival

please be calm my dear even though there are many injuries
welcome the road ahead
a grain of rice is divided in half,
homelands night is wrought with pain
the country is unified but ever separated
mother still sits with the lamp in darkness in that direction
bent-backed father and brother toil in deep jungles
among commendations concealing crimes
peace, happiness to eternity

the road we go is still indistinct and distant
is weary humanity aware of this
though separated from our homeland but not detached
promises that on our return the rain and wind will abate

why is there separation from the depths of my heart
the night is forlorn
Country already parted

of those remaining, who's alive, who's lost
lingeringly flickering a late star
the holy sword sharpened in maternal eyes for a thousand nights in the
past
country lost, you children have to liberate it

a million souls unite to form a torch
history majestically blazes
from now on you are the migratory heron
carrying the warm blood of thousand years the ancestral Lac bird
your soul adrift, still reluctant to part with the homeland
freedom spreads out immensely

Nguyễn Đức Bạtngàn
Excerpt from *Sea Diary* (Nhật Ký Biển)
Translated by Thanh Quang, Indonesia, 1979 – published
online: http://www.saigonline.com/ndbn/)

When we boarded the plane that would take us to England, we joked that at least this time we had proper clothes to wear when we arrived in England, unlike when we arrived in Singapore only wearing our short trousers.

The government appointed three charities to run the Vietnamese refugee reception and resettlement programme. The British Council for Aid to Refugees (BCAR) ran the reception centres located in the south: one in Sopley, Bournemouth and one in Kensington, London. Refugees picked up by the *Ashford* or the *Sibonga* stayed in these camps.

My friend Lockhart worked at the reception centre in Kensington – in the middle of London's West End, on Kensington Church Street. He told me that it was once a military barracks, but then the government leased the property to a company who opened a student hostel on the premises. The UK had very little time to find a place to house the Vietnamese refugees, so they terminated the lease with the student hostel. Lockhart said the accommodation was horrible – it was dirty and there were rats, but the location was good. He said that within a week of arriving, refugees were on the London Underground going to China Town and Soho. The refugees became independent very quickly.

I did not go to Kensington Barracks, but was instead taken to Sopley Reception Centre, located in a former RAF base. Sopley was not what I expected. I thought everything in the UK was modern, made of steel and shiny metal – especially places built by the military. But Sopley was located in the middle of a flat field, and a fence surrounded row after row of square wooden houses. Each house, which actually looked more like a hut, was identical to the next. I think they were built during WWII, and they were very old and run down. Before we arrived the place had been completely abandoned, and the only reminder of the military was the discarded radar listening station. It was desolate.

When I arrived, I was amazed to have several friends greet me having been rescued by the *Sibonga*. Most of the people at Sopley were refugees from South Vietnam. This group heard about our arrival and came to the coach to welcome us. It was a momentous occasion, and it was such a comfort to see familiar faces in this strange new land. My friends took me to their rooms and cooked me a nice meal.

At Sopley, we were all given food that we could cook ourselves, but most nights, Linh and I were invited to a friend's hut for a meal. That week I visited friends, attended English classes, and some local residents donated tickets so I attended my first musical concert. My first Saturday at Sopley, we organised a Mass with a British priest and other Catholics in the reception centre, but mostly I rested. I was relieved that I was finally allowed to stop looking over my shoulder.

Reception

Then the Home Office opened Thorney Island Reception Centre in October 1979. After a week at Sopley, I was appointed as a fieldworker and moved to Thorney Island, a disused Royal Navy Fleet Air base, where I stayed for three years. It had been opened to house the refugees from Hong Kong, and it was the biggest reception centre in the UK, able to house hundreds of refugees.

To get to Thorney Island, we had to cross a causeway from the mainland. We passed rows of terraced housing and a school before getting to the runway. On the other side of the runway was the airbase, which had a very large central building surrounded by housing for staff and families. The central building, once the officers' mess hall, had a large main hall for dining, a canteen, and a large red recreation room with table tennis. One wing had classrooms where we held English classes, and there was also a gym, as well as a squash court – but that was only used by the English staff.

The rest of the main building was given over to accommodation which consisted of small rooms with bunk beds. These once held an officer or two junior officers, but now each room held an entire family. When full, the main building housed around four hundred and fifty refugee families. At the end of each hall were the shared toilets and showers. It wasn't long before every single toilet seat on the premises was broken or missing. This really confused the English staff, until they realised that the Vietnamese, most of whom had never used a western style toilet, climbed up onto the seat and squatted on it.

Streets of houses – formerly the officers' married quarters – surrounded the central building. Each of these three bedroom houses accommodated up to twelve refugees (one large family or several small families). Then the government closed Kensington Barracks, and had to open more houses on Thorney Island to accommodate the refugees who had been housed in Kensington, expanding the total capacity to seven hundred and thirty. This group from Kensington had the hardest time adjusting to Thorney Island. They had such a shock, moving from central London to a remote military base on the coast in Chichester, near Portsmouth. They went from being in the middle of everything, to a place where the nearest village or shop was three miles away. Instead of the late running underground tube and trains, they could now only access an hourly bus service that ended at 6.30 pm.

The feeling of isolation for everyone was worst in the winter when the wind would tear through the Centre and chill us to our bones. I had never experienced such cold before in my life. We were free to come and go, but it was easy to forget this. We were on an island. There was security, and barriers surrounded the premises. For some Vietnamese it felt like a prison; it felt controlled. The guards employed by the Ministry of Defence were bossy, wore intimidating uniforms and some were quite racist.

My first assignment at Thorney Island was to greet new families at Heathrow Airport. I was there to welcome them to the UK and guide them back to Thorney Island. A few of them would run up and give me a big hug; they were so grateful and relieved. I could sympathise with each family member. They were so physically and emotionally exhausted from the long flight, yet anxious to settle into their new life. We were from different parts of the country, but we all experienced the same storm of feelings upon arrival.

But there was one noticeable difference between my friends and I who had been in camps in Singapore, and those who stayed in Hong Kong: luggage. I was only in Singapore for a few months and earned barely enough to send home to my family. Linh and I arrived in the UK with only a few bags of new clothes and other items such as a rice cooker. But each family arriving from Hong Kong had been there for a long time, sometimes for up to two or three years. They had worked hard in Hong Kong and had earned a lot of money, so each family had lots of very, very heavy luggage when they arrived, bringing over things like stereos, videos, and televisions in addition to the rice cookers. Everything!

Then the chaos would begin. We'd gather the luggage and get people to the correct coach. Not everyone on the plane from Hong Kong was going to Thorney Island. Some were expected to go to Sopley while others were to go to reception centres in other parts of the UK, so I had to help find 'our' residents and help others to find the right group to follow. It was hard when family or friends were separated. It didn't happen very often, but occasionally a family would be split between different reception centres. They'd usually be reunited within a week, but they never believed us and were very upset. Once I had 'our' group, we'd begin the struggle to fit all of their luggage onto the coaches.

The drive from Heathrow Airport to Thorney Island was always a disappointment for them. They did not want to leave London. They were not happy to see us drive into the endless countryside. They would say, "Oh, we are going to the countryside. How can we live here like this?" This reaction seems odd to Westerners, but refugees from Vietnam, especially North Vietnam, prefer the city instead of the countryside. Under the Communist regime, people in the countryside had a very difficult time labouring in the fields and struggling with extreme poverty. Under the Communist system, people learned quickly that a city, especially the capital, is a better place to live because those who live in a major city usually have more options for survival. So, when the refugees found themselves carried into the countryside, they imagined more poverty, more hardship, more struggles like they had just left. The families assumed that they'd have to stay in the countryside for the rest of their life in the UK, working in the fields. So I had to explain again, that the Reception Centre was only temporary until suitable accommodation was found, which would usually be in a town or city.

Waiting

All changes, even the most longed for, have their melancholy; for what we leave behind us is a part of ourselves; we must die to one life before we can enter another.

Anatole France

For the residents, life in the Reception Centre was a waiting game. Each family stayed at Thorney Island until permanent housing could be found for them which made the interview with the resettlement team one of the key events at the Centre. Before and after the interview, families had the freedom to fill their time as they wanted.

Each new family settled into the daily routine easily. There was a canteen, with kitchen staff who cooked the meals. It was just like the army. The families had to bring in their own plates or cups and they could eat the meal in the main dining room. But one of the key elements of family life in Vietnam is eating together as a family, so what usually happened was that the kids would collect the food from the canteen and they'd all eat on the floor in their own rooms.

The canteen usually served Chinese food – steamed rice and stir-fry. But because it was mass catered, it wasn't as good as a home cooked meal, and no one really wanted the food. Most families wanted to cook for themselves, so during the Saturday trip to Portsmouth, everyone went straight to the Chinese market to access foods that were similar to those found in Vietnam. Our food is central to our identity and our sense of well-being. Everyone worked hard to recreate food that would seem authentically Vietnamese.

Cooking in the rooms was not allowed, but everyone did it. They'd make their own cooking appliance by using an electric ring from a stove or old hot pot on top of a tin can. Then they'd fix a wire (usually exposed) to the ring and plug it in. The staff were so upset when they'd find these, as they were such a fire hazard, but every time the staff threw away a home made cooking ring, the family could make another and keep on cooking.

The weekly trips to Portsmouth were not just for food. Each resident at the camp received clothing vouchers from the government. This was so that the newly arrived refugees could buy basic supplies, and all of us, even those who came from Hong Kong, needed a few things to help us prepare us for the British winter such as jumpers, jackets, rain gear, boots – equipment we never had to worry about before. As staff, we would take a coach full of refugees to the local discount clothing store and let them shop, but this caused local resentment. They would see the refugees coming out of the store with bags of clothing and accuse the government of being too soft and generous. So, to make sure the new arrivals did not buy anything 'inappropriate' for a 'poor refugee', and that only those who were destitute received a clothing voucher, the staff had to interview the refugees and ask them what they already had and what they needed. The interviews were very detailed: "Do you have any money?", "Do you have any socks?", "How many pairs of underpants do you have?" and so on. The refugees quickly learned that if they were honest, they would not get a voucher at all or only get a small amount, so they began lying.

Between the shared meals and weekly shopping trips, staff at the Centre organised other activities for the refugees. We offered English classes. Next to obtaining accommodation, one of the most important things for the residents was to learn English. The Centre offered four hours of classes a day, which should have been helpful, but none really became very good at speaking English while at the Centre, because they rarely had the opportunity to practice with native English speakers. They did not get to apply what they learned in class because they were too isolated. Refugees housed in resettlement camps in or near larger cities and towns may have received less formal class instruction, but their English was usually much better by the end of their stay because they had more opportunity to practice.

Each newly arrived family had to attend a health check and be interviewed by staff to learn about any special needs which would help staff identify individuals who needed to access special services. This process helped many refugees who were unable to get the right care in Vietnam. The one I remember most was Lục An. He became blind when an American bomb exploded near him. He was eight or nine years old when it happened. In Vietnam, he had not received any formal education, but when he arrived at Thorney

Island in his late teens, specialist teachers were able to work with him. In the end, he spoke better English than the others at Thorney Island because of the special needs teaching methods they used. He was very happy. Lục An became a very good pianist and also learned how to repair pianos as well. And now he is very successful, living on his own and earning quite a bit of money.

There was not much structure to the day for the adults. The children had school, and my friend was in charge of youth activities, organising play schemes and trips for the children. The adults attended English classes and occasionally had an interview with the resettlement team or went to visit a doctor. Yet I remember it being a very busy time. There were so many other things going on. Sometimes the local residents would donate free tickets so that some Vietnamese could attend a local concert or theatre. Local churches would help out and would donate things to the camp. They were very kind. And the Havant Lions Club (a town outside Portsmouth) donated seven season tickets to Portsmouth Football Club. My friend Lockhart used to take about twelve young single men to Portsmouth to watch the match. Seven would go into the stadium with the tickets, then fold the tickets up and put them in a hat and throw it over the wall so the others could reuse the tickets and get in. He told me once that when Portsmouth played Millwall – a team with fans well known for their fighting – the Vietnamese were more mesmerised watching the football hooligans than the football match.

The volunteers and teachers were also very kind and arranged day trips for some families, often to local towns, historic sites, or places with pretty landscapes. I would often accompany the families on trips outside the Centre to visit the local areas of interest. On one occasion we took a group of families to visit London. Many of them wanted to wander around different parts of the city by themselves, so we arranged that the group would all meet back at Trafalgar Square at a certain time to board the coach back to Thorney Island. One family wandered off and couldn't find their way back to the coaches and of course, they spoke little

English. I was at the coach, waiting and waiting for them. When they finally arrived we learned that they couldn't remember the name 'Trafalgar Square', so they told the taxi driver they needed to go to where they have the 'lions'. So naturally the taxi driver took them to the Zoo. It took a while for them to explain what they really meant, but eventually the driver figured out they meant the statues by Nelson's Column, in the front of the National Gallery.

On Sunday, the Protestants would invite the Vietnamese to go to church with them, and I went to their churches a few times. They were always singing. The Catholics also organised a Sunday Mass with either an English priest or a Vietnamese priest, and after Mass the Catholics would all come together and eat a good meal. On many occasions, a Vietnamese priest from Devon would come and join us for Mass. He was a Benedictine monk, and at his monastery he specialised in tasting the wine and liqueur they produced; he really enjoyed drinking his wine. Often before we'd go to Mass, he'd grin and ask: "Hold on, why don't we have a few drinks first?" His Father Superior tried to limit how often he could leave the monastery, but he had to go out to work with the Vietnamese community, and so his Father Superior would in the end relent and let him go, knowing that he would come back drunk. Because he was so skilled at testing the wine, the other Benedictine monks knew that if they lost him their factory would be in trouble, so everyone forgave him.

Compared with the British way of life, Vietnamese is not a drinking culture, yet at Thorney Island, I drank a lot. We like beer but usually, for something stronger, we prefer rice wine. The refugee families received plenty of free rice from the Centre and they bought yeast from the store. It was very easy, and common practice: I even made some rice wine myself. Sometimes, when there wasn't much to do, I would pick a few apples, take rice from the kitchen and buy Chinese herbs. You need to leave it for a few weeks, but then you have some great tasting rice wine. Like the English with their brandy, we believe drinking rice wine can bring you good health. Almost every family made some for the men in the family to drink. The rice wine was in great demand at Thorney Island and when a family learned that they were allocated housing and got notice of a leave date, they would immediately organise a party.

There would also be huge spreads of home cooked food. This was especially true in the officers' married quarters where the family would fill a long table with food and invite all the staff. Amazing food. They'd easily spend £100 for the party. English staff were so concerned that they'd make announcements saying "don't spend so much money on parties, you'll need the money in your new accommodation". What they didn't understand was that a leaving party like this was so important to the Vietnamese. Vietnamese never have empty pockets; they usually used money saved from Hong Kong. They always had money for a feast.

In addition to the leaving dos, we had a few couples who got married while at the Centre. We took them to Chichester Registry Office for the civil ceremony, and it was quite an ordeal. Everyone was dressed up in his or her best clothes, and the couples invited their English teacher and their allocated fieldworker. At the registry office, they were required to say the vows in English, and I found it difficult to explain to the couple what they were expected to say. For example, one phrase they had to repeat was: "I do solemnly declare, that I know not of any lawful impediment, why I, Vương Thành Hoa, should not be joined in holy matrimony to Chu Binh Chi." I had to tell the couple that all these complicated words were old, legal ways of saying: "I'm not related to the person I want to marry and I'm not already married." It seemed quite funny to us that this needed to be said so formally before getting married. The newlyweds would have to have their honeymoon at Thorney Island; usually sharing their room with between two and six other family members.

Administration

Those who lead disciplined and orderly lifestyles they achieve all their goals and progress.

Yajur Veda

When the Home Office opened the resettlement centres, it commissioned a charity to manage the camp, which saved the government money – if they had a local authority to run it they would have had to pay staff a civil servant salary. They chose BCAR (British Council for Aid to Refugees) to run Thorney Island. It was a small charity in the 1970s, what my friend Lockhart called a 'tin pot' charity. Prior to their work with Vietnamese refugees, they helped around four or five hundred refugees a year from all over the world, the largest groups coming from the former Soviet Union and Chile. BCAR was founded and staffed by individuals who once worked overseas in the colonial administrations, usually the military. The management staff were proper, kept a stiff upper lip, spoke the Queen's English, and ran the camp in a military style. They were very well intentioned, and were keen to help anyone fleeing from Communism.

Apparently the officials of BCAR had difficulty recruiting someone to act as the camp leader or administrator of Thorney Island with experience in Vietnam. Unlike America or France, the UK did not have any formal relations with Vietnam, as it was not a former colony. So they hired someone who had experience in Southeast Asia: Major Basil Smith, MBE[4]. He had retired from a distinguished career in the military, and had helped to administer the colony in Malaysia in the 1950s, so the Home Office believed that his familiarity with the customs and way of life of Malaysia would help him to work with Vietnamese refugees. In addition, in Malaysia he had to deal with the Communists. To their minds, Southeast Asia was all the same.

It could have been a disaster, since in many ways Vietnam has more in common with China than with the rest of Southeast Asia. Also, no one at BCAR was qualified to manage such a large resettlement operation, although Basil did have experience working with other refugee groups in the UK – he helped the Asian Ugandans when Idi Amin expelled them in the 1970s. However, the reception situation was very different for the Asian Ugandans, where there was already a large community settled in the UK, so most newly arrived families were able to find extended family to live with and to sponsor them. There were, however, very few Vietnamese in the UK when the Boat People arrived.

Major Smith did a good job. Basil was a tall man with silver hair and thin moustache; he had a long face with jowls that shook when he spoke in his deep booming voice. I later learned that the reason why his voice was so gruff was that he had once been shot in the throat. The scar is still on his neck, and you could see where the bullet had entered on one side of his throat and had come out of the other. He carried himself as if he was still in the military.

The rest of the management team included the Head of the Resettlement Team who was an older man who had once served with the British colonial police force in Hong Kong. The man who ran the stores – the room where we could pick up any bedding or cleaning equipment we needed - had served in the British Navy for years. Basil called him the Quartermaster, as in the military. Brigadier Michael was the education officer for BCAR, and he had also been one of the founders of Peace Studies at Bradford University – a very novel concept at the time. The students had to

---

[4] Member of the Most Excellent Order of the British Empire

do placements of three months, and many came to Thorney Island. This meant that BCAR got cheap labour.

The fieldworkers, all of whom were young, were very different from the management. The management staff were fiercely anti-communist, and still had a colonial mentality towards most ethnic groups; Lockhart joked that their heroes were those who smuggled Bibles into Russia. The younger staff tended to be liberals who were active in the anti-war movement; influenced by all the anti-imperialist, anti-colonial, anti-American protests of the late 1960s and 1970s. They were hippies, and although Hồ Chí Minh was their hero, they were also keen to help those of us who had fled Communist rule.

There were no problems between the groups of staff despite their different worldviews, except for the time my friend Lockhart tried to teach young staff about the Vietnam War. He had realised that many English staff knew very little about the Vietnam conflict, or the reasons why the Vietnamese had fled, so he ordered several movies to show on a 16mm projector in the main hall. The films he ordered were all pro-Hồ Chí Minh and anti-American. After showing it to the British staff, some Vietnamese residents said they wanted to see the film as well. I wasn't there, but Lockhart recently told me: "It was remarkable to see the Vietnamese watching the film; to see their reaction to images of Vietnam getting bombed. Once there was a clip of a bomb dropping in Hải Phòng. One of the Vietnamese shouted 'that's my home!' It was very moving." The next day, Basil yelled at Lockhart for showing 'communist propaganda', and almost fired him.

I wasn't too bothered by the fact that there were two such diverse groups of British working at the camp. I knew that these were their personal points of view. We did not really talk about it, and would only occasionally joke and call friends like Lockhart 'communists'. All of us got along – the anti-communist colonialists, the pro-communist hippies and the anti-communist Vietnamese all became good friends.

There were between five and ten Vietnamese staff. We were

hired as interpreters, and it was not long before some Vietnamese staff complained that although we had been hired as interpreters, we often did the same work as the English fieldworkers. Basil understood and changed our position to fieldworkers as well, but then the English staff became a bit resentful, since the Vietnamese staff could not be given the same kind of caseload because we were needed in so many different capacities. Also, many Vietnamese resisted the cleaning inspections. Each fieldworker was assigned a wing of the compound, and had to make sure it was clean enough for Basil's military-style inspection. The young Vietnamese fieldworkers found it very difficult to tell anyone older than them that they weren't clean enough, because that would be too disrespectful.

Cleaning was a big concern for Basil. Every two or three weeks a new group of refugees would arrive and Basil would make a welcome speech, which I would often have to translate. He would say in a good-hearted, but very commanding voice: "Welcome to Britain. You are now safe." Then he'd become serious and state all the rules that everyone in the Centre must follow: "Staff are here to help you, but we are not your servants. So the rules are: clean this, keep that clean…" Frequently, Basil would walk through the Centre and see something wrong, so he'd call a meeting of all the refugees and repeat: "We welcome you, but this is not clean enough, that is not good enough…" and so on.

After a while I became a senior fieldworker in charge of the Vietnamese staff at Thorney Island, and in addition to interpreting, I had to help to run the Reception Centre. The day-to-day duties included ensuring that everyone was abiding by the rules, and obtaining feedback from the families on what we could do to improve services.

I still remember the time the Director of Refugee Resettlement came from London to Thorney Island to meet Basil. He apparently came with the intention of stopping my work at the Centre, because he had received complaints about me. He told me the complaints were about the announcements I made over the public address speakers, which was a system that could be heard in each room and in each building. I was using the microphone to announce many things, such as "this wing isn't clean enough" or "please stop arguing with one another" or "stop cooking food in your rooms – it is not allowed." I would criticise such things and try to educate the new refugees. I would also remind people: "you need to be gentle, you need to be honest, respect one another" and so on. Remember, with everyone living together at such close quarters, some family problems would frequently arise. Relationships between men and women often led to affairs and jealousy, and there was also some gambling and fighting. The atmosphere often got quite tense.

I must have said something that really upset people, although I don't remember now what it was, or perhaps they felt that the speaker system was too similar to the ones found in Vietnam. Lamp posts in every Vietnamese city announced daily messages about road safety and put out communist propaganda. Whatever the reason, they complained about my messages. When the director came, all the other staff – English and Vietnamese – asked to let me stay, and really defended me. The director decided against sacking me, but he did ban me from making public announcements. I wasn't allowed to use the microphone anymore.

Resettlement

You as a community must do all in your power to be formed in the image of God. And what do we find in God?
We see equality of persons and unity of essence. What should that teach you if not that you should all be one and equal?

Saint Vincent de Paul

The closest village to Thorney Island was Emsworth. It was very small, and at that time only about 700-1000 people lived there all year round. The small village had developed when Thorney Island had been a military airbase, so obviously the village had many pubs. It became a quiet village though, after the airbase closed. I think it was a shock for the locals when all of the Vietnamese came. I heard so many rumours and myths about us. The locals assumed that they were now vulnerable to tropical diseases, fearing that they'd catch malaria from us with the help of local mosquitoes. They thought that we preyed on their pet dogs and cats for food, and assumed that we had risked our lives at sea just so that we could access UK welfare benefits.

There was also a bit of racism. Members of the National Front – precursor to the white supremacist British Nationalist Party (BNP) - occasionally abused some Vietnamese who were brave enough to go to a local pub. On one occasion a few fieldworkers had to take a coach load of families to Deptford, and that same day, the local BNP planned a march against Boat People so the staff were nervous as they pulled into Deptford. A six-year-old black girl came running up to the coach, and the staff hoped this meant that they were actually going to have a nice welcome. But she squinted her eyes, shouted "ching chong ching" then ran off. Luckily, that was the only hostility they experienced that day. The majority of Boat People were not direct victims of racial abuse, but while at Thorney Island many refugees did feel isolated from the host community. They did not have much opportunity to interact with British people while they were there, except for when they spoke to members of staff.

The year the Boat People began arriving in the UK, 1979 was the year Margaret Thatcher was elected as the UK's Prime Minister. Whilst Thatcher was campaigning that spring, she continually brought up the immigration debate, making her famous comment about people feeling "fear of an alien culture swamping their neighbourhoods". She was attacked as racist for these sentiments and criticised for pandering to the 'fear' vote. This was a time of great racial tension, especially in areas with large ethnic groups, manifesting in the Brixton riots of 1980-81.

In this climate, Thatcher was determined not to let Vietnamese live in ethnic 'ghettos', and created a dispersal policy. Vietnamese families were to be housed in cities and towns outside of London and the Southeast, and in order to prevent them from forming communities, there were not to be too many Vietnamese in one area. It was destined to fail. Families were sometimes split up under the dispersal policy and some were even resettled in Northern Ireland during the Troubles with all the violence between the Protestants and Catholics. Lâm Cồng and his family were resettled to Thamesmead in London, but his mother and brother ended up in Inverness in Scotland. Families were dumped in very small towns and isolated from any other Vietnamese speakers. We resettled seven young single men, at different times, in the small village of Ottery St Mary in Devon, and within a matter of weeks, six of those seven had turned up back at the camp with their suitcases, saying that they could not live there. Some areas were not suitable because of unemployment. One man had been a crane operator in the docks in Hải Phòng in Vietnam. He was resettled to the Isle of Dogs, right by the docks and I felt terrible for this unemployed crane operator looking out of his window and seeing cranes and docks that were not in use. Other dispersal areas were inappropriate because of the lack of services. One family dispersed to Wales cried every day because the children had mental health needs but they had no network or support in their dispersal home. Eventually they moved and over time, many returned to London.

Some Vietnamese continued to live in isolation once they had been resettled into their permanent accommodation, while others received a really warm welcome. There was actually a lot of good will towards individual families, since local residents knew about the plight of the Boat People and were sympathetic. At the time, local authorities willingly offered housing to the Boat People, and when they moved in to their new homes, neighbours sometimes welcomed them. Some even had the local press around to celebrate the new arrivals into the community. In one city, the Mayor posed for photos handing the keys of the house to one of the families and welcoming them. This is what I remember most about this time; the UK welcomed the Boat People and wished us success.

It is so different now for the asylum seekers and refugees who arrive in the UK today. They are not welcomed, and there is more racism towards them in the media than there was towards us in the late 1970s and early 1980s. There is more local resentment, there are more myths; today there is more anger.

Tensions

I once read in a report by the United Nations High Commissioner for Refugees that between 1978-79 one million ethnic Chinese had tried to escape South Vietnam, and of those, 50% died at sea, like my friend's wife, who threw herself overboard and drowned. Everyone was so concerned, and there were images on every television around the world of the masses of Boat People trying to escape Vietnam. The mass flight caught the international community by surprise at first, as this was five years after the Communist victory in Vietnam. There had been refugees fleeing throughout the five years, but in 1978 and 1979 the numbers increased dramatically – it became the highest period of refugee flight from both North and South Vietnam because of the war with China and subsequent persecution of ethnic Chinese.

There has always been a love-hate relationship between China and Vietnam. Vietnam resisted the Chinese who continually threatened to colonise the country again, but many of us grew up respecting the Confucian culture. Even when under Chinese rule, Vietnam maintained a strong nationalist identity.

No one should have been too surprised when the Chinese invaded Vietnam in 1979. Both countries were communist at this point and should have been allies, but our long history of mutual distrust meant that old patterns were repeated - China was upset we weren't following their Maoist path or doing what they told us and so wanted to 'punish' us. Vietnamese soldiers pushed out the Chinese soldiers, again signalling to the Chinese that Vietnam was united and strong.

This increased the Vietnamese government's political suspicion of the ethnic Chinese who have long lived in Vietnam. The Chinese community from the beginning established themselves as middlemen, especially in the rice trade. The ethnic Chinese were a part of Vietnam, but usually maintained their own identity and set themselves apart socially as well as economically. This made them easy scapegoats and targets. They were all suspected of intentionally robbing the ethnic Vietnamese and acting as spies for China. Thus, the Vietnamese government began making life very difficult for the ethnic Chinese. Businesses owned by ethnic Chinese were shut down and the Vietnamese government began their programme of systematically forcing the ethnic Chinese to leave. Many crossed into China by land, but many did not want to go to China or to another communist country, so they left by sea in the hope of ending up in Hong Kong.

While the Vietnamese had to leave secretly, the ethnic Chinese were allowed to purchase or build their own ships – often holding up to seven or eight hundred people. The Vietnamese government would make the ethnic Chinese pay for their own tickets – often around twelve ounces of gold per person. Once the ethnic Chinese registered that they were leaving, the government would confiscate anything of value that they owned, including their property and businesses. The government corruption of making the Chinese pay such large amounts of gold when they were forced to leave was not the worst of it. I saw a ship full of ethnic Chinese at a port explode before even setting sail. I heard that this happened a couple times. The explosions could have been accidents, since the government only cared about receiving the money and did not care if the ships were safe, but rumours hinted that the Communists were so angry at China that they secretly set the bombs off intentionally. No one could agree exactly how it happened, but everyone saw the debris and dead bodies floating down the river afterwards.

For almost two years, the only groups to come to Thorney Island were ethnic Chinese from North Vietnam. Most tended to come to the UK via Hong Kong and were resettled in the UK because of this colonial link - an agreement was made for the UK to relieve pressure on Hong Kong. Ethnic Chinese Vietnamese did not call themselves Chinese until they arrived in the Hong Kong camps. This was a label placed upon them by civil servants, and it stuck.

Then, in 1980, two groups of South Vietnamese came to Thorney Island. Those from South Vietnam tended to come to the UK because a British ship rescued them at sea as my boat had been. This would be the first time that large groups from both the North and South had lived together in the Reception Centre. Staff at Thorney Island were very excited to receive South Vietnamese people at the Centre, and were keen to compare the different styles of people and their behaviour. I don't think the staff expected what happened next. A week after the new group arrived, a few South Vietnamese were intensely determined to speak to me, and they declared:

"This is a Centre for refugees, and we don't want the Communists inside the Centre or to use the Centre to promote Communism. This is for real refugees, not for them." The conflict was not so much between ethnic Chinese and ethnic Vietnamese, but between the North and South – the opposing sides during the war. The conflict was continuing here in the UK.

I tried to explain that here in the UK, and in the Centre, there was no North versus South or Chinese versus Vietnamese. I said that we were all refugees in a new land, but they ignored me and went straight to Basil. The new arrivals from South Vietnam repeated:

"We are refugees; we are the real refugees. We are against the Communists, and that is why we fled. We want the residents' committee to be made up of representatives of the real refugees from South Vietnam, not the North."

I advised the staff: "Don't let there be division between North and South. We will recruit some from the South to be representatives on the committee, but we will not replace all of them. That would be very dangerous. We cannot let one part of my country dominate the Refugee Centre." Basil agreed and gradually we made sure the committee had equal numbers of representatives from North and South.

On a basic level, the division between North and South seemed to disappear. The Vietnamese from the South may not have worked closely with Vietnamese from the North, for instance, but the distinction was not strong and not volatile. The only other incident occurred when people from South Vietnam organised a New Year celebration. My friend, Mr Bảy, was one of the organisers who created the programme to include a dancing group, a choir, and a moment to play the anthem and salute the South Vietnamese flag. People from the North and South came together in the big hall to celebrate New Year. When Mr Bảy and his friends played the South Vietnamese anthem and waved the flag, refugees from the North joined in. I was secretly relieved that nothing happened, that it was all very pleasant, and that there appeared to be no tension.

However, I wasn't aware of a few young people who were really drunk. Apparently they went outside the large entertainment room to talk, because it was very crowded, and one of the young men, from the North, swore about the "stupid songs". Later, he claimed that when he said this, he wasn't referring to the anthem or flag, but was simply making fun of the general entertainment. That was not what a few young men from the South, also drunk, understood. They looked over to see who was swearing at the South Vietnamese flag and saw a group of young men from North Vietnam. The rumour spread straightaway:

"Some men from the North swore at the South Vietnam anthem and flag." Some men from the South came to beat up the young man from the North. Of course this young man from the North had friends who were ready to defend him. A huge fight broke out, and one man brought out a knife. Fortunately, the police came in time to prevent any major injuries. Later that night, the Centre moved the South Vietnamese family who had brought the knife out of Thorney Island, to prevent more fighting. They were immediately sent to the countryside.

Culture

Culture is a matrix of infinite possibilities and choices.

Wole Soyinka, Nigerian Nobel Laureate

Thorney Island is where a lot of the initial clashes between cultures occurred and both the British and the Vietnamese experienced culture shock. It wasn't part of my formal job description, but I often found myself acting as a cultural advocate, explaining how and why the Vietnamese did things that seemed bizarre to the British. For example, when the Vietnamese have a cold or fever, they often massage medical oils onto their spine, shoulders, and throat, then use a spoon or something silver to rub, with great intensity, along the spine. It scratches the skin and leaves a bright red mark. Not a bruise, but a deep mark. The Vietnamese feel this is the best way to fight a cold or fever, and use this technique with children too. When they get a headache, they rub their foreheads in a special way that raises the blood to the surface, also creating a strong red mark (sometimes called cạo gió). When the children went to school with these marks however, the teachers became alarmed, and on a number of occasions they called the police, assuming child abuse. The police would come to the Centre and interview the families, accusing them of beating their children. It took a lot of work to raise awareness within the schools that this was a safe treatment and I also had to talk with the Vietnamese

151

about other ways to help treat a child's cold. GPs however, were nervous about prescribing Western medicine because they were worried that the Vietnamese would combine prescription drugs with their traditional Chinese medicine.

I remember once when a woman, whose family was from a rural part of Vietnam, was very pregnant. The health visitor had a hunch that she would have the baby over the weekend, while she was away so she told them again and again to call an ambulance and go to hospital if the woman went into labour. When the health visitor came back the following Monday, she marched in to see the family and found out that she was right: the woman had given birth over the weekend. But the family didn't go to the hospital as ordered, and instead the grandmother had delivered the baby in their room. This was very normal for the family, since in the countryside in Vietnam the grandmother always helps with the delivery. I had to explain to the health visitor that farmers rarely go to hospital for something like that - the Vietnamese see birth as a normal healthy process, not a disease, but the health visitor was very angry.

The British were very curious about some of our Vietnamese customs. For example, even if they are Catholic or Buddhist, on the anniversary of someone's death, the family would build paper models of things they thought the person would want in the afterlife – paper houses, paper cars, even paper money. They would cook lots of food and also offer it to the deceased family member. Then, they would burn the paper models so that the items would reach the deceased in the afterlife. Sometimes family members would jump back and forth over the flame as well.

At other times I was a cultural advocate for the British and had to explain to the Vietnamese how and why the British did things in certain ways, and why they wanted people from other cultures to do the same. I've already mentioned the Vietnamese desire to cook for themselves and eat as a family in their room. I tried to explain the British concern for health and safety issues, but the Vietnamese ignored them.

Vietnamese want to eat fresh animals. Unlike the British, they don't want to eat processed or packaged meat. So, the Vietnamese want to see a chicken running around until it is time to eat it; and surrounding Thorney Island were very large fields full of rabbits. Sometimes, families would catch a few rabbits and bring them to their room and cook them. A few also used some local canoes to catch swans and ducks to eat. How they caught them, I do not know. They were very clever, and I think that they would swim underneath the bird and grab its legs. Members of the coast guard were not happy and would ask us to make announcements demanding that people stop. The camp staff also did not want the families cleaning animals on the premises. I tried to explain all this, but the residents ignored us.

Vietnamese never really ate bread before coming to the UK. They would usually eat rice for breakfast. Most families had rice cookers they brought with them from Hong Kong, so they usually had the equipment to cook rice, illegally, in their own rooms. But little by little, step by step, they began to eat bread for breakfast. In time, they grew to like it enough that they would often buy their own supply of butter and jam. However, one thing never changed - when they ate the bread, they always cut off the outer edge, the crust. It got to the point where Basil wanted me to explain to the Vietnamese that they shouldn't waste food − it was a waste of money. But again we were ignored.

Not all of the staff were worried about it, but Basil also did not like all the gambling. Vietnamese love to gamble, especially with cards and mah-jong. Basil thought gambling was immoral, and he wasn't completely wrong. Wives would often get angry because their husbands would gamble away all their money. This caused a lot of arguments around the camp, but it never stopped the Vietnamese from playing cards at the Centre late into the night.

Another problem angered British Telecom. This was before mobile phones, and in the Centre, they installed public telephones that were coin operated. The Vietnamese figured out a way to make free calls by inserting a coin attached to a string so that after the call, they could get the coin back. I had to make many announcements about this over the microphone because BT could see that many calls were being made but there was no money in the box. Again, most families ignored us.

Even if they struggled to integrate, the Vietnamese were very grateful to be in the UK. This may have surprised some since most did not want to come to the UK in the first place. When they were in Hong Kong, the locals there always said bad things about the British. The UK was always a refugee's last choice. People in Hong Kong would say, "The British are very cold," or "No one will help you," or "Life in the UK is very expensive," or "They are very racist". Representatives from countries like Canada, France, and Australia went to Hong Kong and interviewed refugees to see which ones could come to their country. These countries only allowed the skilled refugees, people with qualifications, to resettle there, and the refugees chosen were thrilled. The UK got all the 'rejects', those who weren't chosen for their skills. Thus for many, the UK was never their choice, and they didn't want to come here. But once they lived here, after their time at Thorney Island and settling into their new home, the families were very happy. Their children were able to go to good schools, they had decent housing, and the NHS was good. They learned that the people in Hong Kong were wrong. Despite the culture clashes, the Vietnamese refugees were meeting so many kind, friendly and helpful people.

Reunited

Loss

By tormenting footsteps

Days followed days

Through my soul of dead leaves

Through my soul blanketed in mist.

Catholic with Confucian Tendencies

When mid-life by gray hair was marked
Regrets came flooding
Sad melody repentance sang
Of the springs forever gone.

Exotic foreign places enraptured the mind
Dressed in glowing academic garb
All bewildered, my poetic soul
Took refuge in the subconscious.

The dry ink-crusted pen
Mirrors feelings in sleep
Yearning for motherland's flowers and grass
Fragrance of poetry.

In this life is reincarnated
Myself a migratory bird
Traversing the immense ocean
The way back unmapped.

Far far away fading sunlight
Deepens emptiness of the heart.
Melancholy drips silence
In longing head bows.

Thành Nhung
The Writers Post, Volume 6 Number 2. Jul 2004
(http://www.thewriterspost.net/V6I2_pp1_thanhnhung.htm)

For most Vietnamese, living away from the home of our ancestors is like being banished to a desert. Everyone I met at Thorney Island was happy for freedom yet pined for the motherland. This contrast often manifested in even greater anger towards the Communists – the evil that ruined our home and forced us to flee.

Like others, I missed Vietnam and my friends yet, strangely, I was not homesick at all. In Vietnam after the war I lived in fear, but at Thorney Island I was very happy - at least during the day when I was working and feeling optimistic about our new future. But at night, when alone in our quiet room, I couldn't stay optimistic. I longed to see my wife and other children. I'm not a poet so I lacked the means to express my feelings. But Vietnam has produced so many beautiful poets and I would spend my evenings listening to Vietnamese love songs and poetry. That way I knew I wasn't alone.

Sometimes the guilt and sadness of missing my family was too much and Linh would come in and find me crying. I didn't want to burden Linh with my sadness so I would send her off to sleep. She was so young, and like the other children she seemed to find the transition easier than us adults. Linh missed her mother and siblings, but she also had so many things to enjoy, to distract her. She had fun running around with her friends. I enrolled Linh at the local primary school because I wanted her to have a more stable education, and I knew that I would be at Thorney Island for a couple of years. She got on very well and had a lot of English friends. In fact, at many weekends and holidays, English families would pick her up and have her to stay with them. When not with friends, she would entertain herself for hours drawing and painting.

I was lucky to get a job straightaway, so every month I could buy things to send back to my family in Vietnam. I would usually send things like clothes, a radio, and other valuable things. We would send photographs and write letters. My wife Điệp would write letters also and tell Linh how much she missed her.

Điệp, in Vietnam, thought we were working very hard and that we were straining to survive like her, she didn't want to burden us or make us worry. She really struggled during this time, and I still feel very sorry about this. Điệp was a teacher, and also ran a shop that sold ice cream and sweets, but even working both jobs she didn't have enough money. She often didn't tell me when she didn't have enough to survive, and because I didn't know, I saved all my extra money for the time she and the other children would be able to join us.

Life in Vietnam was very hard at that time, especially with two children to look after. My wife tried to get money, but it was not easy. Everyone was poor, and everyone was looking for ways to make money, but she really suffered with two young children and with all of the paperwork that was needed for them to join me in the UK. Often when she submitted forms or enquired about the status of her application, she would have to bribe an official which became expensive. There were so many papers needed to satisfy the authorities, but they would never get through. Every time she went, the authorities would say: "Wait for news from the Vietnam Home Office in Hanoi". In 1979 I had permission for my family to reunite with us, a visa, but the bureaucracy in Vietnam wouldn't help. I think the main delay was because of my continued political activity. My wife and I had to wait five years.

Thorney Island closed at the end of 1982 and I moved to London. I was still waiting for my wife and family.

In 1983 I got appendicitis and had to go to hospital, and although I was only there for two to three days, I got my friend to write a letter on my behalf, and also asked the nurse to confirm in writing that I was a patient there. The letters said that I was sick in hospital and needed to see my family. I sent the letters to the Prime Minister, the Queen and many others asking for help to bring my wife and children over. I got a letter from the Queen's secretary saying, "sorry to hear your story". Two weeks later my wife had a visa.

I went to meet my family at Heathrow Airport. I was so nervous, I don't remember the journey to the airport at all. We were all crying when they walked into the concourse. It was overwhelming. So many tears and smiles.

I did not realise that I must have been talking about the arrival of my wife and other children so much, but clearly everyone knew what an important day it was for me. When I returned from Heathrow Airport with my family, many neighbours stopped by to meet and welcome them. It was overwhelming; it was very emotional.

I was so happy to be able to spend time with Tâm and Toàn – they had grown so much in those five years and I had to get to know them again. Tâm and Toàn settled into life in London really well. But Linh struggled a bit. She had to adjust to having siblings again. My wife was very homesick; she had a hard time adjusting to the UK and her sadness caused Linh stress. We were happy to be together, but it took a couple years before we felt truly whole again.

CHAPTER TEN

Advocate

I know how men in exile feed on dreams of hope.

Aeschylus, Agamemnon

"Thành, I have been given a flat in London. I go tomorrow. They keep saying something about signing papers. I'm not sure what they mean. Will you come with me?" A few local authorities around the UK, including London, often came to Thorney Island Refugee Resettlement Centre and offered accommodation to Vietnamese families, but the accommodation was frequently in poor boroughs where no one else wanted to go.

I worked at Thorney Island for three years, and in that time I learned much about housing and the benefits system in the UK. I worked alongside the Resettlement Team, and we would assess new arrivals from Hong Kong, matching them with available housing somewhere in the UK. Once things were in place, a van would take the family to their new home. A fieldworker and interpreter would also accompany the refugee family to help them fill in some forms and hand over the key to them.

Sometimes, when the family first saw their new house, they'd cry. Often, if other Vietnamese were in the area, they'd come round to greet the family and we'd unload the van. Many refugees arrived with nothing but the clothing on their backs, but those from Hong Kong, who could work, were different. These families would move into their flats with TVs, stereos and rice cookers. This caused some resentment with their neighbours if they were being housed in a poor area because the local residents often assumed that the government just gave them free TVs and so on.

Most families were so overwhelmed by the process that they were relieved that an interpreter like me would go with them. We did not simply interpret the words of the fieldworkers, we had to go further and explain concepts and processes to the new families who were used to a Vietnamese way of doing things. Everything was still so new and strange. Everyone I would take from the resettlement camp had a similar look in their eyes at this point: a type of disconnection, as if they had discovered that they were no longer anchored to a shore but were now adrift in the sea again. The camps in Hong Kong and the Resettlement Centres were all new and foreign, but at least they were contained, small and easy to navigate. The endless winding streets of London or Birmingham caused everyone to lose any sense of direction.

Usually someone from the local BCAR (British Council for Aid to Refugees) office would meet the family to help complete additional forms and also help them register for local services, but this was not the only assistance they needed. Nothing was familiar. I understood what the new families were going through - every step of a simple journey was daunting: buying train tickets, finding the correct platform, making sure to get off at the right station. Trying to find basic household items or recognisable food was exhausting. Entering a shop or searching for the Jobcentre made new Vietnamese hyper-alert, anxious even. It wasn't just the flurry of trying to get to an appointment on time, or stress from wondering what the new accommodation would be like. It was fear: fear of getting lost and not being able to find our way. We had no bearings to help ground us. We weren't at home.

My first expedition to London was an overwhelming experience for me — I had as much to learn from the fieldworker as the family we were accompanying, but I became more confident with each trip. Knowing that others were depending on me triggered my determination to learn more about how the UK worked, so I could help other Vietnamese settle into their new life. Depending on the support that BCAR could offer, the Fieldworker and I would stay with each family for one hour or one day before returning to Thorney Island and starting the process again with another family.

After I left each family in their new flat, however, they still would need some help. They would have questions about how to find things that they wanted or needed, such as:

"Is there a Buddhist temple near me?"

"My neighbour is complaining about my laundry hanging on the banister, where else am I to put it?"

"Someone just threw a brick through our window. I don't feel safe here."

In the early 1980s the UK did not have any Vietnamese restaurants. There weren't any shops with Vietnamese food, but after a bit of hunting, I was able to find Chinese markets in many towns around the country where families could go and buy familiar vegetables and rice as well as a few key spices. Before we could even think about the next bureaucratic hurdle, the families would need to equip their kitchens, buy linen for the beds, build an altar for their ancestors to bless their new home – and rest. I would explain all the rules to the families, and I would interpret the family's concerns to BCAR. I was their travel guide, their advocate and their voice.

When families had questions, they called me, because they believed that I understood the UK system better than they did. They hoped that my English language and British contacts would magically right all wrongs, but most importantly, they trusted me. So when I moved to London after Thorney Island Reception Centre closed in 1982, there was an entire community that had come to depend on me for help dealing with daily life in the UK. People found where I was living in Hackney and would come to my flat asking for more help. This spontaneous gathering of Vietnamese families in my home became the birthplace of the Vietnamese Community in Hackney, officially founded on 25th November 1982.

Before long, my work mainly involved assisting those who had moved to London after having previously been housed in a remote city where there were no other Vietnamese for support or friendship. There was a large 'secondary migration' of people who had been given housing in the southwest or Wales, where there were few other minority groups and very little work. They would come to London with their luggage, and find friends to stay with until they could find their own accommodation. A typical family needed help accessing the local services, so, for instance, I would take them straightaway to their local Benefits Office to update their account with their new address and Post Office; I would take the family on the bus so that they could learn which stops to use.

Dealing with any kind of government department was always stressful. I can't tell you how excruciating the wait would be. The family was so nervous – sitting in a bureaucratic waiting room feels the same around the world. Everyone is suddenly drained of optimism and infused with feelings of powerlessness. I would explain what to expect to the family, but there is only so much one person can take in at a time. The loud, crowded waiting rooms were not easy places in which to hold a serious conversation. We would all be so hungry, yet we couldn't leave for lunch and risk losing our place in the queue.

Finally, it would be our turn. I would interpret for the family and the housing department, but I had to do more than interpret the language: it fell to me to explain concepts and ideas to the family. They'd ask:

"Why do they need to ask so many personal questions? I've already told the officers at the camp my story".

"I don't understand, they keep asking me the same question again and again. What do they want to hear?"

"Do I tell them I'm Chinese? Will they still know I'm a refugee from Vietnam?" I became an instant expert on completing the long, tedious forms.

Often, I had to be a bit of a detective to find out a family's core problem. I once learned that an entire family was going hungry. Of course, the children did not understand their father's pride, but complained in front of my friend that they were hungry.

My friend noticed they did not have any food in their kitchen. I went by to see them, but had to be careful how I proceeded because I didn't want to offend the family, or to make the father feel ashamed because he didn't know how things worked in the UK. So I would have to be indirect, "I'm having a hard time finding good *nước mắm*, have you had any luck?" With this particular family it took me a while to realise that his benefits cheques had not been arriving and so they simply did not have any money. He was so relieved when I was able to remedy the situation with a quick phone call.

I'll never forget the time a Vietnamese man called me, really distressed. His neighbour had just punched him in the face, and he had no idea why. The English man, his neighbour, had knocked on his door, said some foreign words and kept pointing and gesturing. The Vietnamese man couldn't understand what he was saying. He just kept shaking his head, which seemed to make the English man angrier. The Vietnamese man could tell his neighbour was getting more and more upset, but couldn't understand and could not find anyone around who could translate. Then, before he knew it, the neighbour punched him.

I went to his house immediately. When I walked into his flat, I noticed that there were beautiful flowers all around the room. A few of the flowers were arranged in a lovely wreath shape. Then it struck me. I went to the neighbour's flat and explained the misunderstanding. It turns out that the neighbour had recently lost a family member and many friends and relatives had brought flowers. He had left them out in the front yard area by the street so they could be taken to the church for the memorial service. When he came back out a few hours later, they were gone. I was eventually able to smooth things between the neighbours, but I'm not sure if he ever forgave that Vietnamese man for assuming the flowers were out front to be thrown away.

Vũ Khánh Thành

Windfall

Tomorrow I will be home

Tomorrow I will be home and someone will ask
What have you learned in the States?
If you want to know give me a broom
I'll tell you, I am a first class janitor

I wash dishes much faster than the best housewife
And do a vacuum better than any child
Everyday I run like a madman in my brand new car
Every night I bury my head in my pillow and cry

The speech art becomes a physical exertion
The more you talk, the more muscle you get
And your mother tongue is used only for cussing
Or at best to pen verses on nights of despair

In the States I learn the meaning of vastness
But love here seems the size of a toothpick
Such naturalness they appear like kids
But my soul is aged by a thousand years

The big lesson I learn since coming to the States
Is this boundless craving for my land
How I hate those damn fellows who have despoiled it
Made it a million times worse than when we got thrown out

Should life change all over once again
And heroic me become the saviour of the Fatherland
I will set up a thousand re-education camps
Throw everybody in there to learn about Love

164

The old war will be seen like the last 'kiep'
Even reactionaries cannot last more than a hundred years
We'll all be friends, no enemies or puppets
The victors will feel glorious and so will the defeated

Cao Tần

(Translated by Nguyễn Ngọc Bích; War and Exile: A
Vietnamese Anthology, 1989 p212-213)

My work with the Vietnamese had at this point been voluntary,
done in my spare time. I was taking English lessons so that I could
continue to improve my own command of the language. I was
enrolled at the School of Oriental and African Studies (SOAS) in
London to study for an MA. In Vietnam, I studied Confucian
philosophy, but SOAS did not have a professor who specialised in
Confucian philosophy so, for some reason, SOAS instead offered
me a place to study Buddhist Archaeology. I decided to give it a try,
but I only lasted a year. The entire experience was incredibly
frustrating – my English was still not very strong so I would take a
month to read a book that my peers would read in a week. But the
main obstacle for me was my own reluctance to put my time and
energy into the coursework. It was hard to refuse to help a
Vietnamese family who came to me for help on the grounds that I
had to read about the symbolic interpretations of an ancient
artefact in Thailand. The degree would not serve any purpose
except to give me an MA. It would not help me secure a job, nor
would it give me any greater insight into how I could help the
Vietnamese in London.

While studying at SOAS, I was required to work. I registered
with a cleaning company so I could work in the evenings. I would
mop, dust, and empty rubbish bins in business offices and
buildings at the university in the evenings, so that I could have my
afternoons free to attend class, leaving my mornings free to
volunteer my time in the community.

I juggled these three worlds for a year, and at the end of it some friends and I decided to organise a Vietnamese New Year celebration. This was my first experience of fundraising. We went around shops in Hackney asking for donations. Some would give us a few free items like plastic forks or coloured paper. I remember being so grateful when a local butcher gave us £5. We added these donations to contributions from the Vietnamese community itself, and I approached Hackney's Town Hall. Somehow I convinced them that it would be a great idea to host the celebration in the centre of Hackney. So, in February 1983 we held the first annual New Year's celebration in Hackney, which we ran annually for about 20 years. The main festivities included music, dance and fashion shows, but we also had exhibits with photographs and artwork, as well as pictures of projects that were currently happening within the community. It was a great way to bring the Vietnamese community together, as well as an opportunity to let the locals get to know us and learn more about Vietnamese culture.

Gradually, the needs of the Vietnamese community changed. After finding their feet in Hackney, men and women wanted my help in finding a job or an English class that fitted into their work schedule. Other families were worried that their children were forgetting how to speak Vietnamese. Each day brought more and more people to my flat asking for assistance. I was beginning to feel like my old self again. I had a purpose and a focus. However, having so many people coming to our flat was becoming too much. We did not have enough space and my family had no privacy. So the next year I set out to find premises for a proper office. From my flat, we initially moved to the recreation room in Wally Foster Community Centre – a one-story dark brick building with heavy wooden doors facing a large park. We were only able to use the room during the day because in the afternoons the young people in the area would come to the Centre for youth programmes. So at the end of the day, we had to put everything back to normal – the ping-pong table and the football table had to be placed back in the centre of 'my office'. This meant I had to bring all my files back to my flat each day on my motorbike.

In 1984 I continued to meet many dedicated people fleeing Southeast Asia, who also found that many within the community needed help. We pooled our resources and created the organisation Vietnamese, Laos and Cambodian (VLC). I quit SOAS and became the chair of the steering committee. At this same time, Wally Foster Community Centre staff found they could no longer afford to let us continue using their space. Yet there was still a need for our services. So VLC moved back to my flat.

However, we could only do so much. All of us who volunteered at the VLC needed to work in the afternoons or evenings so that we could earn an income - I was still a cleaner – and this limited how much time we had to give. We had no funding – no money at all. Paper supplies, phone calls, bus fares – all came out of our own pockets, and we had reached the limit of what help we could offer for free. I enquired about funding from Trust for London – I heard that they gave small grants to community groups – and someone who worked for Trust for London came to my flat to explain the grant programme. She helped me to complete the simple one page form, and was so kind; I couldn't have done it without her help. In 1984 we were awarded £5,000. This was a huge windfall for us, and I knew it was mostly luck and good timing that had brought this funding to us. The process made me aware of how little I understood about how things are done in the UK. I realised that I needed someone to help with fundraising and all the bureaucratic duties that come with running a charity – someone who was familiar with the system. We needed someone English.

Foundations

An Việt = 'well-settled'

Mr Thống was a community leader in Bristol who was very successful. He had received substantial funding grants, and his advice centre was growing and able to offer a diverse range of services. Mr Thống introduced me to Paul[5], an English man who was helping him with his community group. I presented Paul my written plan for a community centre in Hackney and asked him to review my ideas. He seemed interested in the proposal, so I asked him to help us make it a reality. Paul travelled from Bristol to London two days each week to develop projects for us. I still worked as a volunteer, and used all the money we received from Trust for London to pay him for his part-time work. To support my family, I carried on with the cleaning job.

We needed new premises; Homerton House Secondary School was the only place willing to offer us free space. The school centred around one large high-rise building, which looked impressive from the street, yet when I walked inside, I realised my impression of the school was wrong: this was a tough school, full of tough students. The room they offered us was tiny – it was not even a proper office, it was a small space where all the electrical and gas meters were held. The room was just big enough to fit one small desk, and there weren't any windows. I accepted it gratefully, and we moved there in April 1986. We gave ourselves a new name: An Việt Foundation.

Today, people conduct extensive research into the factors that help or hinder 'integration' – the buzzword on every modern government's mind. With all the influx of immigrants in every

---

[5] Name has been changed to protect identity

nation, leaders are continually struggling with how to ensure the new residents contribute to the society and economy. The UK is no different. But when the Vietnamese first arrived, the ideal of social 'integration' wasn't talked about much. There was more of a focus on making sure basic needs were met and then letting everyone get on with it.

After a while, we began to see that there were basic issues that needed to be addressed before anyone could feel truly settled: a house, a job, and a place to go where we could honour our unique culture and traditions. At An Việt Foundation we continued to provide advice and information, host Vietnamese cultural events, and began a youth play scheme.

Another group we who noticed were struggling were the elderly. This was very hard for me because I was raised to respect and care for my elders. In Vietnam, there was such pressure and expectations about how to respect the elders in a family that if a neighbour didn't think you were doing a good job or didn't care enough, they would intervene and complain to others. This would be a great shame for the family.

Despite this deep tradition, elder members of the families living in the UK were becoming more and more marginalised. They weren't just isolated from the wider community, unable to communicate with English speaking neighbours, these parents and grandparents were growing more and more isolated at home. The younger generation had to go out and work long hours and the grandchildren found that they struggled to communicate with their elders. It wasn't just the language; it was the competing demands of traditional Vietnamese way of doing things and the new British way. So I also wanted to find a place where the elderly could gather and socialise.

Around 1986-1987, we estimated that 75% of Vietnamese in the UK were unemployed, and this greatly concerned us. As Vietnamese, we had such a welcome from the British government and neighbours, but there was also resistance when it came to offering jobs. There were some who blamed us for the poor economy, saying we were taking all the jobs - despite our relatively small numbers in the country and the high levels of unemployment in the Vietnamese community. At the same time, these same people would complain that many Vietnamese were receiving welfare benefits. However, I don't think the high level of Vietnamese who were unemployment was necessarily due to discrimination. I think it was the recession at the time leading to generally high unemployment, as well as poor levels of English and lack of UK diplomas or accreditation. I knew the Vietnamese are good workers, they just needed help getting started in our new home. Helping Vietnamese find jobs became another high priority for us.

Paul's first success was to obtain a small sum of money to develop a few programmes. His support was invaluable – he understood how things worked in the UK and helped us navigate the system. He was a funny man though: he chose to sleep in the office we had in Homerton House School, as he didn't have another place to live. The office didn't have a bath so he smelled. But we needed and trusted him so quickly got used to his lifestyle.

We used the money Paul raised to open a class teaching English as a second language (usually referred to as ESOL) in the mornings. That didn't come close to meeting the demand as our office could only hold a few people at a time, but as there were hundreds of other English language classes around London, we weren't too worried. What we couldn't find, however, was a place where Vietnamese children could continue to learn how to speak, read and write in their native language. Parents were proud of how quickly their children learned English at school, but didn't want them to stop speaking Vietnamese at home. If the children weren't taught Vietnamese, parents feared the children would lose the ability to communicate with their elders. So at Clapton Girls School on Saturdays we offered two or three Vietnamese language classes at different levels, which funders called 'mother-tongue learning programmes'. The classes were a great success but when Hackney Council declared that they could no longer afford to pay overtime for the caretakers to open and lock up for us on Saturdays, we had to move.

Classes

A different language is a different vision of life.

Federico Fellini

It wasn't long before Homerton School realised that the demand for our services was growing, and that we needed more space. So the next year, 1987, the school kindly offered us a portacabin – a stand-alone box room on wheels in the school's car park. The portacabin was large enough for me to keep files and offer a chair to visiting families. I no longer had to carry all the paperwork back and forth from my flat to the office on my motorbike, and we could hold small classes there. This was great progress for us; it made us feel more settled and gave us room to offer a more professional service. Everything, however, was still being done on a voluntary basis.

The demand for mother-tongue classes grew quickly, so we moved the classes to the VLC community centre, a centre founded with money from the Greater London Council (GLC). In the mid 1980s Margaret Thatcher closed the GLC, then run by Ken Livingstone, so that the government could run London directly. Before being handed over to the central government the GLC gave away all of the spare money in its budget as grants to local community groups; they preferred the money to be spent instead of just being absorbed by the central government. I seized this opportunity and applied for money, since I wanted a meeting place or venue for celebrations and events via the VLC. We received £100,000, which we used to purchase an old chapel and convert it into what became the VLC Community Centre.

I also submitted a second proposal for a media resource centre that would have printing equipment, as I often had to go to a local printing company to make and copy textbooks and materials for the mother-tongue classes. The staff at the Centre helped me to complete the application form for GLC money, and we asked for £50,000. I waited and waited, but I never received a letter from the GLC. When I enquired about the status of the application, I was told that it had been approved but, because they never received a response from us, they put back the money. Such a shame.

I was still an active supporter of the VLC but was no longer on the management committee. I approached them about the Vietnamese language classes and they were very open. There was enough room at the VLC community centre to allow us to offer thirteen classes, and we could therefore teach children from age six all the way to A-level. It was very successful and there were enough students for the Department of Education to allow young Vietnamese students to sit the exam for GCSE and A-level Vietnamese.

CHAPTER ELEVEN

Housing

God loves to help him who strives to help himself.

Aeschylus, 525 BC - 456 BC

As I mentioned earlier, the resettlement policy of the British government in the early 1980s was to disperse the newly arrived Vietnamese around the country, based on where local authorities offered accommodation for refugees. However, once dispersed, many of the Vietnamese felt isolated and alone. They didn't feel at home, even in the nice properties in the countryside, and they moved to London.

I remember this period clearly. Many Vietnamese became squatters, breaking down the doors of empty flats and moving in, living there illegally. This was especially common in the London borough of Hackney, which, at that time, was a very rough borough - white people didn't want to live there. That is why Hackney Council committee was one of the main local authorities to come to Thorney Island Refugee Resettlement Centre to offer us accommodation, while other wealthier London boroughs offered none. Now, many in the Vietnamese community feel that Hackney opened its heart to them. The council's offer was fully appreciated, and I often say that Hackney today has become the "safe nest for the drifted Vietnamese birds".

Over time, more and more Vietnamese moved to Hackney to live. Eventually, the Hackney council agreed to consider the squatters as homeless and offered them accommodation. Today, Hackney is home to the largest Vietnamese community in the UK, an estimated 4,000 Vietnamese in the borough.

After this second migration from around the country back to the capital, London authorities, including Hackney, were very slow to offer permanent housing to the Vietnamese. In addition there was the natural growth of population within the Vietnamese community, as well as the arrival of more Vietnamese from Vietnam or Hong Kong through family reunion. This meant the housing needs of the community continued to grow. The local authorities and other housing associations tried to respond to the need, but there was never enough accommodation. There always seems to be a shortage of housing stock; this was the case then and is still the case now.

I kept hearing people mention 'housing associations' and even worked with a few and thought this might be an answer to our prayers. Housing associations are basically not-for-profit landlords – businesses, trusts, or charities that maintain affordable homes for people with housing needs. Some rent the properties and provide additional support to the tenants, such as care for those with mental illness, while others help people purchase affordable homes. What if we started a housing association that would support the housing needs of the Vietnamese community?

I asked Paul to find information on how to set up a housing association, and he also conducted research into housing association law. Paul's help was essential. After all our research, I was able to set up An Việt Housing Association in 1988, which started off with letting one property from a housing association. It was a 'short-life' property, meaning that the housing association that owned it was waiting to demolish or refurbish it. This housing association let us manage the property and fund other projects from the rent paid by the tenants. This simple start helped me learn how to run our own housing association and how to manage properties.

One year later, we were the first Vietnamese housing association officially recognised by the Housing Corporation - the government agency that oversees housing associations in England. We received great support from them, which was vital, as it is the primary source of funding for housing associations. It is also the regulatory body.

Here in the UK, housing associations provide new homes for people who need them. Most associations are small and own fewer than 250 homes. However, the top 10% of associations, many with over 2,500 homes, own 80% of all the sector's homes. These larger housing associations have more assets and more money; it is easier for them to stay leaders in the sector as they have a stronger ability to purchase and develop further housing. Thus housing associations obey that invisible law of power: the big get bigger and the small get smaller; the rich get richer and the poor get poorer.

Still, we had defied the odds. First, my wife Điệp became the first Vietnamese qualified housing officer and started working for us. Second, we had acquired 176 properties within three years of founding An Việt Housing Association. This was unheard of for such a small housing association, even during times when funding from the Housing Corporation was generous. Most other housing associations run by minority groups tended to focus only in one region, often in one borough of a city, whereas An Việt was the only minority housing association that operated nationally. We had properties in cities around the UK where there was a large population of Vietnamese, with twenty properties in Birmingham, fifteen in Bristol, sixteen in Southampton and eight in Northampton.

My goal was not just to make property available to Vietnamese, but also to empower the local communities around the UK. I wanted the Vietnamese to manage their properties themselves so I tried to provide support and advice to the Vietnamese property managers in the hope that they would learn. I wanted the Vietnamese community to be independent and self-reliant. I didn't want us to be a burden to our host country.

A key feature of housing associations is that a committee, or board of management, made up of volunteers – often tenants, representatives from local community groups, business people or politicians – has overall responsibility for the work of the organisation. An Việt was no different. The management committee met regularly to make and approve all decisions, but as director of the association and secretary of the management committee, I did much of the day-to-day work.

I tried very hard to encourage the younger generation to participate in An Việt Housing Association, as they were fluent in English and also had professional skills. In those days however it was too early for the young generation to be involved. They had just finished their studies, maybe had new jobs, and didn't care about community work. Some also felt that the older generation did not act professionally, in the UK manner, as they had been taught, and, if someone from the younger generation did come to join the management committee, their Vietnamese was not very good. It was very difficult for the older generation to work in harmony with the younger generation.

I could have asked some British people to join, since they were willing to help, but the Vietnamese members of the committee at that time said that it would be difficult for them because they didn't speak English very well. In the end, the committee resisted having native English speakers on the Board. So instead, I reported everything to the management committee so they would know what was happening and why. I didn't mind this extra work.

An Việt Housing Association made good progress in providing for housing needs. At that time, the management committee was quite good and very stable, and all the members were Vietnamese. I trusted everyone on the management committee - many already were, or quickly became, friends and one was a relative of mine. We had a shared vision – we were very committed to developing housing for Vietnamese people and others who were in need. I was committed to running it in a proper way – not just according to the Housing Act and the instructions of the Housing Corporation – but according to the Confucian virtues of *Te* (good governance) and *Yi* (righteousness; the moral disposition to do good). With these strong foundations, I believed that An Việt Housing Association would have a positive, lasting impact.

Employment

I have not seen a person who loved virtue, or one who hated what was not virtuous. He who loved virtue would esteem nothing above it.

Confucius, Analects

An Việt Foundation continued to operate as before, providing advice, youth programmes, services for the elderly and assistance with job hunts. But in 1989, the government changed the welfare benefit rules. It instituted "actively seeking work" regulations among other things. Quite a few Vietnamese were threatened with benefit suspension if they fell foul of this new regulation. This meant that many Vietnamese would stop receiving money from the government unless they could prove they were doing their best to find employment.

I was personally determined to help people into work; it angered me to see adults who were given a second chance, unable to do anything with it. So An Việt Foundation stepped in and made a deal with the local Restart Team – the government's enforcers of the "actively seeking work" scheme. We agreed that, rather than immediately cutting off someone's benefits, Restart teams in Hackney and surrounding boroughs would refer

Vietnamese and other Southeast Asian refugees to An Việt Foundation for assistance. In turn, An Việt Foundation would report any employment-seeking activity (or lack of it) to the Restart Team.

This formalised our employment and training project. This also made us quite unpopular with many within the Vietnamese community. We were honest with the refugees about their requirements and what impact this would have on their lives, and explained their options to them. We offered help and support in finding work. The practical support involved exploring career ambitions, educational background, individual strengths and weaknesses and creating a job-hunt plan.

Naturally, some Vietnamese did not like this and did not want to participate. A few of these individuals were too frightened to enter the UK job market – they wanted to work but lost all hope and confidence after many employment rejections, or because they felt they were unskilled or still couldn't speak English confidently. For these individuals, much of our work focused on building up their self-esteem and setting realistic expectations. We were quite successful in the end, helping many find jobs that led to self-sufficiency.

However, others did not want to participate in the Restart scheme because they simply lost the desire to work. They expected to live on welfare benefits for the rest of their life. They had become dependent, and did not have any dreams or ambition. When they were referred to An Việt Foundation, they expected us to falsely amend our records so that their benefits would not stop. Of course, we refused, and, of course, this upset many people.

Entrepreneur

Believe me, he who does not think of the wants of the poor is not a member of the Body of Christ. For if one member suffers, all suffer.

St. Alphege of Canterbury

At An Việt Foundation, we knew that the road to self-sufficiency for many Vietnamese was to help refugees to start their own businesses. Vietnamese have always preferred to work for themselves, to have family owned businesses with relatives as staff you can trust. A few were naturally entrepreneurial and went ahead and opened their own businesses, like Mr Nguyễn Đức Cung[6]. Cung volunteered his time to help with An Việt Foundation, and was also part of the management committee from the beginning. When he wasn't helping at An Việt, he was working behind a stall he had in Hackney Market. Cung was a bit of an artist: he made large figurines of animals out of clay and painted them. He sold them as decorative items that people could put in their gardens. He was very resourceful and was eventually able to sell his stall in Hackney and move to Covent Garden.

On the side, tourists paid him to tell their fortune. He dressed in traditional Vietnamese clothing, burned incense at an altar – all to make him look mysterious – and charged £5 to read palms and, even with his broken English, say a few things about a tourist's future. He eventually made a fortune doing this over the years. He recently stopped and used the money to open a mini-market, the first Vietnamese mini-market in Hackney.

Many Vietnamese wanted to run their own business like

---

[6] Name has been changed to protect identity

Cung, but very few had the money to do so. Some Vietnamese got jobs in the catering industry, working in take-away restaurants, however not everyone wanted to do this kind of work and there was a limited demand for staff in this industry. Despite the number of jobs in London, finding employment for Vietnamese was not easy. Cung and I went around Hackney and surrounding areas enquiring about the types of job opportunities that were available; we focused on low-skilled manufacturing jobs, but few seemed willing to hire Vietnamese refugees.

Then we found something that would work. We stumbled on it by accident, when we found ourselves in a huge warehouse. I first noticed the noise, a loud hum, which men were continually trying to shout over in a language I did not understand. It felt hot and musty, despite the cold outside, and there was a smell of damp. Then my eyes adjusted to the light and I saw racks and racks of clothing and fabric. It was a clothing manufacturer. The Turkish owner was desperately looking for help – his factory cut fabrics to specified patterns, but they were always short of people who could sew the fabric into a garment for sale. I told him about all the Vietnamese refugees who were willing to work hard, but didn't speak any English. English wasn't needed for this work. It was a great match.

Before long, Cung and I had met most of the local Turkish, Jewish, Cypriot and Greek manufacturers in the Hackney area and asked them if they would be willing to hire or work with Vietnamese. This became an easy way for Vietnamese to enter the job market, as the work was simple to learn.

Most Vietnamese involved in clothes making worked from home, and they were paid horribly low prices. For instance, they might be paid just 20p to sew a complete shirt. To do the sewing, all they needed was a commercial sewing machine. How much money they earned depended on how many garments they could sew in a day.

Nonetheless, some were able to make a decent living over

time. At first, they found that when they bought enough cloth for a promised one hundred shirts, they would have some fabric left over. They would then get a design from the showroom and cut the cloth themselves before sewing as usual. They would then sell the clothes at markets for a cheaper price – the only difference being the lack of a label or brand name. Many Vietnamese were able to make some money this way; their income was equivalent to slave labour, but many felt that it was better than nothing. They would work very hard, often starting their day at 5am and working on till midnight.

Over time, some who worked in the clothing industry wanted to open their own clothing business, and we would help them get started – find an accountant, register as a limited company, apply for enterprise allowance and so on. We would also help them to contact the showrooms so they could go and purchase pre-cut cloth to make into garments. They would go to the showrooms, and negotiate on the price they would accept for taking home a piece of cloth that was already cut for assembly and sewing.

For investment capital, Vietnamese needed around £10,000 to £20,000 to take over a small workshop. Vietnamese would never consider borrowing money from the bank. Instead, some would work hard and save, others were able to borrow money from relatives, and others would obtain the money using the traditional *choi hui,* where ten to twenty individuals each deposit a set amount of money each month and then, using a rota, take turns withdrawing the needed money. For example, if twenty people each paid in £1,000 each month, then each month, a member of the group would receive £20,000.

The enterprise thrived. The small workshops employed around 400 people by late 1989 and increased dramatically through the 1990s. The clothing was for UK factories, but also exported to other parts of Europe. There were Vietnamese communities living in Eastern Europe and at the time these countries were still under Communist regimes. When communism collapsed in the early 90s, the Vietnamese communities there also started making clothes. These communities then competed with the UK Vietnamese community for the clothing market. However, those living in countries like Poland or Czechoslovakia had an advantage because the fabric was cheaper there – in the UK we were importing fabric from Eastern Europe.

Ironically, when Eastern Europe became part of EU, the clothes making industry collapsed in places like Poland and Czechoslovakia, because of competition from Vietnam itself. When clothing factories closed down, the Vietnamese started to open nail salons. I don't know if the Vietnamese nail salon phenomenon started in the US or Europe. I presume it started in the States because the Vietnamese community in the US settled down very well and there was a great need, especially for young women, to find good employment. It spread very quickly and was very successful everywhere.

With nail salons, families can be independent and can get money straight from the customers without any intermediary (which was also the case in the clothes making industry). I don't know how it got started but once some Vietnamese became successful then the news quickly spread around the community. Starting a nail salon takes money, which a young person or a new arrival wouldn't have, so it was the clothes makers who saved money who could invest in the salons.

Vietnamese now dominate the nail market, nail salons are almost exclusively owned by the Vietnamese community. For most, it started with owning the nail salon, but then Vietnamese started opening and running the supplier businesses (varnish supplies) and also the nail schools. This meant that the Vietnamese were involved in, and controlled, the whole 'chain'.

At An Việt, we were the first to open the nail training centre in London for Vietnamese. We asked people in the college to come here to An Việt to teach and this arrangement lasted for about three years. At the time we were involved, there were still very few

Vietnamese nail shops. After training at our centre, they got a certificate so they could open up their own shops, so An Việt was part of the first movement for nail development in London.

Other successful businesses included take away and fish & chip shops, self-employed house repair and decoration, and cleaning contractors. These were usually small enterprises with family members as cheap, trustworthy labour. Even as the younger children became educated in the UK they would help support the family business by working there and providing help with translation and paperwork. If the business grew and needed more staff, the owners would hire close friends or contacts made through the community.

When the clothing factories closed, some people opened mini-supermarkets that sold Vietnamese food, especially in London where there was a large community. Some are still very successful; they order products straight from Vietnam to sell in the UK, including vegetables and sometimes even dog meat. They hide it from the border/airport security who check 'declared goods'. Someone told me it is not easy to bring dog meat here, but sometimes officers don't pay enough attention so they can get through. When they are able to get dog into the country, it is usually given and sold to friends secretly, but not in their shop because they know the news would spread and the police would come.

It is helpful having Vietnamese food shops, especially now that Vietnam is more open, and it is easier to access and serve authentic Vietnamese food. I buy everything here in London at these supermarkets. It is easier for me because if I tried to import directly from Vietnam I'd have to go through so much paperwork.

Irony

Those who profess to favor freedom and yet depreciate agitation, are people who want crops without ploughing the ground; they want rain without thunder and lightning; they want the ocean without the roar of its many waters. The struggle may be a moral one, or it may be a physical one, or it may be both. But it must be a struggle. Power concedes nothing without a demand; it never has and it never will.

Frederick Douglass

While An Việt Foundation worked hard to promote self-reliance among the Vietnamese community, the government was indirectly promoting a different message. I'm not referring to the message coming from the benefits offices, and employment branches of the government. They were very clear about their desire for us Vietnamese to be self-sufficient and stand on their own two feet, because this meant that they would pay taxes.

However, when the government was ready to fund projects for refugees or other communities, they gave the money to a couple of central, national agencies run by white people.

An Việt Foundation and other Vietnamese self-help agencies were much more successful, yet we operated with only the help of volunteers and a miniscule budget. The British Refugee Council was too large, bureaucratic and remote to make the impact that we could, since we were situated next door to the refugees. We argued that it was time for the national agencies like Refugee Action or the British Refugee Council to withdraw, and that the Vietnamese self-help groups should be recognised, properly resourced, and supported by local and central government.

We highlighted this discrepancy at the 1989 An Việt national conference, which celebrated the ten-year anniversary of the Geneva Convention, where Britain was pressured into resettling additional Boat People. Our conference was hosted by Vietnamese, was for Vietnamese and was about the Vietnamese. The consensus of the delegates at the conference was that the time of the national refugee resettlement programme was over. We sent the conference reports and letters to leaders in the Home Office, but only received a patronising reply. The Home Office stated that it had created the national resettlement programme to develop Vietnamese self-help groups, and therefore they were happy to see we had made 'considerable progress'. They did not recognise that agencies like An Việt Foundation made this 'considerable' progress without the benefit of the money given to the national refugee programme. They could not comprehend that we were competing against agencies like the British Refugee Council or Refugee Action for funding to achieve similar aims – funding that the big refugee organisations usually received but small ones like ours never saw.

As insulting as the Home Office reply was, it made it very clear how the system worked - that the bigger the charity is, the more funding they will receive; the more English people running the service, the more effective the service appears to the funders; the more a community needs to be 'empowered', the more they need others to do it 'to them' or 'for them'.

I found the funders' view patronising. I was angry. But I also recognised that I could not change the way the system worked, so if I wanted to continue serving the Vietnamese community and fostering independence, I would need to find a way to work within the system.

Fraud

Rather fail with honour than succeed by fraud.

Sophocles

In Vietnam, fraud, lies, corruption, disorder, pettiness all existed; there were many people at all levels of society who were ignorant of the virtues that can lead to peace and prosperity, just as there is in every society. But in Vietnam, family, friends and mentors - inside the seminary and out - made it easy for me to take shelter in the philosophical and moral teachings of the church and the ancient sages like Confucius. We had a common grounding and ideals which we were striving towards, a common language which we all spoke regarding how man should conduct his life.

Something happened when the Vietnamese separated from the homeland. It's as if all of that was thrown away. We couldn't see familiar leaders exhibiting the ideals of virtuous behaviour; all our wise elders were now sweeping floors. Perhaps some felt this gave them permission to abandon propriety, or perhaps, they thought first of their own survival and hoped that later, in the future, they'd have the luxury of contemplating justice, order and truthfulness.

Perhaps that is how so many Vietnamese justified not working within the UK system or obeying UK law. Or, perhaps it is the Western view that money can fix anything, including unemployment. There were national programmes to support employment, but even though these national programmes had a £32 million budget, they failed. The employment schemes for example, sponsored by the national programme, were standard for all British. Therefore it did not take into account the unique difficulties faced by refugees. For instance, the national programme encouraged middle-aged Vietnamese to train for clerical and administrative jobs, ignoring the fact that many still only had a basic understanding of English. But that wasn't the largest problem.

An Việt conducted further research into employment in the Vietnamese community living in five north London boroughs. The survey threw up continued large-scale unemployment – for heads of the family it was around 78%. We also learned that a considerable number of Vietnamese in the survey area were claiming benefits to which they were not entitled – usually by not notifying the government about any earnings, even if negligible. Also, some who weren't receiving benefits often failed to declare tax on their earnings. We knew that if word got out, the Vietnamese community and other minorities would be further ostracised and could stir up hatred against them.

We also knew that all of these issues were interconnected, and that much of the problem stemmed from the instability of their income. Members of the Vietnamese community who were able to find employment tended to work making garments in their homes or working in a Chinese owned business where they were paid cash-in-hand. This meant that they did not have an employment contract, so the workers were vulnerable to exploitation and unfair dismissal. Garment work was all or nothing, and often there were times when no work was available. When they were paid – the money was negligible. These were not stable jobs or regular sources of income. Hence, most families depended on benefits for stability.

I also suspect another reason why the Vietnamese were reluctant to pay tax is related to the reality of war-torn Vietnam. They didn't trust any government, or corrupt official, not to take more than their fair share. In addition, few understood UK bookkeeping and tax law and were afraid of being punished for sending inaccurate returns – or of being suspected of inaccuracy even when truthful. Vietnamese never use banks: again they don't trust them, because of the experience in Vietnam. So all cash goes into secret hoards in the house. The government, therefore, does not know how much money they have, and they have savings ready for the next flight and escape. All this relates to the Vietnamese fear that the UK will want to throw them out of the country despite their refugee status. A refugee never settles, and refugees often need to be selfish. Only by being completely selfish will they survive.

But I knew that a deeper source of the problem was the Vietnamese feelings of 'victimhood'. It all began as a survival technique in Vietnam where we had to flee persecution. Our government took away our rights, our individuality and our nationality, and the Vietnamese authorities inflicted emotional, and often physical pain. Our very humanity was taken away; we became non-beings, without worth. Suddenly, at the height of our misery, the British government gave us sanctuary: a house, money – a sense of self-worth. Whilst receiving this gift from the government, many Vietnamese became dependent on it; if any part were to be taken away they would lose a proportion of their fragile sense of worth. A refugee's feelings towards government are ambivalent – he trusts no one in authority and is fearful of the state. But, through the benefit system, the hand of the state, his sense of self-worth is reinforced and he becomes deeply dependent on the physical fortnightly proof of his continued worth.

To my mind, it was this time of uncertainty, of moral chaos, when families were separated from their ancestors that we needed to cling to the Vietnamese core belief in righteous behaviour: to help others, to speak the truth and to act with honour. This included honouring the rules of our new home. So staff at An Việt Foundation applied for funding to expand our employment work. We believed that a programme, led by a Vietnamese community group could reach and help Vietnamese to become confident and legitimate earners and taxpayers. We hoped we could remind the Vietnamese of their proud heritage and strength and find their feet again.

Our success came from the fact that it was difficult for the Vietnamese to pull the wool over our eyes, and we were able to work with the Vietnamese sympathetically. In this way we could effectively encourage and assist Vietnamese to join mainstream society and become taxpayers. They knew we wouldn't let them get away with fraud; that they had to actively seek work or their benefits would stop. However, our prime motivation was not to prevent anyone getting caught for fraud, but to remind everyone that the Vietnamese brought skills with them, and thus did not have to depend on catering or garment-making to survive the rest of their life. We wanted to lead by example and to pass on confidence. We hoped that many would find their own internal sense of worth that did not depend on the government, and we hoped that once people felt good about themselves again, they could then reach out and help others, restoring balance to the community.

I'm proud of the successes in the community. I'm very practical and want to help people to do good work. Lao Zu asks us to distance ourselves from life, but Confucius encouraged us to engage with life and change things for the better.

Growth

It does not matter how slowly you go so long as you do not stop.

Confucius

An Việt Foundation continued to expand, and the mother-tongue classes opened in other parts of the UK, including in Thamesmead, Derby, Harlow and Birmingham. We carried on with English classes; employment and education assistance; support for the elderly; youth programmes; and still hosted local festivals.

With all this growth, An Việt Foundation needed more space. I called Hackney Council to ask for information, and explained that I wanted to know how we could find an office for our community group. What followed was very strange. Usually when I called the council, I would get a receptionist who seemed determined not to connect me to a staff person who knew what they were doing. This time, however, my call went straight to the right person. I don't know who picked up the phone, but he said: "Yes, we have a very good building in Englefield Road that has been empty for nearly ten years." I couldn't believe it. He then said, "If you want to have a look, I'd be pleased to arrange for someone from the council to meet you there to open the door for you." Of course I agreed.

It was a typically grey, rainy day when Paul and I met the officer at the building. I was early and had to wait for the officer to show up. While I waited, I explored the grounds a bit on my own. There was something different, unusual about the building that I could not place: it did not look like a house, nor did it look like an office. There was a brick and iron gate in the front with some overgrown trees and shrubs, and I could tell that the building had been vacant for a long time. There was a lot of rubbish that had been thrown over the gate, a few of the windows were broken, and the paint was peeling off.

The officer arrived and invited us in. When I first stepped in, the first thing I noticed was the size of the rooms in the building. There was so much space. The man gave us the basic tour: "This building was built in 1930. As you can see, this is where the laundry facilities were…" I wasn't sure if I heard him correctly, but I didn't say anything. Paul and I simply followed him down the dark corridor where he pointed: "This side was for the women and that side was for the men."

Paul looked just as confused as I was. We walked into the 'men's side' and saw taps for water, and huge baths surrounded by shelves and clothes racks. The entire floor and wall was tiled.

"What kind of building was this?" I finally asked.

"This was a public bath house, sir," he replied. "The

residents of the area would come here to take their baths since they didn't have bath rooms in their homes. They would come here, wash their clothes, wash themselves, then go home and return the next week to do it all again."

An old bathhouse for an office space? Why not? I thought. If anything, the public baths were actually too big for us at that time. I immediately informed the council that I was interested. And what luck. The council accepted the feasibility study that Paul wrote, and helped us to apply for funding from the Department of the Environment's Urban Improvement Grant. We were given £250,000 to convert the building. It took two years to finish the building works, but the entire process was fraught from the beginning.

I was so naïve. The walls that went along the building and all the walls separating each bath were built with marble, and each bath door was made of a heavy solid wood. All of this marble and wood was incredibly valuable. I noticed the builders taking tremendous care with the marble, cutting it into even squares with great concern and attention, stacking the marble in a specific place at the back of the building. I had no idea how valuable the marble was, nor that the builders would want it. Then one night, they brought a lorry, and took all of the marble away; they must have sold it for 100% profit. I knew the doors were valuable, and there were hundreds of them, so I asked the builders to put a lock on the wooden doors to the boiler house at the back of the building. I then locked it and controlled it to keep it safe, hoping to sell the doors and thus raise more money for An Việt. One morning, however, I returned to work to find that the lock to the boiler room had been broken. All of the doors had gone. I can only assume that it was the builders.

During all this, Paul was able to work full-time as administrator for the Foundation. He had done really good work for us since he began, but working with him became more and more of a challenge. He worked very hard, but he had nowhere to live in London. Paul often slept in the office, which at that time did not have a bath or shower. It wasn't just his smell, which was bad enough, but every room he worked in would end up incredibly dirty – he'd leave a trail of dirty dishes on the tables, food crumbs on the floor, and used tissues behind the desks. Every day I would have to clean up after him.

Over time, I realised I might not be able to trust him. When refurbishing the building in 1991, we received funding from the Department of the Environment, but the funding did not cover all of the estimated costs. Paul told me and Hackney Council, that we had been awarded £25,000 from Tudor Trust to cover the rest of the costs. Only later, when the building works were almost done and all the council money was about to run out, did we learn that Paul never actually applied to Tudor Trust for the money. Was that intentional; did he lie to me? Or was it a mistake? Perhaps he forgot.

In the end we did receive £5,000 from Tudor Trust as well as a series of other small grants, which enabled us to finish the building. However, the only reason that we were able to complete the project was because Clare came in, replacing Paul when he disappeared again.

Paul's disappearances had both occurred during the Christmas season. He would disappear for months and I would have no idea where he was. The first time, I called Mr Thống, the man who introduced us, to ask if he had heard from him. Mr Thống became worried as well, promised to look for him, and searched inside some of the temporary flats owned by his housing association in Bristol. When he entered one of the empty flats, he was shocked to see piles of wine and beer bottles scattered everywhere. Mr Thống had a suspicion of what must have happened and when he called the police, they told him that Paul had been admitted to hospital. When Paul recovered, he came back to London and continued to work for me.

Over Christmas 1991, Paul didn't show up for work, and I didn't see or hear from him for several weeks. No one knew where he was, but remembering what had happened a year earlier, I looked for him in one of An Việt Housing Association's short-term flats in Finsbury Park: I found him on the floor like a dog, and I couldn't stop coughing because of the smell. Paul was sprawled in his own vomit, surrounded by bottles of wine, beer and liquor. He recovered, and returned to work for me again four or five months later when we moved into our new premises. I didn't care how Paul spent his free time, I was used to his nomadic lifestyle and hoped he'd continue his good work for An Việt. We also still needed someone who was British who could help us.

Changes

For a just man falleth seven times, and riseth up again...

Proverbs 24:16

In the early 1990s I was busier than ever. I volunteered at An Việt Foundation, I worked as director of An Việt Housing Association and I was part of a Vietnamese Catholic Charity. At that time the Vietnamese community was very organised, and in those days every London borough had a Vietnamese community organisation. I therefore created the Vietnamese National Council to act as an umbrella group for all of the smaller organisations. I wanted us to have a more unified voice so that we could have a stronger lobby and increase our chances of gaining political recognition and obtaining funding.

Day-to-day life at An Việt was quite chaotic, but I liked it that way – it meant that we were reaching more and more people. The phone was always ringing, and people were constantly coming in and out of the office. There were always ESOL students walking around, asking for reimbursements for their travel to class – a perk of the funding award. Vietnamese clients could walk in for advice and assistance. Accountants, students, local politicians all came through our doors. The more diverse our funding stream, the more monitoring visits we had. Volunteers came and went.

When we moved to the new building, we first used the area at the back as a factory. It was a place where we let Vietnamese run a small clothing factory, so that they could gain experience before setting up on their own. Five families paid a small fee to An Việt so that they could learn about clothes-making here in the Centre, before moving on to open bigger clothes-making factories elsewhere. We also had a printing press.

We still had our youth play scheme, and new projects included a computer-training programme, printing services and certificates in catering and food hygiene. We also still provided advice, hosted cultural festivals, and provided two English classes a day in the Centre.

Yet sadly, at this same time, while many of our services at An Việt Foundation were growing, the need for the National Council declined. Many Vietnamese community organisations failed not long after they started, and only a few such as An Việt, and those in Tower Hamlets, Southwark and Kingston still exist. But outside London we still have strong Vietnamese communities in cities like Bristol, Birmingham, Nottingham, Northampton and Manchester. All of the others closed down, mainly because of funding problems. Often, after receiving funding from a local authority or a trust, the community group would recruit Vietnamese staff, and that, in itself, was a good thing. However, people were frequently hired because they were a relative or friend, not because of any particular skills they had.

I recognised that our English was not very good and that we didn't understand the systems for running a charity in the UK. For this reason, we have always hired English staff to raise funds for projects and to coordinate and network with outside bodies. I tried to hire Vietnamese staff who had the necessary skills for the job, not just individuals I knew or who were recommended by friends. If they lacked some skills, I hoped training would help. But, I discovered, as many managers have around the world, that despite our best hopes and intentions, job interviews often don't reveal who is a person of integrity, who really shares your vision of serving the community and who will stab you in the back.

CHAPTER TWELVE

Accusations

To put the world right in order, we must first put the nation in order; to put the nation in order, we must first put the family in order; to put the family in order, we must first cultivate our personal life; we must first set our hearts right.

Confucius

The problems at An Việt Housing Association began late in September 1992, when the chairman and Paul went to the Housing Corporation with an urgent request for a meeting. The chairman had apparently found a letter in one of the training classrooms in Southwark. In the letter, an anonymous man stated that I had promised to give him a housing association property if he paid me £500. He claimed that he met me at a McDonald's at 12.30 pm where he gave me the money. He was upset because he still hadn't received a property and was asking for his money back.

I had heard whispers before that I accepted bribes. These rumours were common among members of the community who didn't understand how the housing association chose which family would receive a property. I knew that these stories stemmed from misunderstandings, jealousy and often desperation. Because I knew the truth, I never worried about it.

Unfortunately the Housing Corporation believed the letter. No one at the Housing Corporation asked me for an explanation or questioned whether the letter was genuine. Instead, the Housing Corporation immediately froze the funds of An Việt Housing Association, and reported the alleged crime to the police.

Once I heard about the letter, and the way in which Housing

Corporation had learned about it, I knew immediately what was going on. About a month earlier, the chairman had come to me and casually complained about how he was having trouble finding someone to repair his roof. I didn't think much of it at the time, and simply said that he could look in the Yellow Pages to find someone qualified, or that he could ask around in the Vietnamese community to see if there was anyone interested in the work. Later on, two men who worked for An Việt Foundation – let's call them Mr. Tho and Thi (Thi is my cousin, who at this point was a member of the committee) - came to see me in the office. Mr Tho had been working with a family that was struggling. I genuinely meant it when I said, "I am glad to have you here to help, your expertise is greatly needed."

"Thank you." I knew from the look in his eyes that something was on his mind, but I realised that it would take a while to learn what it was. I made us some coffee and we talked about family in Vietnam and the latest scandal to make the Vietnamese newspapers.

"I'm tired of hearing the chairman complain about the leaks in his roof cousin, aren't you?"

I paused. I knew that we were getting to the real point of the visit. I replied carefully: "He did mention something the other day. I recommended that he find someone in the community who could do the work cheaply. Has he found anyone?"

"No he hasn't. The chairman keeps complaining that his wife is very angry because of the leaks. I wish we could do something to help them to resolve the issue once and for all. The chairman complains he can't afford the expensive roofing costs of this country." Mr Tho rolled his eyes as he spoke to emphasise his dismay.

"An angry wife makes all men miserable," I agreed, "but there is nothing we can do."

We all quietly sipped our coffee while I waited for his next move.

Mr Tho pretended that he had just come up with a great new

idea: "Let's tell the chairman to go ahead and fix his roof. He can then give his receipt to you and you can have the housing association pay the bill." Both Mr Tho and Thi got very excited, as if this was the perfect solution. They quickly began making further suggestions on how we could get the housing association to pay.

I interrupted them abruptly: "No, it is not allowed. Never. I can't do that." They both looked genuinely shocked. In Vietnam, this became a normal way to do business. I spent the rest of the coffee break explaining British laws and the importance of running An Việt Housing Association in accordance with the Confucian principle of Yi (righteousness). I reminded him of the corruption we had just fled and that we now had a chance for the Vietnamese community to run businesses ethically. It fell on deaf ears.

One night Thi came to my flat at 11.00 pm. Only my wife Điệp was at home. Thi told Điệp that I should give the chairman £5,000, and that if I gave him the money, the chairman would drop the charges of bribery. My wife said: "No." I knew that I didn't have to worry, and that the police would not find any evidence. So of course I didn't pay him, and of course I was freed of the allegations made against me.

I'm not sure why Paul got involved – he had left the organisation earlier in the year. Perhaps Paul was still not happy with me for refusing to make him director of An Việt Foundation when he returned from his long absence. In the past he was reliable, but since the previous Christmas, he wasn't the same. We all make mistakes. However, Hackney Council's Partnership and Co-ordination Office said they would not fund us if Paul had anything to do with the project because of the issue with the Tudor Trust. I appreciated all his work and skills, but couldn't have someone with a bad reputation become director.

And I guess Mr Tho was also not happy with me - I assume that this was because I also wouldn't let him use housing association funds for personal use. I had bought a car for the housing association because staff had to drive widely in order to visit all the properties. I had to take the new car to the garage to install an alarm, and Mr Tho came with me in his own car. He got the garage to install an alarm in his car as well, and when it was time to pay the money, he asked me to put his car on the bill, at a cost of £150. I said "No" and explained that this was a company car, but that his car was his own personal one so he had to pay with his own money and not housing association money. He didn't understand. Mr Tho was Treasurer for the housing association.

But the most unbelievable supporter of the malicious fraud was Thi, my cousin. He was a civil engineer, having re-qualified in this country; he had worked for a while in the building industry but was out of work at that time. Why did he join the chairman, Paul and Mr. Tho in their conspiracy to overthrow me? I later learned that they all intended to install Thi as director of An Việt Housing Association – that explained everything. It was a nasty betrayal. To not just disrespect, but to lie and deceive a family member like that is a deep hurt to the Vietnamese. Love of family, loyalty to one's family, is central to everything in Vietnam.

That might be why Thi assumed I'd let him get away with it, but I couldn't. When he came to challenge me, he said "I am your cousin, you're supposed to help family. Why won't you support me and approve me as director?"

"We're not in Vietnam, we have to follow the English rules. The law says that staff can only use money from the housing association for expenses related to the work. If you, Paul and Mr Tho were in power, you'd use the money for your own benefit and destroy this project."

"How dare you insult me! I work hard for the housing association and so deserve to be paid. We all do. We want to help the community so we would never do anything to destroy the project. The housing association is doing well."

Thi must have expected me to back down once he showed his anger. He still didn't understand. Even if he only took £25, it was still wrong. "No matter how small the amount, it is illegal to use funds of the housing association for personal use. £50 wouldn't destroy the project financially, but it would destroy our reputation and we'd have to shut down and lose all the funding if they found out." I was so angry. "I can't let you be director. You want to continue doing things in the way you did them in Vietnam. If I let you do illegal things, I would be destroying myself as well as the housing association."

My words stung. I had insulted him. "Cousin, you are betraying your family by not helping me". He was shaking with anger.

"No". I stood my ground.

"You are no longer my family," he said as he walked out the door.

Since then, I have never seen Thi. He now lives in Australia, and I have totally cut off my relationship with him and his family. That hurt, but I had no choice.

Thi's actions were hurtful, because he was family. But otherwise, allegations made against me never really make me nervous. I could no longer deny that I was surrounded by staff who put their own interests before those of the community. This is not foreign to any manager so I simply intended to be more cautious who I trusted in the future. I kept on working as normal.

Referrals

The universe would not be rich enough to buy the vote of an honest man.

Gregory I, (Saint Gregory)

All housing associations receive referrals from the local authority, and An Việt was no exception. We were a housing association set up by the Vietnamese, for the Vietnamese community, but because we were a housing association registered with the Housing

Corporation, we had to take referrals from the local authority and give out property based on need. If a property came up that had three bedrooms, for example, then An Việt Housing Association had to take the referrals that met the three-bedroom criteria (such as a large family with both sons and daughters who needed separate rooms), and choose three families with the most need. Of these, the housing association was to visit the families and based on the letting policy, decide which of these families best met the criteria. At An Việt, if we found that two families were of equal need, and one of them was a Vietnamese family, we were able to give preference to that Vietnamese family. However, if one family came out as the most obvious in need, regardless of ethnic background, then that family got the property. I found that occasionally some members of the management committee, the very ones who approved the letting policy and knew all this, had a difficult time believing that the procedure would or should actually be followed.

During the war, in Vietnam, anything could be bought. Bribes became standard ways to influence decisions. The Vietnamese still constantly assume that people in high positions use their contacts with the government to get what they want. That is the way in Vietnam and it was part of the mentality of the Vietnamese on the management committee. To their mind, they assumed that I used contacts between the local authority and An Việt to give tenancy agreements to friends or family. They never noticed that my close friends and family did not have An Việt housing. Instead, in their mind, they wanted to use their position to get property for their friends or family.

Usually, it was the members of the community, those who were in need of housing, who assumed that I allowed bribes to influence my decisions. This was how things were done in Vietnam so this is how many assumed things operated here in the UK. There was once a man who had a family greatly in need of housing: a property came up, and his family was one of three visited by An Việt as potential residents. He and his family were interviewed. He failed to get the property however, and was furious. The man went to the house he assumed he should have been offered to find out who had bribed me. He knocked on the door, but when he saw who answered it he understood and felt better about it. It was a family he knew, a family that had a much greater need for housing than his own family – they had more children and had been homeless for seven years. Only then did he believe my claim that I never took bribes, but he had to see it with his own eyes.

The irony is that the very same people who wanted An Việt to take bribes to influence decisions on who got a property, accused me of taking bribes for the same reason. These committee members told the Housing Corporation that they didn't know how I made decisions on who received a property, implying that I was being deceitful, but that was totally rubbish. I was not involved in the selection of tenants and they knew this. They knew that, according to the policy, new tenants were to be selected by a panel. This panel was made up of three individuals: one was a committee member, another was the housing manager and the third one was the housing officer. I was not part of the panel and I had their signatures to prove it.

In the investigation, the police found that someone giving a false name and address had written the letter. After further investigations, they concluded that the letter was 'malicious fraud'. The case was dropped, and I was very pleased.

Not long after the investigations things at An Việt were back to normal, the chairman, Tô Cao Huề[7], came to tell me that his wife did not want him to be chair anymore, saying: "She feels it wastes a lot of time."

I leaned back in my chair. I knew this was the Vietnamese indirect way of making a point. I knew the game, so I replied: "How can she say that all of the work you do for the housing association is a waste of time? You are the chair. We have so much work to do to keep this association going."

---

[7] Name has been changed to protect identity

"Yes," he replied, pausing to take a deep breath. "She doesn't understand all that we do or how hard this job is. All she knows is that I am often away from home with all the late meetings."

I nodded in agreement so he would know he could continue.

Mr Huề then went on: "You know how women are. Perhaps if you offered something, like a holiday in Paris for a week, she might consider letting me continue as chair."

I was almost surprised by the audacity of his statement. "You know I cannot do such a thing. I can't use funds from the housing association or the Foundation to buy personal things." He must have assumed that I would actually comply, and he must also have assumed that I was keen for him to remain as chair. Only that can explain the startled look that appeared in his eye when I said: "I understand your desire to make your wife happy. I know you don't want to keep making her upset by working extra hours here. If your wife does not want you to help anymore, you can simply sign a letter stating that you are resigning."

I guess he knew that his hidden threats wouldn't work. Mr Huề signed the letter of resignation, which I happily presented to the Board.

Recommendations

Why slap them on the wrist with feather when you can belt them over the head with a sledgehammer.

Katharine Hepburn

When the police investigations had been concluded, the Housing Corporation sent their own audit and evaluation officers to evaluate the work of An Việt Housing Association. They were specifically forbidden to investigate the allegations, and they were instead to simply check that we were working efficiently and ethically. Up until this point, we were trusted to get on with it; we were praised for our growth and success, but now we had the attention of the Housing Corporation and they must have been worried we were taking them for a ride.

The audit and evaluation officers came to An Việt five times and looked through all of the paperwork, including all documentation and files. Sometimes the visits were planned and scheduled, but on other occasions they were surprise visits. In the end, they found no evidence of negligence or mismanagement. In the report of their findings, the audit and evaluation officers said they were impressed with An Việt, noting that we had made great progress as a young housing association. This was good news.

The audit and evaluation officers also said, however, that there were still areas that needed improvement. The report was clear that these issues needed attention, but were not insurmountable. One of the officers said that these issues were not unique to An Việt and, in fact, were common concerns for small housing associations – especially those run by minority groups who might be inexperienced in housing. I was aware of the reality for minority or refugee groups – we came from a different culture, and had different ways of life and often didn't totally understand UK professional policies or laws.

To remedy this, the audit and evaluation report recommended that the committee members should receive more training in their roles and responsibilities, and that someone with more experience in UK housing matters should be appointed to the committee. I welcomed the suggestions – I was well aware of the shortcomings and agreed that it would be helpful to have some more experienced members on the management committee. But I was shocked when the Housing Corporation went beyond the recommendation of the report and co-opted four individuals with housing experience onto An Việt's management committee.

These new British born and raised, experienced members of the management committee worked really hard to help An Việt

Housing Association. They worked closely with us to strengthen our policies and share good ways of working. We learned a great deal and made great progress in a short period of time. But this wasn't good enough. We were late submitting one of our reports. The Housing Corporation said we had failed to comply with our end of the requirements and so the Housing Corporation was "going to have to take action".

This was an understatement, as the Housing Corporation transferred around 45 units – schemes not yet approved – to An Việt's development agents (all of them white housing associations), and this left An Việt with even fewer properties. The Corporation withdrew An Việt's right to nominate tenants to 'our' schemes, which meant that we could no longer recommend Vietnamese tenants for units that we didn't fully own. The Housing Corporation also advised all of the regional directors not to provide An Việt with further allocations of property. A contributor to *Black Housing* in April 1993 likened the Housing Corporations actions to "a sledge-hammer being used to crack a nut". Without access to properties, housing associations do not have development funds, so this undermined our ability to stay solvent or to make progress.

At the time I had no idea that this was just the beginning. Once a bureaucracy decides it wants something from you, it won't let go. The acts of a few foolish partners at An Việt started the involvement of an entire government body in the day to day running of our housing association. And trying to be heard, to use reason, to negotiate with a bureaucrat is as easy as lighting a candle in a thunderstorm. But I was not going to be swayed from my original dream to help the Vietnamese community. I was going to try to continue working as normal and learn what I could from the new members of the management committee.

Canteen

Man shall not live by bread alone.

Deuteronomy 8:3

I was so busy with some exciting new projects at An Việt Foundation that I didn't have time to sit around worrying about the dramas occurring within the housing association. An Việt Foundation was moving from success to success.

An Việt Foundation was well settled into the new building by April 1992 and the clothes-making workshops, printing press and catering/food hygiene training were still going strong. We also noticed that the new building gave us space to expand our project for the elderly in the Vietnamese community. My friend Dân became the coordinator for the elderly project – all the old ladies loved him because he would flirt and make them laugh. For a while we offered dance classes: they loved to learn ballroom dancing, and I don't think they realised they were exercising. Most of the time however, the elderly preferred playing mah-jong or Chinese chess. We also provided a video and TV for them to watch Vietnamese soap operas and films, as well as Vietnamese newspapers to read, and we would often organise Vietnamese festival celebrations at the Centre that would involve the elderly.

The elderly seemed to love the expanded services since it meant they could get out of their small flats and interact with others. When someone on my staff commented on how many of the elderly did not really get to eat lunch while their family was away at work, we all began to worry. Good nutrition is vital to health and well-being and eating traditional Vietnamese food, we knew, would be important to the elderly who were sad at being so far from home. Since our new facility had more space, we knew it would be easy to create a kitchen space to cook and serve food. So we opened a canteen to serve a hot lunch to the elderly. We also hoped that we could use the working canteen as a work placement for those who went through our catering/food hygiene course. It seemed like an enterprise that would benefit everyone.

The canteen started out serving basic dishes such as phở – a traditional Vietnamese soup. My wife did all the cooking. It took a few tests to discover which recipes everyone liked and, of course, all the old ladies had suggestions and ideas on how to improve the food. Phở is a Vietnamese staple – in Vietnam everyone ate it. Even if someone was too poor to open a shop, they could make phở and carry it around the city in a big pot over their shoulder and then sell it on the street. Phở is becoming quite popular in London. I recently heard about an English man who opened a place that sells phở in London. I guess he learned about it when travelling around Vietnam. I tried it but didn't really like it; it has a different taste than the one I'm used to. It didn't taste Vietnamese. But it is popular with the British and I think he wants to open more.

Back then, our canteen served phở regularly and soon gained a good reputation. All the staff and volunteers for the An Việt Foundation and housing association ate there as well.

Funds

There is no dependence that can be sure but a dependence upon one's self.

John Gay, English poet and dramatist

Owing to reductions in the grant money available for housing development, the Housing Corporation in 1992 began changing the way in which it funded housing associations. With hindsight, I am not surprised that this happened. In the beginning, the government funded 100% of the money needed to build properties. Later on, with public spending under pressure, the government reduced the grant for housing associations from 100% to 70% and then down to around 50%. The larger, more established housing associations were less affected, as they had the ability to borrow money from banks.

Based on the need to restructure the funding of housing associations, the Housing Corporation also re-evaluated its Black and Minority Ethnic Housing Association Strategy (BME strategy), and set new targets for the number of registered associations, investment levels, and homes to be developed. This 'review' of the BME strategy was debated in the housing sector, often heatedly. The larger minority associations were fine with the changes, but they were not being threatened financially by the reduction of grants from the Housing Corporation, and remained optimistic about attracting private funding.

In the review, the small housing associations – usually run by minority groups – often received "grade D" or worse, which meant that the Housing Corporation did not believe they had much of a financial future. Without continued corporation funding, the smaller housing associations would not be able to develop future housing, so we were all threatened with losing our independence. This change to the funding strategy outraged many minority housing associations. Minority groups were disproportionately affected by the Housing Corporation's funding changes. I was not the only one who felt it was wrong to judge minority housing associations solely on their borrowing power on the day of the review.

The Housing Corporation used this review as the basis of a new policy – funding for the smaller housing associations would be dependent upon the creation of 'group structures'. The group structure was a way to help the smaller housing associations to benefit from the borrowing power of the larger ones. The plan was for a small association to be 'parented' by a larger association, which would borrow money on the smaller one's behalf. Then, the parent association would keep the ownership of the properties until the small housing association could buy the properties back. In order to pay back the loans it had indirectly borrowed from the bank, the small association could use the money it received for rent from the tenants and could draw from its reserves.

An Việt was small, and after the allegations against me, it had now become vulnerable and exposed, and had drawn the attention of the Housing Corporation. We were perfect guinea pigs for this new policy. The writing was on the wall. An Việt was going to lose its independence.

All the members of the management committee agreed that this change came during the Tory years when public housing was not a priority. The Tories didn't care. They cared even less about minority housing associations. I often found myself debating this issue with some of the newer members of the management committee.

One of the men would state: "The Housing Corporation is wise to push for fewer small housing associations. Today, minority housing associations are so fragmented." I would reply: "Small minority housing associations, run by the community, are well situated to meet their community's needs."

He would say: "The former funding structure actually encourages splintering because associations got money if they represented a small ethnic group."

I would say: "The way the Housing Corporation looks down on small minority housing associations, is a little bit racist or colonial. It doesn't understand that 'black' or 'minority' are not a homogenous group and that communities have different needs".

But regardless of how either of us felt, the Housing Corporation was moving forward with its plan to reduce the independence of smaller minority housing associations. An Việt was a small association, as far as the Housing Corporation was concerned, An Việt did not have much of a future without becoming part of a group structure.

The new management committee, which no longer had 80% minority representation, voted that, in view of its problems, An Việt should join a group structure with a larger housing association. At the same time however, the Vietnamese committee members were questioning the conduct and motivations of the newly co-opted committee members. Three months after being appointed by the Housing Corporation to strengthen the management committee, no measures had been taken to improve management competence. Steps to improve the skill set of the Vietnamese members were thwarted, and I was frustrated - the Housing Corporation was saying one thing and doing another. Ten months after the audit and evaluation report recommending training, An Việt Housing Association was being pushed to become a subsidiary. I guess they assumed that now that some English people were on the board, there was no need to train or support the Vietnamese members. The Vietnamese members were starting to feel more like tokens.

I also began to question the overall aims of the Housing Corporation – were they really committed to developing a strong and financially viable organisation? As much as I agreed with 'group structure' in theory, I was wary about how things were heading in reality, and I didn't want us to lose our goals or sense of purpose. I wanted the Vietnamese community to become more empowered, not more dependent.

Negotiations

In spring 1993, An Việt had to decide what housing association we would 'merge' with. This wasn't easy. The large white housing associations were national, and this was something that we wanted. However, many within An Việt believed that a minority organisation would really help other minority organisations. For example, the really large associations clearly wanted to take over An Việt completely. One plainly stated they wanted to replace all of the Vietnamese committee members, leaving only three Vietnamese members who would only be used as 'interpreters'. I wasn't interested, and their proposal was rejected out of hand. In the end, we decided that what was most important was to join with a parent association which, regardless of whether or not it was national, would work towards empowering An Việt, had the capacity to monitor and support An Việt, and to give us access to private funding. In July 1993, An Việt chose Kuumba[8] to become An Việt's parent association.

It took a full year of negotiation before the two associations agreed on how they would work together. Kuumba and An Việt drafted a blueprint, but the Housing Corporation rejected the proposals because they gave An Việt too much freedom and independence. The Housing Corporation wanted Kuumba, being our 'parent' organisation, to have full control over An Việt. I was furious - the immediate elimination of our autonomy by an outside entity felt just like the Communists taking over all enterprise in Vietnam. It was too similar, and I did not like it.

Consequently, I did everything I could to resist accepting the Housing Corporation's new requirement that we should become a wholly owned subsidiary of Kuumba. I had lived under bureaucracies long enough to know that once a subsidiary of Kuumba it would be very difficult to retain our identity and become independent again. What was so infuriating was that I could not only see, but feel, how every change the Housing Corporation forced upon our internal policies was another nail in the coffin.

Only a year earlier, an independent body had recommended some training and the formation of links with a larger, more financially secure association so that the management committee could gain more skills and experience in housing issues. Now we

---

[8] Not the organisation's real name

were being taken over and made puppets and the Housing Corporation had no desire to negotiate. I resisted signing the agreement to become a subsidiary of Kuumba to the point that the Housing Corporation threatened to withdraw all funding. This ultimatum, forcing us to accept the changes, was like the Communists threating Father Hiệu with the death penalty – sign a confession or die; I had to sign the agreement or An Việt Housing Association would die. But unlike Father Hiệu, I had the freedom and power to keep fighting.

Intentions

He did not say: You will not be assailed, you will not be belaboured, you will not be disquieted, but He said: You will not be overcome.

Blessed Julian of Norwich

The committee of An Việt Housing Association appointed a new chairman – another person they hoped would help teach us how to run a charity in England. This new chairman – let's call him John – was British and had extensive experience working within the housing sector. This meant John had experience with British bureaucracy, and he could understand the way the Housing Corporation worked.

John assured me that all minority organisations struggled the way we were – they grow as an organisation, then state institutions want to control, monitor and ensure they comply with policy. He had experience helping these small associations to make the steps from a community-based organisation, to dealing with the state.

John was keen to make the group structure work. He recognised that there was no precedent for this - we were doing something new; trying to get separate organisations to work together just because the Housing Corporation was forcing us to do so. John knew both housing associations had a lot at stake and needed the group structure to succeed. An Việt was committed to its independence. Kuumba was seeking to uphold its reputation, and establish itself as professional after its own run-in with fraud. There were big risks on both sides, but John believed that the biggest risk was to An Việt – he kept warning me that the Housing Corporation could close us down.

John worked hard to support An Việt but he didn't believe me when I tried to warn him that Kuumba's motives were changing from 'capacity building' to more predatory intentions. An Việt was small, but we were the first minority association to become national, with properties in Southampton, Bristol, Birmingham, and Manchester. I began to suspect that Kuumba intended to use us to enable it to become a national housing association as well.

My suspicions were confirmed when, in January 1995, the housing association's London office asked An Việt to transfer newly completed properties to Kuumba. Luckily the property in question was in Northampton, and the Housing Corporation's East Midlands office recognised that this property request was not appropriate. That office refused to force the transfer and we were able to hang on to the property in Northampton. But Kuumba was not deterred. They then focused their energy on the London region, their home ground. The chair of Kuumba was good friends with the director of the Housing Corporation's London office. Not surprisingly, this director supported Kuumba and declared that Kuumba would be allowed to have ownership of An Việt properties.

This type of backroom negotiation and pseudo-nepotism again reminded me of the corruption in Vietnam I thought I'd left behind, and the old anger I felt towards those who abused their power for selfish gains, the rage I felt towards those who ignored the needs of the poor, returned again.

I had lived in the UK long enough to know philosophical debates would not change anything. Only legislation could enforce change. An Việt then sought legal advice, which supported our argument that the transfer of property was illegal and unnecessary. Kuumba's reaction? Systematic colonisation of An Việt Housing Association.

It began with a closed meeting between the chair of Kuumba and John, the chair of An Việt. John said that he went into the meeting ready to argue about Kuumba's attempts to get some of An Việt's properties transferred to it, but he came out of the meeting saying the opposite. After the meeting, John began arguing that because we did not fully own the properties – which was technically true since we still owed money on them – they would be better under the group structure. He believed it would be best if Kuumba took on the properties so that it could acquire development money on behalf of An Việt.

I was well aware that the other housing associations that owned the properties in question weren't putting money into An Việt, but that didn't make me agree with John. I did not believe Kuumba's explanation that it wanted to take over some of the debt so that it could have development money for An Việt. Kuumba wanted the properties for its own development, not ours.

Perhaps John had good intentions. He felt that things would get worse for An Việt. He may have thought that cooperating with Kuumba was the only choice, but John didn't understand my problem with the property transfer. He failed to understand that stripping us of our assets would take away any chance we might have for future independence. We would be tied to Kuumba forevermore – it was a one-way street. We would never be able to untangle ourselves from the parent organisation.

An article in *Black Housing*[9] magazine, the one that included the sketch depicting John as Judas, noted that in order to fully understand the concerns, one has to remember the history and nature of the black housing association movement. The author explained that: "unlike a number of white associations which were

---

[9] *Black Housing*. August 1995. Vol 11, no 3. p.6

formed either by wealthy philanthropists or benevolent employers, the black housing association movement was forged in the various communities of black people throughout the country." And these communities are often concentrated in certain towns and cities, so their "initial strengths lay in the community activism at a local level." And community based housing associations are set up by groups with a common identifying factor. In the case of An Việt, it was race, language and a shared traumatic past.

To ignore this principle, especially when justified by another minority association saying: "we are all black anyway," is not acceptable continues the author. "No community should have their identity subsumed within a larger amorphous collective." Which is exactly what Kuumba had done with An Việt. Reading this article was such a comfort on one level – someone out there understood why An Việt was so determined to keep fighting. At the time Kuumba was one of three organisations considered leaders in the black housing association movement, but many small minority housing associations saw them simply as "big, bad predators", and did not trust them. Kuumba had gained a reputation for developing aggressively at the expense of smaller housing associations. An Việt was therefore not the only small housing association to feel bullied by a larger one. Other housing associations felt swallowed up by the parent associations like Kuumba, but apparently I was the one putting up the biggest fight.

And where was the Housing Corporation in all this? All I know is that they failed to create or enforce any accountable leadership to deal with the predatory threats of the larger associations. I've read many articles, and spoken to others in the housing sector who questioned the role of the Housing Corporation as I do. Unlike the private sector where funding institutions like banks rely on separate bodies to supervise regulation, the housing sector places both funding and regulation in the hands of the Housing Corporation. And many in the black housing association movement have witnessed inconsistent rulings by the Housing Corporation.

This reminder that An Việt was not alone, and that other small housing associations were also struggling to maintain their independence, gave me strength to keep on resisting the takeover. When this struggle with the bureaucracy of the Housing Corporation and the merger with Kuumba began, I tried to keep working properly within the system. But now things had got so out of hand I honestly felt that the government was acting unjustly. That was when I knew I had to keep fighting for what was right just as I've done all my life. I fought a powerful General in Vietnam, I was going to fight the Housing Corporation here in England.

But the more I resisted, the more aggressive Kuumba became. They created a new order that I, the director, could not send letters to external agencies, such as the Housing Corporation or local authorities. They wanted me out of the way. They dismissed some of An Việt's staff or members of the management committee, two of whom were not given reasons for their dismissal. I couldn't help but notice however that next to me, these two were the most outspoken critics of Kuumba's attempts to take over An Việt's properties. This meant that now Kuumba had the upper hand on the committee. So much for Kuumba trying to help An Việt by passing on their experience and expertise. They were going to make sure they ran this Vietnamese housing association their way without any voice or objection from anyone in the Vietnamese community.

Protests

Bureaucracy defends the status quo long past the time
when the quo has lost its status.

Laurence J. Paul

We were determined to resist what Kuumba were doing. In reaction to their increasingly hostile actions, some of the remaining Vietnamese members of the management committee called a special committee meeting in April 1995. We wanted to fight the loss of our autonomy just as the Vietnamese had done for millennia. The Vietnamese fought the Chinese and French coloniscrs, and I was going to fight this colonial attack as well.

The next week, fifty Vietnamese tenants and members of An Việt marched in protest before a committee meeting about the threatened property transfers and the dismissal of committee members. They called for Kuumba to withdraw from the group structure or for the Housing Corporation to take action to resolve the dispute. The Housing Corporation did not respond.

The chairman of the Vietnam Refugee National Council announced the formation of the 'An Việt Justice Campaign Group'. This group was made up of former management committee members of An Việt and many outside supporters of the housing association. This campaign group formalised our resistance. We organised protests at every opportunity and, if we learned of a conference relating to housing – whether it was in Birmingham, London or Bristol, we'd organise people to deliver leaflets.

Kuumba felt that I was going too far in organising protests, but what else could a small, marginalised group do in the face of Kuumba's strong-arm tactics and excessive bullying? Kuumba wasn't going to let us continue. So on 3rd and 4th May 1995, Kuumba sent bailiffs with a court order to force their way into An Việt's offices and take all our equipment. They forcibly removed housing association files, documentation, even computers. I remember that day – it was really traumatic. The bailiffs came with removal vans and threw every piece of paper and bits of computer into boxes. They cleared everything out of our offices in Dalston and shipped it to Kuumba's top floor office in Haringey.

After completely replacing the management committee with Kuumba 'yes-men' and moving An Việt's office to its own premises in Haringey, Kuumba dismissed me. The last three remaining Vietnamese staff stopped working for Kuumba in protest. This meant that there were still no Vietnamese staff at the housing association that had been created to help Vietnamese.

In the meantime, the tenants were suffering. Richard, who was housing administrator for An Việt at the time, stepped up as interim director after they fired me. He was livid about the condition in which Kuumba had left An Việt. In essence, An Việt Housing Association had ceased to operate for a few weeks, yet there were constant phone calls from tenants needing repairs, or with housing benefit problems. But, when he went to Haringey, the entire office had been piled into one open plan room. The door could hardly be opened against the weight of the things that had been dumped behind it, and he had to climb over piles of filing cabinet drawers; heaps of papers; and unconnected bits of computers. It was a complete mess, because the removers hadn't boxed anything up in a proper manner. Ian, who was housing manager at An Việt and worked under Kuumba until leaving earlier that year, volunteered to come in and help Richard get things up and running again. Ian and Richard worked evenings and weekends to get it sorted enough to find tenant files so that they could assist them.

Until this time, most of the campaign had been requesting intervention in the transfer of properties to Kuumba so we could one day soon be independent again. However, discontent was growing over the general management of An Việt since Kuumba had become involved. For example, Ian was dismayed that none of the new staff hired under Kuumba's term had the skills or had received any training to do some of the basic tasks needed to run a housing association. Also, because none of the new staff came from the Vietnamese community, all of them had to rely on the one Vietnamese-speaking member of staff to interpret. For Ian, after nine months under Kuumba, nothing had improved.

Yet even a complaint from a white man did nothing. The Housing Corporation was silent. When something happened we'd write letters of complaint, but we were ignored. The Corporation had washed its hands of us. I wanted it to do a proper job, to intervene, and it should have listened equally to both sides instead of blindly supporting Kuumba. But, to listen to our side would have been to admit that the group structure wasn't working, and this was something that the Corporation couldn't face. It had invested too much in its plan for it to back out now.

Letters

Cuoc Chien Dau Nay

Cuoc chien dau nay chua phan thong phu
Ta van con day va sai thep con kia
Chet choc tham cam, cot nhuc chia lia
Ta van song va khong he lan lu
Ta muon noi voi loai da thu
Khuc hat khai hoan ta se hat thien thu!
Nguyễn Chí Thiện (Flowers of Hell, 1996, p404)

This Fight

It is not yet over, this struggle;
Here I am still and there, the iron and steel,
After so many silent deaths and the loss of loved ones

I am still alive and far from being lost:
To the beasts I simply want to say
That the Victory Song will be mine to sing till eternity!

Nguyễn Chí Thiện (p404)

The momentum was not moving in a favourable direction for An Việt. The Housing Corporation was 100% behind Kuumba, and saw my protests and appeals as annoying disruptions. An Việt's management committee was made up of only Kuumba supporters. I was no longer employed by the association and no longer had access to the files or documentation. I'd fought more frightening foes in Vietnam but, for the first time, this fight was personal. An Việt Housing Association was something I had started from nothing. I refused to give up.

During this time, over a hundred tenants and members – many of them leaders in the Vietnamese community – wrote letters to the Housing Corporation. Some also wrote to MPs, local authorities and to the Minister of Housing as well, demanding justice. Still this did not work. We went further.

In July 1995, three other members of An Việt wrote to the National Federation of Housing Associations requesting arbitration. It declined the request, so in October 1995 the chair of the Vietnamese Refugee National Council wrote to the chair of the Commission for Racial Equality asking for them to intervene in the dispute. As there had been no apparent breach of the Race Relations Act, they declined. In December, a tenant applied for legal aid to take Kuumba to Court, but the application was refused, as "there would be no personal benefit from such action". Because these steps didn't work, we went further.

The campaign continued. We approached Sir Timothy Stocks[10], patron of An Việt. He in turn agreed that An Việt could approach

---

[10] Name has been changed to protect identity

Sanctuary Housing Association, to put forward a proposal for it to become the parent organisation of An Việt. In March 1996, Sir Timothy hosted a meeting between the chair of Sanctuary and the chair of An Việt about leaving Kuumba and joining Sanctuary. In the end, Sanctuary declined, but this still did not deter the An Việt Justice Campaign Group or me. We went further.

Eventually, help came. At last someone read one of our letters. Someone actually listened to our story. Mr Smith, MP (Member of Parliament), got involved, and wrote a letter to the Housing Corporation asking about the transfer of properties. There was no reply so Mr Smith wrote a second letter, again asking about the transfer of properties. Then suddenly, we received a reply that casually stated no transfer of properties had occurred and that as far as the Housing Corporation was concerned, properties developed by other associations on An Việt's behalf would be transferred to An Việt provided they could afford them. Just like that. Finally, a minor victory.

While the properties were safe for the time being, the concerns about Kuumba's management of An Việt, the properties, and thus the tenants, still remained.

So in late November 1997, the chair of the Vietnamese Refugee National Council, wrote to the Department of the Environment – the ministerial body responsible for the Housing Corporation. He requested a meeting to discuss the dispute between Kuumba, An Việt and the Housing Corporation. We received a reply from the MP, the Minister who headed the Department of the Environment, stating they supported the actions of the Housing Corporation. This made it clear to me that the Housing Corporation did not worry about going to Court. So we went further – we appealed to the High Court, requesting judicial review.

The entire time, people questioned me, wondered why I bothered to continue fighting. They would tell me: "No one can beat the Housing Corporation." Or they would remind me, as if I had no idea: "the Housing Corporation manages millions of pounds from government to deliver to housing associations; it is very powerful."

I remember once when I was meeting with a colleague who asked me: "Why fight? You can't win," I replied:

"Did you know that today is 30th April? Did you know that you and I are meeting on the same date the Vietnamese lost our country under the Communist regime?"

He sat quietly – I could tell he did not understand my point. I added: "You must understand. We risked our lives to come over here. We had nothing to lose, we were only asking for justice. And that is all we want today. We want justice but the Housing Corporation ignores us." I was laying all my cards on the table during that meeting, which was a very emotional meeting. It was a difficult situation for him because he worked for the Housing Corporation.

I tried to explain to him how the conflict with the housing association put me in an untenable situation. On the one hand I was being asked to act as an obedient employee, while at the same time witnessing attempts by both the Housing Corporation and Kuumba to wrest control of property from An Việt and pass it to Kuumba: attempts that legal counsel had advised me were totally illegal. "I am following this advice, and my own personal and political conviction in order to defend the housing rights of my own community so I can sleep peacefully at night." I didn't give up.

In the summer of 1998, I wrote an affidavit requesting judicial review, helped by a friend of mine. On paper, I lamented that an exercise that started out as an attempt to improve the capacity of the members of a housing association to manage their own affairs, had resulted in an entire community being without a voice in their own housing matters. I wanted to make it clear that An Việt recognised that we suffered from a lack of management experience and had made mistakes from time to time. However, I also made it clear that independent studies and reviews of its work always maintained that these problems were surmountable and that any short-term lack of capacity should have been overcome by encouragement, training, support and understanding. Then I got to the point: the Housing Corporation had a moral, professional and legal responsibility to undo the damage it had done. I was granted leave to go to the High Court.

Judgement

There are some defeats more triumphant than victories.

Michel de Montaigne

My request for judicial review was successful and in March 1999 the High Court granted me leave to bring the Housing Corporation to Court. I felt like David taking on Goliath when reading my statement to the Court. I did not hire a barrister to represent me, as past experience had taught me that barristers and solicitors were very narrow, so on this occasion I represented myself. To help, I put everything in writing. I hoped that if the three judges had something to read, something to follow while I spelled out my arguments, it would make it easier for them to understand me.

The vast old Courthouse, every surface made of heavy, dark wood, reminded me that I was in the heart of a former colonial power that – like the French – claimed to spread democracy and civilisation but often at the expense of the little men like me. But this was Britain, where human rights, justice, and the right to a voice are sacred. Looking at the judges in their black robes and white wigs, I could not tell which Britain would emerge in the Court – the coloniser or the humanitarian. The Court started at 10 am.

I read my statement, which told the entire story from the beginning. I made sure to emphasise how things had been done illegally from the moment the Housing Corporation got involved, going through every detail beginning with the Housing Corporation's ultimatum to become a subsidiary of Kuumba.

As I read, I continually glanced up to look the judges in the eye. The entire time, they looked back. They were actually listening to me, and I was finally being heard. I could see in their faces that they also felt a little bit of sympathy for my case. I was very moved. I was also encouraged, so I continued reading my statement.

Then it was time for the Housing Corporation's barrister to speak. After much grovelling to the judge, he rebutted all my statements by quoting past cases that did not seem relevant at all and then asked the judges to set the case aside. Almost every comment the barrister made, I disagreed with. I raised my hand again and again, as if I was a keen student in a classroom, wanting the judge to call on me to speak. Finally, a clerk or assistant to the judge whispered to me, with a smile on her face: "Sir, you have to wait to speak when the judge asks you for a reply."

Finally, I was able to speak again. "The cases put forward as precedent aren't relevant to this case."

The barrister's turn: "Your honour, if the Court agrees to allow An Việt Housing Association to break free of the group structure and no longer work for Kuumba, this would create a precedent for black and minority groups in the future to get out of the group structure system imposed by the Housing Corporation."

My turn: "There is nothing wrong with the group structure in principle. Except in reality, when small minority housing associations are forced into a group structure their rights and freedoms are removed. Small housing associations can be effective because they are able to work closely with the tenants. When the voice of the small housing association is removed and all power stripped, this ability is lost. Group structures should be equal partnerships where both associations learn from and assist each other."

The barrister's turn: "Your honour, at the end of the day it comes back to the core issue, An Việt Housing Association's appeal was made out of time. They missed the three-month deadline to seek judicial review. There is nothing else to debate. The appeal must be set aside."

My turn: "Your honour, let me repeat myself. I already explained how we were given permission by the Housing Corporation itself to negotiate a new parent organisation. It was the Housing Corporation's suggestion and they agreed this. This was a time consuming endeavour and no decision from our newly chosen parent organisation was reached until the quoted deadline for appeal had passed. So I tried to negotiate a resolution to our problems with Kuumba and the Housing Corporation at three stages. First, I approached the Housing Corporation for them to help resolve the dispute. None of my requests received replies from anyone in the Housing Corporation. Second, I sought mediation. In addition to my appeal for a different parent organisation, I approached the Registry of Friendly Societies who were unable to help. I finally approached the MP who was head of the Department of Environment, Transport and Regions – the department responsible for the Housing Corporation. This MP wrote to tell us he supported the decision of the Housing Corporation on 1st June 1998."

I told the court that I decided to appeal only when every possible approach and every level of housing control had been explored. "What I am trying to say", I concluded, "was that I began to pursue this matter legally immediately following the MP's letter, when the highest authority on housing matters ended the process, therefore my appeal has been done promptly and within the time limit specified."

Then it was time for the Housing Corporation's barrister to speak. He said matter-of-factly, "The Housing Corporation is an independent agent of the Housing Department. Therefore, the Housing Minister, the MP Mr Vũ refers to, is a politician, and not someone with the authority to give the 'final word' on Housing Corporation matters and hence his letter cannot be seen as the start of the three-month time limit." He concluded, pushing his glasses so they did not fall off his nose, "Thus, Mr. Vũ's case is out of date and therefore the judge must set it aside."

I stood up. I was no longer reading from a statement. "In the British legal system, a minister of the government must be a MP, a 'Member of Parliament'". I spoke as clearly as I could, I wanted to make sure the judge understood me. "Thus, a Minister, like this MP, has two hats. With his first 'hat', he is the representative of his constituents; he is a politician. But, when he joins the government, he also wears another 'hat' as a minister of a department." I paused. My point seemed so obvious: "The Housing Corporation is an agent of the Housing Department. So the Housing Minister must have the final word. "Therefore," I concluded, "my appeal to the court was within the three months' time limit."

Our trial lasted from 10 am to 1 pm. The entire morning, I was amazed at how poor the barrister's arguments were. To my mind, it was ridiculous, even silly, to base their case on potential expenses or the fact that other minority housing associations might not want to comply with forced group structures. But I wasn't sure whether the judges would agree.

The judges didn't announce their verdict until 4.30 pm, having discussed the case in private for a long time. In the end, I failed. The official wording of the verdict was that the judges had "set my case aside."

Afterwards, the An Việt Housing Association changed its name to Liên Việt Housing Association. It remained a subsidiary of Kuumba. They owned fewer properties. No one at Liên Việt would speak to me about the status of Liên Việt except to state confidently that they are doing really well.

But I knew that wasn't the case. Liên Việt Housing Association never developed much since the late 1990s, and lost links with the community since becoming part of a group structure. A colleague who is still working in the housing sector once told me that all the protests and resistance An Việt put up saved some other smaller organisations, and said that my determination and persistence had achieved a larger impact. Because we put up such a fierce fight, the Housing Corporation can no longer actually push smaller associations into the three big ones any more.

I did the right thing. It wasn't for my own glory that I fought the Housing Corporation and Kuumba, but for the community. In my mind, I felt that we had lost everything in Vietnam: we had lost our country, and we had lost money. We accepted losing the life we had had in Vietnam in order to come here to rebuild our life. I didn't want to do anything stupid, just to do my best. So if somebody tried to help us, to help us build anything, I was very grateful. But I didn't fear anyone who might have wanted to destroy it. Kuumba didn't break An Việt or me.

But the entire ordeal helped me see that I no longer wanted to continue working in housing. An Việt was still expected to be a subsidiary of Kuumba and to have a close working relationship with the Housing Corporation. That was my biggest headache and I saw no need to continue working for An Việt Housing Association if Kuumba was going to be part of the work. I preferred instead to continue my work with the Foundation.

Which I did. An Việt Foundation is still running today. But Kuumba isn't. In 2008, Kuumba collapsed. Financial mismanagement and greed destroyed them in the end. They continued to buy up housing aggressively, but over time, they couldn't pay back the loans with the money raised from rent and so eventually Kuumba was taken over by a parent organisation.

I knew justice would prevail.

CHAPTER THIRTEEN

Service

An Việt Foundation was also going through some big changes while I was off fighting the housing association. We continued to offer English classes, then taught by an English woman. She taught NVQ level 2 English – she was very highly skilled, and had lots of experience. She also took the students on trips around London, which the students enjoyed. At the end of each course, we often had a party for the students – they brought ethnic food and An Việt supplied food as well as some beer and wine. We also hired in music and dancing. We once had a professional Turkish dancer come. She was so beautiful.

Over time, fewer and fewer students were attending the mother-tongue classes. Parents often were too busy to bring their children to class. The students themselves were less and less interested, which saddened me greatly, but, one of the most difficult challenges to keeping the classes running was recruiting qualified teachers. We could only afford to pay £5 per hour, which was not enough money to motivate a teacher to spend three hours every Saturday teaching students – it did not even cover all the time it took to prepare the lessons. Over time the number of classes reduced gradually so that eventually the A-level and GCSE certificates ceased to exist. There weren't enough students to take the exam.

And fewer families were able to support themselves in the garment making industry. There was less demand because it was much cheaper to buy clothes assembled overseas. The costs prohibited many families from competing with the overseas market. As mentioned earlier, many Vietnamese began working in the nail salon industry – quickly dominating the market.

But the biggest change came around 1995 or 1996 when An Việt created a new service to address a growing problem in the Vietnamese community – drug addiction and all the side effects including drug dens, theft and deaths. We all knew that the drug problem in the Vietnamese community had begun in Hong Kong, and that the problem did not disappear when people left the refugee camps. Several Vietnamese repeat offenders were arrested, but criminal acts involving shoplifting and burglary continued. The UK had never faced drug problems with other ethnic groups originating from the Far East, who are well known for their family values and industry, and Vietnamese in the 80s did not present this type of social problem. But then the UK government resettled large numbers of Vietnamese refugees from Hong Kong prior to the handover of Hong Kong to China.

In the camps in Hong Kong most of the adults were too confused and worried about their own fears to exert any real discipline over young adults, and there were many unaccompanied minors in the camps who were especially vulnerable. The camps in Hong Kong were cramped, noisy and lacked any real means of controlling order. They were also open – residents could come and go freely. Individuals over seventeen years old were allowed to work in Hong Kong and earn income.

Finding a job was easy in Hong Kong and the Vietnamese refugees helped with the local labour shortage. Hong Kong was also called a "city that never sleeps". Drugs, particularly heroin from the Golden Triangle, were easily available and cheap. They were smuggled into the city and supplied by organised gangs known as the "triads".

In the late 1990s, I hired Mr Tran to be the Drug Worker for our project. Mr Tran had worked as a translator with UNHCR for a year, and then had worked as a Drug and Harm Reduction Counsellor with *Médecins Sans Frontières* in Pillar Point camp. He was ideal for our job, not only because he was Vietnamese, but also because he had worked with this issue in the Hong Kong camp where the drug problem originated.

Mr Tran gradually discovered, during his work in the camps, that the clients he saw who used drugs had strikingly similar backgrounds. 99% were male, and were from rural fishing and farming villages in the coastal regions – most notably Hải Phòng, Quảng Ninh – and the central area. They grew up in an open, carefree, close-knit environment with a large network of extended family and friends, but with little education. Many arrived in Hong Kong between the ages of fifteen and twenty-five, on their own without parents or siblings. They were, therefore, without any support network that they could trust, nor did they have anyone to discipline them. Those who had jobs could easily fund their habit.

These youths were often lonely and incredibly vulnerable – easily drawn to any group that showed interest in them, including drug dealers and gangs. Sadly, those who wanted to quit using drugs found it difficult because of the prevalence of drug use in the camps, and thus experienced difficulties in making new friends in that environment.

Mr Tran said that around 1995 it would have taken a newly resettled Vietnamese refugee a year to find connections to the drug network but, with the passage of time, London had established drug supply facilities set up by the Vietnamese drug users themselves. By 1999, a previous drug user (who had temporarily detoxified himself to pass the medical exam for resettlement) would probably be able to resume his habit within two weeks of arrival, without speaking a word of English.

Most of the Vietnamese who came to see Mr Tran used heroin or crack cocaine; the heroin users often used methadone to sustain their daily need. It was sad to see how drugs ruled the lives of some of these men. Some had families that they were struggling to support, and felt great shame – they were 'reluctant' users. Others belonged to a syndicate that shoplifted, dealt in stolen goods or sold drugs to support their habit.

In Hackney a few drug users purchased their drugs in local pubs, snooker clubs, or even shops. However, most Vietnamese apparently preferred 'drug dens', which were normally run from council flats. Mr Tran conducted a study in Deptford and found that the dealers preferred corner flats because of the 'lookout' they provided. Anyone who entered the flat had to pass the security checks carried out by guards, who were often drug users themselves. Mr Tran described the atmosphere as similar to a coffee shop or a laid back social club. It felt very lazy with regular 'customers' chatting, some snoozing on the sofa or sitting on the floor injecting themselves. There were often stolen goods on sale in the corner of the room. The council flat often belonged to a drug user who owed a large debt to the dealer so received no payment for helping with the den. After about three months the police would raid the premises, and then the entire operation would transfer to a new council flat and begin again.

The biggest challenge for anyone wanting to help the drug addicts was encouraging them to access support or help. Vietnamese drug users were extremely wary of anyone in authority, and assumed that officials all worked for the state – even the staff of British charities. But more significantly, both in Hong Kong and in the UK, the needs of the Vietnamese drug users were not identified nor addressed by society or the government. In Hong Kong, for instance, there were some recreation centres for rehabilitating drug users, but rarely did any Vietnamese utilise them. In the UK, Mr Tran found that Vietnamese did not know of any drug programmes available in their area. Those who were referred to a rehabilitation clinic often failed to complete the treatment. Almost all programmes were based in English and were designed around individual and group counselling sessions, which the Vietnamese found intimidating or inaccessible. They simply were impractical. At An Việt, we were more successful. Mr Tran was able to gain people's trust, which meant that when someone was ready to quit, they felt comfortable turning to our drug project for help.

Restaurant

We never really intended to open a restaurant. We had always had a programme for elderly Vietnamese in the area, a dedicated space where they could come to meet friends, since many were feeling very isolated. When we realised that many were so lonely and they didn't have access to have regular meals, we created a canteen that served the elderly a hot lunch. The canteen was a small project, located in the front of the building at that time, and took up about half the size that the restaurant is now. Before long, some local residents came in and asked us if they could sample some of our authentic Vietnamese food. As the word spread, more and more came in wanting to eat at our canteen.

At the time, our head chef for the elderly project, when he saw how many English people seemed to want to try the food, he encouraged me to open to the public.

So I approached An Việt Foundation's management committee, and we all felt that this could be a wonderful opportunity. We agreed to move the elderly activities to the back of the building and use the canteen to serve the local residents. But we had no experience in running a commercial food service and needed to find someone to manage it. It was difficult, however, to find someone to take on the day-to-day operation of the canteen. When I approached professionally trained cooks or people with catering and food service experience, they decided that our canteen could never be successful because we were located in a residential area. Even my friend, Mr Pham[11], when I first asked him, said that he couldn't do it. "I live all the way in Harlow, in Essex. It will be hard for me to drive to this quiet street and cook all day, and anyway there won't be any customers. If you move to a main road, then perhaps I'll think about it," he said. I was having so much

---

[11] Name has been changed to protect identity

trouble finding someone to run the canteen that I went back to visit Mr Pham in the hope of persuading him, but in the end, I was able to persuade his daughter, Trinh[12]. She had just graduated from university and had been applying for jobs, but had not been successful. She was feeling bad about herself after all the various rejections, but I knew that she was smart and talented. To my mind, it would be a perfect solution to both our problems – she would have a job and feel good about herself if the restaurant was a success, while I would have someone I trusted in charge.

Trinh's husband also agreed – he had experience working as a waiter – and shortly after meeting with them we were open for business. They did not have much in the way of overheads. The equipment was already there, and the rent was only £100 per week. When we started, we only had ten dishes on the menu, but they learned how to prepare and serve these dishes very quickly, and then began to learn about how to do catering and provide other services often expected of restaurants. My friends, Mr and Mrs Pham, helped their daughter to run the canteen for three years.

In spring 1996, we sent the family a letter asking them to renew their contract, their 'license to occupy' as we did every year. This time they did not sign the contract. We weren't too surprised. We knew our arrangement was that they would work in the canteen and gain experience and job skills so they could one day work in the restaurant business in London.

But we were truly shocked when one day I received a letter saying that the entire family was leaving; they were no longer going to run the canteen. They gave us no notice as we had agreed and told me they were all in poor health and couldn't run the canteen after the end of the day.

I was so upset. My friend had stabbed me in the back. I knew immediately they were opening their own restaurant now that they felt they had enough experience after working at our canteen, but that is not what bothered me; we always knew that would be the

---

[12] Name has been changed to protect identity

case. Instead, I was angry that they had kept it a secret from me and had then left without any time to find a replacement. We would not be able to open the restaurant the next day. Then I learned that this was their plan all along. I found posters around the canteen that read: "This canteen is closing down forever. We are relocating to Kingsland Road." They also distributed cards and flyers to customers alerting them that the canteen was moving.

I called an emergency meeting of the management committee. We all agreed to let them go, and not to take any action against their breach of contract. However, we did have to send them a letter threatening action if they did not change the name of their new restaurant. While in our building, the restaurant was called 'Việt Huê Canteen'. But when they opened their new restaurant down the road, they named it 'An Việt Canteen'. That was the name of our Foundation and we were perplexed why they would want to do such a thing. Our question was answered soon enough; we discovered that the reason for their sudden departure and name change was because they had not been paying tax for the past three years and Inland Revenue was beginning to ask them questions. They thought that if they changed the name, either we would be the ones to get in trouble or the taxman wouldn't find them. They were wrong.

The committee instructed me to find someone else to take over the canteen immediately. We felt that it was vital to open as soon as possible – if we waited a few months to find someone to take over, then we risked losing our customers. We also risked losing the income generated from the canteen, which now paid rent for the building, while extra income went back to the Foundation to fund the community centre and the elderly activities. We had also learned there were other, indirect benefits to having a canteen besides the extra income. The restaurant is one way to introduce Vietnamese culture to the local residents. Also, having the restaurant directly below the Foundation, we were able to raise awareness about the work we did to serve the Vietnamese community. All of this helped to raise the profile of the

Vietnamese community. We also liked having a place to feed visitors and volunteers. We might not have had money to pay many of those who helped An Việt, but we could show our gratitude by providing an authentic Vietnamese meal.

I decided to call Mr Bảy, who had been a very good friend of mine when we were in Thorney Island Reception Centre. He had been working for a long time at a Thai restaurant in Richmond, and when I reached him, he had just arrived back in England after a month long holiday in Vietnam. I insisted that he come to be our head chef and to open the canteen without delay, and he agreed.

When Mrs Pham and her daughter Trinh heard that Mr Bảy had agreed to work for us, both of them came to An Việt and found my wife. She was back in the elderly centre, cooking lunch while the elderly played Mah-jong and chatted. Mrs Pham and Trinh shouted at her:

"What are you doing asking Mr Bảy to cook for you?" My wife was surprised to see them but was even more shocked when they began accusing us of forcing them out of the canteen. "You kicked us out so you could take over the restaurant!" they yelled. Điệp calmly explained:

"Don't you remember, you wrote to An Việt saying that you were going to vacate the canteen? You didn't even give us any notice of your plans to leave. You left us no choice, so we had to find someone to replace you quickly." Mrs Pham and Trinh began to protest again but Điệp simply said: "when you left, you gave the restaurant back to An Việt. What we choose to do with the restaurant now is no longer your concern." Mrs Pham and Trinh were raising such a fuss that they apparently disturbed a few of the older people in the room. A fierce old woman who regularly came to An Việt was very upset. She scolded Mrs Pham and her daughter saying:

"Get out, you are disrupting my game," then kicked them out like naughty children.

Mrs Pham and Trinh did not let this stop them. As soon as

the canteen was opened again for business, they placed new posters and flyers all over the area, including cars, accusing us of kicking them out, asking customers not to eat in our canteen. She even shouted at me in the Dalston market one day when I was there with Mr Bảy, but by this time I had had enough. I looked her in the eye and said that she already was losing her reputation within in the Vietnamese community, so if she wanted a fight, I could give her one. She finally stopped, but by this time, many customers believed that we had kicked them out. To the local residents, we looked like the bad guys, not them. It took us at least a year to recover and get enough customers. We made no profit during that time.

Death

By the second year the canteen was doing really well. We knew that it could be even more successful if we had more space. We received help from friends in drafting a proposal, and made an application to the council requesting permission to become a proper restaurant. Hackney Council began the usual procedure for this type of application, and for us, since we were in a residential area, a notice had to go out to our neighbours asking for their views on whether or not the council should give us permission. I knew that the same neighbours, who had fought our proposal to convert the building from public baths – which were falling apart from neglect – would also fight our proposal for a restaurant. Furthermore, unlike the previous time, there was now a Conservative councillor in the Ward who I believed would side with our neighbours and help to reject our application. There were eight councillors and we needed a majority vote to get permission for a licence, I knew that it would be a close vote, so rallied as much support as I could before the meeting. Four voted to reject the application. Then four voted to approve it. It was down to the LibDem councillor who was chairing the meeting to cast his vote. Our future was in his hands.

It was a narrow victory, but we were given permission to obtain a licence and become a restaurant. Mr Bảy stayed with us, and success grew from success. He was an excellent chef. We were even written up by Time Out magazine, whose critic was excited by the quality of our food. The staff were so proud, but Mr Bảy remained as modest as ever. One of the staff joked with him about how good a cook he was, and teased him, saying: "the Ghost of Hell heard your name and one day he will invite you to come and cook for him". Mr Bảy simply replied: "I don't care. I'm enjoying cooking, so I don't mind". Today, what is amazing to me is that the restaurant remained successful, even after Mr Bảy died.

To everyone, his death was sudden. He was young, only 53. The Vietnamese feel that this is a very unlucky year, but I don't know if Mr Bảy also believed that 53 was unlucky. I do think, however, that he knew he was going to die. Just before Christmas 2000, Mr Bảy suddenly approached me with a request for time off, so that he could go to Vietnam immediately to see his mother. At first I resisted, as Christmas would be the worst possible time for him to leave, since it would be almost impossible for us to find a replacement. I asked if he could wait until after Christmas before going, but he replied: "I have to go to see her for the last time". I knew that his mother was ill, so I assumed that she had got worse and was expected to pass away soon. So Mr Bảy went to Vietnam for one month over Christmas. He then returned to London and worked in the restaurant as head chef as normal. In April 2001 he approached me during one of his breaks, and said: "I am here to give you one month's notice. I cannot work for you anymore".

"Is this a joke?" I asked.

"No, it is not a joke. I will leave at the end of this month."

I wondered if this was his way of putting pressure on me to increase his salary or something. "If you have decided to open your own restaurant, I respect your decision. But, if you are leaving because you are not happy here and you want to work somewhere else, please tell me. Perhaps we can negotiate?" And I meant it. I really valued Mr Bảy's work. He was so conscientious and cared about the restaurant; he welcomed comments from customers, and if there was a complaint, he did not take it as a threat but instead wanted to know how he could improve the service. I did not want to lose him. But he said that he had to go, even though: "I like to work here. This is the first time in my life I have worked for someone for four years". When he said this, I hoped that this meant that we could raise his salary or do something else and he would stay.

The next week, he reminded me that in three weeks he would go, but I still thought it was a joke. The following week, he again reminded me, pointing out that he would now be leaving in two weeks. At the same time he told his staff in the kitchen that he intended to cook a very special dish for everyone. He wanted a party to say good-bye. When I heard this, I finally had to admit that he might actually be serious, and so I spoke to him again: "Are you unhappy in any way? Is there anything we can do to convince you to stay?"

"No, no, no," he replied, "I really want to work for you but I have to go." Then he left the room.

The final week arrived quicker than I would have wanted. I learned later that, on the Wednesday of his final week, the lady who had delivered the Vietnamese tofu to the restaurant for many years came and spoke to Mr Bảy. They were friends and he often gave her a bowl of traditional Vietnamese soup when she came by. This week, when she dropped off the boxes, he came outside to bring her a bowl of soup and said: "This is the last bowl of noodles I will cook for you. Next time you come, I will not be here". The lady looked at him in surprise and asked: "Why, what happened? Is something wrong?" But he said nothing and walked back to the kitchen.

The next day, Thursday, Mr Bảy came into my office. "Mr Vũ, please give me my P45." I couldn't believe it. "What? Why do you need your P45? I only give staff a P45 when they stop working here." I guess I still didn't want to believe that he was actually going to leave the restaurant. He replied saying: "I need the P45 because I don't want to work here anymore. I have to go."

"Please tell me." I asked, "what can I do to make you stay? Do you want more money?"

"I like working here, but I can't anymore," he replied, before going back downstairs.

I went to my wife. Perhaps she could get more information from him, learn why he was leaving, and if we could get him to stay. I said to my wife: "Talk to him. Find out why he is leaving." She went to see him immediately. By then however it was the end of the day: the restaurant did not have many customers, and the kitchen staff were preparing to leave. My wife invited him to sit at the table to tell her why he intended to leave at the end of the week. He said again: "I like working here, but I have to go". Then suddenly he put his head down on the table.

My wife said that at first she was shocked. It must have only been a second before she realised that something was very wrong: something about the way he was slumped on the table told her that he was not just tired. She shook him cautiously: "Are you okay, what happened to you?" she asked. She jumped up and ran to the kitchen where Mr Bảy's cousin also worked, and told him to come out and see Mr Bảy. When she returned to the table, followed by the cousin and other kitchen staff, Mr Bảy was still slumped on the table. They moved him to the floor to try to revive him, and someone called an ambulance. The remaining two customers came over to offer their help, and someone called Mr Bảy's wife and family.

By the time the ambulance came, he had woken up, and the paramedics placed him on a trolley. Mr Bảy's family arrived as he was being wheeled into the ambulance. His family, my wife and my family all followed the ambulance to the hospital. The doctor who saw him when he arrived assured us that he was fine, but they just wanted to run a few tests. Then, however, completely unexpectedly, Mr Bảy suddenly died less than an hour later. A blood vessel had burst in his brain. As soon as the nurse broke the news that he died, Mr Bảy's daughter turned to my wife: "It is all your fault. You forced my dad to work too hard. You killed him."

When I looked in the kitchen the following day, a strange sensation came over me. In the four years that Mr Bảy had been with us, the kitchen had never been so clean. He must have asked the staff to clean everything; even the cleaning cloth was folded nicely. I can't explain why this realisation filled me with such sadness as well as apprehension. What was Mr Bảy thinking before he decided to quit? Was there a link between the timing of Mr Bảy's death and his decision to leave our restaurant?

While I was replaying my final few conversations with Mr Bảy in my head, my wife called Mrs Bảy. She wanted to offer her condolences:

"I am so sorry for your loss. Mr Bảy's death is a shock to all of us. My entire family is very sad."

Mrs Bảy began to cry: "I can't believe he died. I don't know what to do."

My wife Điệp tried to comfort her: "We are all here for you. Let us know how we can help you through this sad time." Mrs Bảy and my wife continued to talk in this way for a few more minutes, with my wife expressing her sorrow and sympathy and Mrs Bảy agonising over the death of her husband.

Then suddenly, Mrs Bảy was very angry. She shouted: "What are you saying? How can you talk about the restaurant at a time like this?"

Điệp was baffled, since she couldn't recall mentioning anything about the restaurant during their conversation: "I'm not sure what you mean. I was just saying that how much I am going to miss Mr Bảy because he was such a kind, considerate man."

But Mrs Bảy didn't believe her: "You just said very clearly that even without him, the restaurant is still running as normal and customers continue to come." My wife was even more confused.

She tried to explain and calm Mrs Bảy down: "Actually, we are all so shocked and sad by his death, that we will probably close the restaurant for a couple months. I would never say on the day after his death that the restaurant is fine. Even if that were true, that would be a callous and horrible thing to say. I would never say that. All I said was that we are all so sad to lose him." It was very strange. My wife told me about the conversation and I agreed: it was very odd. But we forgot about it, assuming it was her grief that had made Mrs Bảy so confused.

My entire family grieved Mr Bảy's death. We all prayed that week, both at home and at work. Staff who had worked with Mr Bảy also joined us in the prayers, including the lady who delivered the tofu. We all talked about him, shared anecdotes from our times with him, and reflected on his last few weeks with us. We all agreed that Mr Bảy must have known his life was coming to an end.

Điệp was so affected by Mr Bảy's death that she became depressed. My wife tried to run the restaurant after he died but she couldn't so Linh, my eldest daughter, stopped working as an architect in order to help me look after the restaurant. She and I did everything to keep the restaurant running, including the cooking. It was a very difficult time for everyone. I know Linh found it hard to transition into this complete change of career. But after four years at our *Hương Việt,* she started her own restaurant which became very successful.

Ghosts

My family was not allowed to attend Mr Bảy's funeral. We sent flowers, though, and we tried to reach out to the Bảy family but they wouldn't let us. I think Mrs Bảy resents us because she had always wanted to open a restaurant but Mr Bảy had always refused to do so. But I do know that the Bảy family still blame us for his death. I think Mrs Bảy also believes that we heartlessly only mourned Mr Bảy's death because it inconvenienced the running of the restaurant, but this is far from the truth. We miss Mr Bảy, and are still sad that he died.

We do have clues, however, that Mr Bảy never really left us. For example, it is traditional for Buddhist families to place a photograph of the deceased, surrounded by incense, in a Buddhist temple, so that the Buddhist monks can pray for the dead. I learned that one night, a few weeks after Mr Bảy's death, his daughter had a dream. In this dream, Mr Bảy told her that he didn't want his altar to remain in the Buddhist temple any longer. Mr Bảy told his daughter in this dream: "Take me back home." He didn't want to stay in the temple because it was too noisy, so his daughter went to the temple to bring his photograph back home.

But most of the signs that Mr Bảy was still with us occurred in the restaurant. For example, we had two Chinese gentlemen who helped in the kitchen. One day, shortly after we reopened the restaurant, they went to the back of the restaurant for a break. It was later in the afternoon, the time between lunch and dinner when we were closed. A few minutes later, they came running through the kitchen shouting that they had heard a strange noise. "Oh, I don't want to stay here," they cried, "ghosts, ghosts!" I laughed at them at the time, but now, I'm not so sure.

Then there was the visit from my friend, Mr Quang. He came to London in 2001, not long after the 9/11 bombings in America. Mr Quang lives in Texas, and, although he's not a professional fortune-teller, he does know *feng shui*. He is very good, and has a real gift. He came to the restaurant and immediately said:

"Oh, the restaurant has a strange feeling."

I asked him: "What do you mean, what is strange?"

Without hesitation, he replied: "I feel that there is a spirit here".

I was often sceptical about Mr Quang's beliefs, so I questioned him. "Tell me, what do you feel? Did something happen here?"

"It is not a bad feeling. In fact, it is good," he stated.

Now I was curious: "Really?"

"I think that someone is here trying to protect you. I think

243

something happened in this restaurant, but now someone is trying to help."

I was amazed. I quickly told him the story of Mr Bảy and his death. He smiled. That seemed to explain the sensations Mr Quang was feeling. "I think you had a good relationship with this head chef of yours. His soul is still around here and he is protecting you."

"How so?" I asked.

"I think your restaurant will run as normal and that customers will always come back to you. The customers will be very happy to be here."

But the strangest sign that Mr Bảy is still around the restaurant occurred three years after his death. It is the Vietnamese custom that each year for three years, relatives of the deceased, usually the spouse, have to pay respect to the family member. At the end of the three years there is a big ceremony. Although we weren't related to Mr Bảy, my family also paid its respects to Mr Bảy for three years after he died. There were nights during this time when I would wake up with a very strange feeling, a sudden urge to go to the restaurant – even if it was after midnight. But when I arrived, I could not see or hear anything wrong. It was very strange. Then, one Sunday afternoon, I was sitting in my office. The restaurant was closed as usual and no one else was in the building. Mr Tuan, the cleaner, had already left a few hours earlier. At 3.00 pm I heard a very loud noise coming from the kitchen. It was very noisy, and it sounded as if someone was cooking, frying some meat; the sizzling sound couldn't have been anything else. No one could be in the building so I was confused. I went downstairs to the kitchen, but no one was there.

I had a feeling that it was a spirit, and I felt that this spirit was Mr Bảy. I thought he was trying to tell me something, so I burned some incense and said to him that I would try to find out what was wrong. Then I prayed and paid him respect. The next day I called my friend Mr Quang: I trust his wisdom about things like this. I told him what had happened, and he said that it might be that Mr

Bảy felt that he had not been paid enough respect. I was curious as to what this could mean. My family had paid him a great deal of respect, including the burning of incense in front of his altar. So I called Mr Bảy's sister, and learned that his sister was also concerned about Mr Bảy. It was the end of the three years – which should mark the end of the mourning period – but Mrs Bảy had not taken any steps to build a tomb for Mr Bảy as tradition dictated. This explained why Mr Bảy was trying to communicate with us. He was upset.

So Hương Việt, the restaurant, has a protector – Mr Bảy. My daughter is so convinced that he protects the restaurant that she has a photo of him in her restaurant and she prays to him for protection as well. And I believe this. What else explains the success of the restaurant? We have been through four head chefs since he left, many of them terrible cooks, yet the customers still come. After so many bad chefs coming and going, I wanted some stability and consistency for the customers, and I thought about how to do this. I know that most good Vietnamese chefs don't have any specific qualifications – they learn their skills by practice, by training under someone with experience – so why couldn't I do it? I spoke to a friend who knew the restaurant industry, and he told me the basics about running a restaurant and about how to prepare food in advance. After two nights with him, I opened a few Vietnamese cookbooks and experimented. I tried to prepare sauces, marinades, and tried cooking a few recipes. After a few weeks, I was confident that I could prepare the staple sauces and marinades for the cook. My intention was that, even if we continued to have a high turnover of chefs in the restaurant, they would all use the same sauces and the same marinades. All they would have to do was cut the meat and vegetables, fry the food, and present it.

For a long time, it worked. Until I retired from the restaurant in 2015 I worked all day on Sunday, when the restaurant was closed, to prepare the sauces, marinades and dishes for the whole week. I also went in every morning at 6.00 am to prepare the restaurant for the day, before going upstairs at 9.30 to work for An Việt. I've never told anyone my recipes for some of the sauces and marinades – I think I'll keep these a secret.

CHAPTER FOURTEEN

Hackney

Hackney, a borough in the east end of London, has been a poor area for a long time, and the multiple '£1 shops' and cheque-cashing businesses only hint at the poverty. These stores aren't found in more affluent areas of London, and many chain shops weren't interested in investing in Hackney until quite recently. A visitor to the area may not realise the extent of the hardship in Hackney however, because there is a vibrant atmosphere on the High Street. The shops and restaurants reflect the diverse communities that have made Hackney their home – hairdressers with displays of colourful hair extensions in the window, take-away shops that sell goat curry or jerk chicken, and clothing stores that sell three-piece suits in fabrics and colours not sold on Oxford Street. For such a diverse area – over 40 languages are spoken in Hackney – there is relatively little racial tension. Turkish barbeque cafés are often full of Vietnamese customers; Vietnamese often run nail shops that are popular with women from Eastern Europe and Africa. People from all over the world shop in the Arabic or African food stores because they enjoy the variety of fruits and vegetables that can't be found in mainstream British food stores. There is a large Jewish, Turkish and African-Caribbean presence in Hackney. Hackney Council has always welcomed the Vietnamese community and supported us.

Today, 2015, most of Hackney is seen as trendy and house prices are still rising. Yet for most of my time in the area, Hackney was a poor borough. It was a rough borough – high unemployment, dirty streets, a high crime rate, and rampant drug use. It was often the little things that bothered me about Hackney –

trouble renewing the lease on my building, parking nightmares, noises at night from fighting teens. Prior to the 2002 elections, the Audit Commission rated London Borough of Hackney as one of the worst in the country. I've lived in Hackney for nearly half my life, and it is home to the largest Vietnamese community in the UK. I think many people who have lived in Hackney for some time have loved it as a home, but they also assumed that nothing could be done to improve it. It has been poor for so long that I think many people just stopped trying or caring.

To make matters work, there were often allegations of fraud or corruption within the council. Then I read in the papers that there was an estimated £40 million deficit in Hackney's budget, but later reports said that it was no more than £17 million. The most disturbing thing to me was that no one knew exactly how large the deficit was. I couldn't believe it, and thought that this was very strange. Most of this money had been lost because of incompetence and mismanagement. They were having to spend more money on compensation claims than repairs to the streets. Because Hackney was bankrupt, the Borough Treasurer issued a Section 114 order – a complete freeze on any spending until a budget cut was agreed. Rubbish wasn't collected, classes at school were cancelled because they couldn't hire supply teachers, and repairs to council property were left undone or incomplete.

Even when this emergency was resolved, there were still so many other problems. Charities were suffering because community grants were cut by almost 80%. The management service was very poor on the council estates. But one of the worst problems was the benefits system. This was because, in the late 1990s, Hackney Council had hired a private contractor to handle the council's revenue service. The contractor however proved to be totally incompetent. For instance, there were thousands of people waiting to have their housing benefits claims assessed and processed and so they hadn't received any payments. These same people were given eviction notices because they were in arrears.

To most residents, it appeared that it was simply bureaucratic ineffectiveness that made every step in dealing with Hackney Council so difficult. But there were so many people to blame for the failures, from councillors who failed to act, to incompetent staff working for the council. Many of these problems stemmed from a lack of money, and Hackney's budget was a total mess, even before the deficit. Then there was also the internal political conflict. The 1998 election left no party in control: it was a "hung council". I read that the dispute was personal; that opposing sides hated each other. The result was that there was no administration and no decisions could be made. To my dismay, reading these reports felt like déjà vu – I'd read similar stories and experienced similar dysfunction in war-time Vietnam when there was constant in-fighting for power in the South Vietnamese government. And of course I'd fled the Communist regime that disrupted every aspect of life with their corruption and lack of competence.

Eventually, the problems became so bad that people began to demand change. There were protests in late 2000, and like the protesters in Hackney, I too wanted a change. I knew so many people who were having problems with the council, and I don't like seeing other people struggle. I don't like undue suffering, suffering that wouldn't take place if things were run properly.

I wanted to help tackle the problems, and after twenty years it was time for me to give something back to the community. So I decided to run for local government. I had experience of working as a councillor in Vietnam so I believed that if I were to be elected, I could use this experience to help.

Campaign

Around ten years ago, I wrote to the Tories, asking to join the Conservative Party. I received no reply, and assumed this meant that they did not care. The Liberal Democrats have a good name as well, but they were not a strong presence on the council, and this prevented them from being in touch with the working class people in the way that the Labour Party was. I felt that the Labour Party was more in touch with people compared to the other parties, and here in Hackney, most people have supported the Labour Party for a long time. The majority on the Hackney Council were Labour. So I turned to the Labour Party.

Once I announced that I was standing for election with the Labour Party, things became very busy. Most of my time and energy went to the campaign, which was very hard work. I campaigned with the rest of the group from the Labour Party. We would get in a car or van to visit an area of Hackney; we'd go door-to-door trying to talk to people. So many times, we climbed up and down the stairs – even down to the basement flats – knocking on doors. We did this three or four nights a week for several months. It was exhausting. Many people would slam the door on us. They were not interested in listening to politicians giving political commentaries or making promises. I found, however, that when I introduced myself, telling them I was one of the Vietnamese Boat People, that I had been in Hackney over twenty years, and then asking them to support me, they were usually very interested. They'd listen to me.

This gave me the impression that people were looking for somebody like them, who knew their problems, who had experience in life. This was especially true of other refugee groups: they knew I understood their hard life. I believe that is why many people supported me. People wanted to listen to something different; and were fed up with promises that never happened. Also, I think the Vietnamese community has a good name in Hackney, and we are seen as good neighbours. After over twenty years in the borough though, we have never had a Vietnamese candidate. This was the first time, and I believe that's why many people supported me.

I did not get many votes from the Vietnamese community however. Getting the Vietnamese to vote is very difficult. Remember, they were under a Communist regime for many years, and this did not allow them to join parties or organisations. That is why the Vietnamese rarely want to join any campaign or organisation, even a voluntary organisation. In Vietnam, under the Communist regime, the Party appointed the candidates that the people were expected to vote for, and they could only vote for the candidate of the Party. This means that now they are very cynical, and don't believe their vote matters. Few Vietnamese in London, especially in Hackney, are registered to vote. In my ward, Dalston, out of eleven thousand constituents, there were just forty-five Vietnamese registered to vote, and in the end, only fifteen of them voted.

I'll never forget the actual day that they counted the votes. I was with the other candidates in the Ocean, a big assembly hall in Hackney. All night they would make announcements and update us on the news. I was so anxious that I could not sit still; I had to keep moving – pacing back and forth, walking around talking to people. But, as the evening wore on, my anxiety gave way to optimism and anticipation. Based on the trends appearing with the other wards, I had a feeling that the people in Dalston would be more in favour of the Labour Party. So, I began to get very excited and was hopeful that I would be elected. At 11.00 pm the chief officer, the returning officer, announced that our ward had three councillors, all Labour, including myself. I was very, very happy. Not only had I just become the first Vietnamese councillor in the UK, but I was now the first Vietnamese representative in Europe. It was a very good day.

It was also a good day for the Labour Party, which won an overwhelming majority in Hackney: forty-five seats compared to nine Conservatives and three LibDems. In my eyes, almost all of the new councillors were committed to improving Hackney. The deadlock of the previous council ended with the 2002 election, and so we had a group of committed councillors who were able to work together to make changes and improvements.

Because I had to work so hard during the campaign, I did not have time to worry about whether or not I was actually ready for the job. I was never really anxious about it. Some of this is because I had previous experience as a councillor in Vietnam. But mostly, I felt confident because of the support I had from the Labour Party. Their people were very organised, offered lots of material, briefings and training for new candidates to prepare them. Then, once we were elected, they provided thorough inductions for new councillors, introducing us to every department within the council and informing us of the code of conduct and other internal policies. They offered training on budgets, finance and how the council operated, and they hosted an away day so that we could have an opportunity to talk, to learn and to ask questions. Also, I was too keen to get to work to be nervous. I had many goals and lots of things I wanted to accomplish during my tenure as a councillor.

Personal

I think it was around this time, when I felt busier than ever, that I had to spend a great deal of time fighting for my own safety. I usually wouldn't have let this bother me, but things got out of hand. I first met Nguyễn Chiến[13] when he appeared in my office at An Việt Foundation in 1998. I had never seen the man before, but suddenly he was accusing me of trying to kill him. "You didn't think I'd find you, did you?" he screamed at me with a look of smug satisfaction. "You think you are safe here, pretending to be a good man. I know who you are."

I was so confused. "Who are you?" I asked.

"Don't pretend you don't know me. You know exactly who I am. You tried to kill me," he replied. He had a manic look in his eyes. I still had no idea who he was or what he was talking about. All I knew was that I had to calm him down so I could get him to leave safely.

---

[13] Name has been changed to protect identity

"You tried to kill me," he repeated.

"I've never tried to kill anyone," I said, as I slowly stood up.

"Yes you did. On the battlefields in Vietnam. You tried to kill me because I was fighting with the North Vietnamese Army and you were for the South."

He said it all so fast, I wasn't sure I was hearing him correctly. I had never been a soldier; during the Vietnam War, I was a Philosophy lecturer. I tried to reason with him. "I never tried to personally kill you. In any case, we are both now refugees here in the UK and we should concentrate on our new lives and not dwell on the war." Eventually he calmed down and left.

I didn't hear from Chiến for many years after the occasion. I forgot about him that very afternoon, and then I stood for election. A constituent received a letter from Chiến that said I was not to be trusted, that I was a burglar, a murderer and a mafia leader. In the letter he also said, "Thành has been trying to kill me for ten years. I am in great danger."

I, in fact, was the one in danger. At first the attacks were indirect: I had to hide my car because he slashed my tyres so frequently (I've had to change my tyres twenty-eight times); he spread car oil over the front of the An Việt building, cut the lights to the building, and damaged the locks. He even stole my milk bottles on random mornings. Then one day, Chiến ambushed me outside my restaurant. He punched me in the head, but when I began to fight back, he ran off. A few days later, as I went to get my car from its hiding space, I heard my name shouted from above. When I looked up, he was on a balcony directly above me. He dropped chilli oil and threw a coat rack down at me. Luckily he missed. I used my mobile to call the police. He ran off and disappeared, but the police caught him, arrested him, and he was sent to prison.

It had been a funny story until it became serious. Once he assaulted the husband of one of my staff. The police placed cameras around my house and the restaurant. Throughout all these ordeals over the years, I had him arrested several times. He was also sectioned in a hospital at one point, but overall, the police seemed unable to do anything to prevent the harassment, and he continued to slash my tyres. A fellow councillor and the Mayor wrote to the police on my behalf, requesting action. Eventually, the police got Chiến to sign an 'acceptable behaviour contract' in which he promised not to harass me anymore. But, because this was not legally binding, I also took out an injunction. After that, I had no more problems for a while.

Councillor

My job was very simple: I represented the people of Dalston in the London Borough of Hackney.

Sadly, the people who had suffered the most from the chaos of the previous administration were the individual residents of Hackney, and as a new councillor I received many letters from people complaining, expressing their concerns, and asking for help. The first year or so, when I received a letter, I often went to visit the person at their home. I think people liked this, as I was able to speak to them directly and answer their questions. But this became too difficult to keep up, since I simply didn't have time to visit everyone – mostly because of the meetings.

Nearly every month we had a full council meeting, which normally lasted for about three hours. We also had a monthly, or sometimes fortnightly, Labour group meeting to discuss within the Labour Party all the things that related to Hackney Council, and this was usually held prior to the full council meeting. On top of all this, each councillor also had to join a committee such as the Planning Committee, the Learning/Education Committee or the Regeneration Committee, and each of these committees held a monthly meeting as well. In the beginning, I joined the Planning and Education Committees. There were simply too many meetings however, and I always became very depressed by all of the clients who needed assistance with their own planning applications, so I moved to join the Regeneration Committee. I also had to attend committee meetings hosted by representatives of the three estates in my ward. These were held every quarter, and on top of these we had Neighbourhood Committee meetings. Sometimes there were sub-committee meetings to target problem areas such as drug dealers, prostitution and anti-social behaviour in our ward. And finally, every week the councillors for Dalston had an open office for 'drop-ins', and the three of us took it in turn to be there. But that was not all: we also had a Labour Party Branch Meeting that met once a month. In addition, we also represented the council at the housing association meetings. The councillors also had to join the school governing body in our ward, which met regularly, and every quarter there were requests to help with Labour events like a by-election, where we needed to help the Labour Party deliver leaflets or newsletters door-to-door. I also had to attend many training seminars such as project training, finance training, budget setting. So on top of my full-time job, and the restaurant, I had to attend meetings three or four nights each week on average. And the paperwork – letter writing, performance reports, progress reports – was endless.

I sometimes felt like waving a white flag in surrender: it really was a full time job. We worked very hard, but even so, I enjoyed it. I felt that those meetings and committees kept me in touch with the people. At the meetings we made great progress towards improving people's lives in Hackney at a very basic level. This is especially true with the estate committee meetings. The people in the estate come together to ask the council to improve their environment: rubbish collection, the noise nuisance in their area, drug dealers on their estate, teenagers fighting, or small things like repairs. At these meetings, we collected all the information and then wrote to the directorate asking for a statement on how they planned to tackle the residents' concerns and problems. Often the response was weak, the questions went unanswered, or actions weren't taken.

But over time, I saw enough development to keep the residents engaged – they weren't giving up, and continued to strive to improve their living conditions. To witness this first hand, and to be part of it, I found rewarding. Those were moments when my enthusiastic idealism from my young days as a councillor in Vietnam returned. These minor victories served as small reminders that, as citizens in a democratic country, we could make a difference and could institute change.

However, it wasn't long before my optimism was drained. I found it difficult to have the impact I wanted because of all the protocols and systems that were already in place. The bureaucratic hurdles in Hackney's local government were vast.

Take parking issues as an example. Even before becoming a councillor, I was frustrated by the parking regulations in Hackney. I felt the parking restrictions were excessive, and hindered a needed increase in business development and regeneration. When meeting with residents across the borough, I heard similar complaints: too much resident-only parking in areas where residents have off-street parking, lack of parking space for visitors or business customers or employees, and large commercial areas that restricted parking from 7am to 11pm. In fact, I came to believe that one of the most unpopular Labour Party policies in Hackney was the change to parking regulations. In most boroughs, parking tickets have become a huge moneymaking racket. When I became a councillor, I learned that Hackney actually lost money on its parking policy because the extra-long hours of restrictive parking meant it had to pay for more wardens.

Even with this contentious issue, I saw direct progress. I wrote a strong proposal to Mayor Pipe and the other Labour councillors with recommended changes to Hackney's parking policy, but unfortunately the policy of Ken Livingstone across London in general was to try to limit the number of vehicles on the road. Some councillors were anti-car and wanted restrictive parking to encourage more use of public transport. We now have a new parking policy, which began in March 2005. The new parking regulations weren't as good as I expected or hoped for, but they were an improvement.

While some residents' concerns related to the community at large, like rubbish collection or parking, many people in Hackney had their own individual problems with the borough. They often needed the intervention of a councillor to have these problems finally resolved. Some wrote to me, others emailed me and some visited the surgery the councillors held once a week. Members of the Vietnamese community were an exception. They never came to the surgery to see me or the other councillors. They have never recognised the role of the councillor, or what their local government representatives could do for them. Instead, the Vietnamese came to see me at An Việt Foundation, just as they'd always done.

I did my best to investigate and advocate on their behalf, but what I didn't like about being a councillor were the occasions on which I'd try to help someone and I wouldn't get a response from an officer or from the council. It made me think that there were those in local government who weren't actively trying to improve the situation or to help someone out. Take Mr Achara's[14] case. He came to see me at the councillor surgery in mid-February 2004. He was 70 years old at the time, but appeared much older. He was weak and frail, and struggled to walk into the office. He was diabetic and was in a great deal of pain because of severe arthritis in his hips, knees and hands. He came to seek help because he had received a letter threatening bailiff action for failure to pay his council tax, and was trembling with anxiety. He had been asked to re-apply for Housing Benefit and Council Tax Benefit several months earlier, but since then had not received any payments. He therefore found himself unable to pay his rent or council tax. I requested an investigation into his case, and was given an appointment for an interview in early March. The following investigation found that Mr Achara's council tax benefit

---

[14] Name has been changed to protect identity

entitlement had not been correctly transferred from the old computer system to the new one, and this meant that his council tax account was incorrect. Hackney noted this error and promised to stop any bailiff action. They also found that Mr Achara's housing benefit cheques had been sent to the wrong bank and assured him that this had been corrected. Such incompetence and inexcusable mistakes should never have happened, but I was at least relieved that Mr Achara's nightmare was now over.

We were wrong however. In April that year – the very next month – Mr Achara received a letter from bailiffs saying he owed over £4,000. He returned, asking for more help, and this time he was desperate. "I am suffocating," he gasped. "I don't have that kind of money. I can't meet my obligations. I don't know what to do. My heart won't stop racing." He was living in a state of never-ending panic. He told me he was unable to stick to his diabetic diet because he had no money. He couldn't afford to go to the dentist. He needed help. He tried to get debt counselling, but most charities only helped with credit cards. He tried to apply for a loan to pay the council tax, but was denied.

I was shocked. I wanted to find out how Mr Achara's debt had become so large. It turned out that the council was claiming that he hadn't paid council tax since 1993. His case has been outstanding for ten years? I couldn't believe it. While this financial fight was happening, Mr Achara's son, who was depressive, was depending on him for help, and a beloved family member had just died. The man was crumbling under the weight of his burdens. Mr Achara's health was so poor that I knew he didn't have the strength to fight this alone. I wrote a letter in mid-July demanding a full investigation. I continued to pursue his case, continued to stay in touch with him until finally his case was resolved.

Then there was Ms Harris[15]. She had been trying to get mortgage relief for almost a year – this is a type of income support for homeowners who are in temporary receipt of benefits to help

---

[15] Name has been changed to protect identity

them meet their mortgage payments until they are on their feet again. Mortgage relief is normally straightforward and simple to process. But not in Hackney. Ms Harris tried many times to have the local Department for Work and Pensions (DWP) send her the necessary forms, but they never arrived. When she finally received the form and took it to her bank, the DWP claimed they never received it. She would try again and again to hand in the necessary forms but, at the same time, the staff at the DWP were continually changing their minds about what paperwork was actually needed. Back and forth she went, each time feeling more and more helpless against all the bureaucratic excuses given to her for the delay. Meanwhile, all this time, while she was chasing forms that seemed to go missing, the bank was threatening her. Even when all the paperwork had been collated, she still never heard a reply from the DWP. She was about to lose her home, and was desperate. Only when I got involved did she finally receive her mortgage relief and was no longer threatened with losing her home.

Sadly, these stories were not uncommon. Councillors intervene, the problem was investigated and a resolution was agreed. But often, nothing happened. The political schisms, incompetent staff – both within the council and within companies outsourced to help – and financial mismanagement became a curse for many residents of the borough. The elderly Mr and Mrs Hunt[16] were also pursued by bailiffs for council tax payments. Each time they tried to renew their council tax benefit, they were asked to provide evidence of their pension. Their daughter would take all the relevant paperwork to the council, since their knee problems and advanced age prevented them going themselves. Nothing changed. They continued to receive letters requesting information regarding their pension followed by threatening letters from bailiffs. Twice the Hunts were able to have the recovery action against them stopped, but then the entire cycle would repeat itself. I got involved. The mayor got involved. This was 2003. As far as I

---

[16] Name has been changed to protect identity

know, the case is still unresolved.

A recent case involved a disabled man who needed a ramp to be built to his door, but nothing was done about it. Finally, he took it to court, the judge ruled in favour of the man, and Hackney council was told to build this man a wheelchair ramp. I don't know if the ramp was ever built.

Yet, Hackney has made many improvements. Being able to have such a direct impact on someone's life, being able to help someone, was what I loved about being a councillor. I loved helping people to fight for their rights, a basic tenet of a democratic country. That is why I know that the improvements in Hackney will continue.

Planning

The welfare system was not the only outlandish mess we inherited that term. The Planning Department of Hackney Council was notorious for being difficult to deal with. The average turnaround time for planning permission in Hackney was one year, while in other councils it was an eight to ten-week process. The Planning Department did all that it could to make commercial and large-scale applications a priority, and this wasn't necessarily wrong, but it left the smaller scale commercial or private applications to be dealt with on an extremely ad-hoc basis. It shouldn't take someone over a year to get permission for a simple loft conversion.

And when residents lodged complaints about the service, they often encountered rude, unhelpful staff, if they received a response at all. What frustrated many people was the unknown, the inability to get any kind of information about their case from the Planning Department. Hackney relied on a culture of "it is at the bottom of a very big pile" or "we have just moved buildings and the files have been lost" or "we are very understaffed". They continually hid behind excuses, never taking responsibility or admitting unjustified delays or incompetence. They seemed to think that if they said:

"that's not what the computer says" or "you aren't in our system", that meant that somehow it was not Hackney's fault. Residents could never get a straight answer or get anyone in the Planning Department to take action. The department could not be held to account, which was unacceptable. Residents, as well as fellow councillors, had been complaining about the Planning Department in Hackney for years. As usual, councillors blamed much of the problem on the financial chaos from the 'hung council' years.

Mr Singh's[17] story illustrates what I mean. Mr Singh owned the Post Office across the road from my office. He was awarded a Conservation Area Partnership Grant of around £60,000 towards building a new shop front and making some repairs to his store. This was in 2001. Late in 2003, Mr Singh came to me requesting assistance, as he was still waiting for the funds to come through. Over the course of two years, he had called, written letters, but had received no reply or advice about what he needed to do to claim the grant. The project manager for the building works also appealed to the Planning Department for information, but without any luck.

I wrote a letter to the Deputy Mayor of Hackney, and she agreed that this was one of the worst cases she had come across. The Deputy Mayor started a full audit investigation into the matter. The auditors found serious 'weaknesses' in how the Planning Department had been handling the grant, which was a polite way to say that the council shouldn't have lost all of Mr Singh's paperwork. The Deputy Mayor personally visited the site to see things for herself, and contacted the heads of all the relevant teams within the council. She told Mr Singh that the grant would be paid once they could verify that the project was complete.

I thought the problem would be resolved quickly and completely after such a strong response from the Deputy Mayor, yet around ten months later I received another letter from Mr Singh. The building work had been completed, but he was still

---

[17] Name has been changed to protect identity

waiting for someone from the Planning Department to visit the site, to verify that all the grant conditions were met before he could get paid. He was still waiting for the money. I had to write again to the Deputy Mayor to inform her that after all her previous efforts, the project had still not been completely resolved. Mr Singh was a victim of the disorganisation from the previous council that still hadn't been sorted out, and despite great improvements recently, he is still waiting for a resolution.

I'm also awaiting a resolution. Before I became a councillor, An Việt enquired about buying the property we are in now, but nothing happened. Then I became a councillor, learned how the system worked, and spoke to people in property management. After a year, still nothing happened. When the new chief executive arrived he intervened on our behalf, but still there was no reply. The Deputy Mayor got involved, and the office in charge of property wrote a letter to me full of promises to look into it "by the end of the week". That was in October 2005. It is now 2015 and I'm still trying to buy the building.

The negative impact of the delays in planning applications had repercussions beyond nightmares for residents and small business owners. Few companies or entrepreneurs have the stamina and commitment to do business in Hackney when there is such a long waiting period before work can begin. Instead, most investors, especially those who have knowledge or past experience of the Hackney 'system', invest their money elsewhere while the borough lounges at the top of the government's list of deprived areas. A strong Planning Department is vital to a borough; it brings in money to the council.

When I and other new councillors joined Hackney in 2002, we were almost lost on where to begin. Improving the services of the Planning Department seemed a daunting task: the problem appeared almost too big. Everything was in chaos, and even the meetings called to discuss how to make improvements were a joke. Often, relevant staff didn't attend the meetings and, when they did, they were often unprepared.

But I had an idea of how we could begin to step forward. The Community and Environment Directorate was too big, and its remit was too broad. Both the Mayor and Deputy Mayor of Hackney agreed that there was a great need to improve this directorate's performance and that it was simply too large and unwieldy to provide the needed focus. I recommended that the council split the Community and Environment Directorate into two. In the end, they agreed. Now instead of one oversized directorate we have the Culture and Community Department, which focuses on cultural services and community partnership, and the Planning, Transportation and Environment Department.

I waited so long for the Planning Department to get its act together so that the borough could move forward with large-scale investment projects. I was always thinking of the future, and I had an idea. Prior to London's hosting of the 2012 Summer Olympics, I submitted a plan to Hackney Council's Regeneration Committee to build a "Little Vietnam" in a site used during the Olympics. I had a vision of a village centred around a large temple or tower, a place where the community could come together for ancestor worship. The tower could also act as a community centre, a focal point for the Vietnamese community where they could gather for cultural celebrations. I also hoped that around the tower we may be able to have lots of shops. I wanted the village to look like a real Vietnamese village. We would have set up one committee to run the tower centre, one for community activities, and another committee to oversee the business area.

Nothing came of my proposal but I still dream about it. I still have the architect's drawings. Hackney has changed recently. It's become a trendy place for young people to come for music and places to eat and drink. I think the train line built as part of the Olympic regeneration has helped.

Volunteer

One of the key differences between a communist country like Vietnam and capitalist and democratic countries like the UK is the role of the voluntary sector, or the not-for-profit services. In communist countries, the State is seen as the sole provider of all basic needs from health care to housing. Thus, there shouldn't be a need for a charity to provide a service – the elderly, the sick, the poor should be able to turn to the State for care and help. What this usually meant was that everyone lacked.

But in capitalist countries, everyone is expected to take care of themselves. This means those who are financially able can make decisions about what services they want based on value for money. In countries like the UK, which recognise that not everyone is able to stand on their two feet at all times in their life, core services like health care and education are provided, however, there frequently the poor, the distressed, the lonely and the struggling often have needs that aren't met by the central government. So charities have always been present to help these who fall on hard times or who need a bit of help.

Over time, the people have demanded more from the State but it is difficult to balance the need for a free economy and free choice with the need to provide care for those less able. So many western governments give money to charities to provide specialist services. Combined with the spirit of giving from the public, this allows an organic growth of services to meet the ever changing needs of a modern, growing community.

But today's modern world means that those of us who wish to provide help need more and more money to do so. Very few of us can afford to raise our own family and dedicate our entire day to serving others. So charities need to have paid staff as well as volunteers. We need office space with computer and phone equipment and lately, we all need to gain specialist skills, continue training, and prove we are actually doing what we say we're doing. All this means that the State has had to create another huge bureaucracy to maintain, fund, and monitor the charity sector.

In Hackney, this was yet another bureaucracy that was a chore to deal with. And this was an area in which I knew I could make the greatest impact – the council's relationship to the community sector. There are hundreds of community groups in the borough, and the more support they were given, the more services they could provide to Hackney's poorer residents.

These residents, many from minority ethnic groups, sometimes needed specialist support and services. A mainstream, national charity might not understand the needs of the Turkish/Kurdish community in Hackney, but the Dey-Mer Turkish and Kurdish Community Centre provided a safe meeting place for members of this community. The Asian Women's Advisory Service reached out to isolated Asian women who might not have trusted or have been allowed access to government services. There was also the Hackney Chinese Community Service; The London Irish Women's Centre; Lubavitch Youth (which served Jewish young people); North London Muslim Community Centre; Simba Community Alliance (which provided advice to the African community); and the Turkish Cypriot Community Association. Not to mention the specialist community groups working with the disabled, the elderly or disadvantaged youth.

I wanted the council to recognise the importance of voluntary and community organisations, and I also wanted it to understand the complexities and obstacles of sustaining a charity in today's environment. The London Borough of Hackney budgets large amounts of money for voluntary sector funding in the borough, around £2.15 million in 2003/4. However, many of the smaller charities have trouble accessing this funding. One of the core problems was, not surprisingly, Hackney borough itself. Hackney Council did not have a central, clear goal or vision around the voluntary sector. So it seemed to get involved in many enterprises – often initiated from within completely different teams within the council. This meant that there was not a centralised monitoring or funding policy. This had multiple repercussions: some funding sources were swamped with applications while others remained virtually unknown; funding grants were awarded on an ad-hoc basis; and organisations often had to complete multiple, redundant funding applications or reporting forms. It was a mess and it was frustrating.

Funding is always a struggle for charities. Some of the larger charities have entire teams of energetic young people who work full time writing grant applications and hosting events to raise money. But in Hackney, most of the smaller charities doing a lot of the work on the ground don't have this luxury. And so the chaos of applying for any funding provided by the council often hampered the ability of the voluntary sector to provide much needed services. I felt that I was well placed to voice the concerns of many of the minority charity organisations regarding the council's voluntary sector grants. I could personally relate to the difficulties these smaller organisations faced in applying to Hackney Council for funding because I myself had struggled with the process at An Việt Foundation for over a decade.

Hackney Council allocated grants to black and minority ethnic groups, but to me the problems faced by minority run organisations were not something that could simply be fixed by throwing money at them. We needed support in actually securing the funding. I still have problems with the long and time-consuming grant applications, which are difficult to complete, especially because they are written in a style of English that is hard to understand if you are from a different culture. Even if you are fluent in the language, bureaucratic English is a dialect unto itself – full of jargon, buzzwords and acronyms. Furthermore, questions on the application forms expect a certain type of answer, and if you are going to stand a chance of providing a strong funding application, you have to be able to discern what the funders actually want to hear. This is why minority groups like the Vietnamese often score low on applications: it is because of the difficulties involved in making applications, and not because of shortcomings in the project idea. I've also found that in order to present value for money, minority groups often present lower budgets than may be realistic, leaving out necessities like pay increases, recruitment costs and so on. This frequently happens due to a lack of 'self-esteem', resulting in a belief that they can access funds only if the bare minimum is requested.

I've long been annoyed by the tedious demand to complete multiple applications for a single grant – for a National Refugee Forum grant I had to complete four applications in eighteen months – and for years I've found that the lack of long-term funding made it impossible for me to do long-term strategic planning. I may learn of a need within the Vietnamese community, but without the security of funding that will last beyond a year, it is hard to justify hiring new staff to deliver services for such a short time. Besides, by the time the community came to learn about a new project and came to trust and rely on it, the funding would end. Funding that is only guaranteed for a year at a time hinders sustainability, which is a goal of all funders. For small community organisations that develop to meet a specific need of a group, like An Việt Foundation, these challenges mean that staff and volunteers spend more time on paperwork and applications than providing the much needed service, and they often find their funding is cut before they've had a chance to secure additional monies to keep them up and running.

I wanted increased accessibility to funding opportunities for minority groups. Thus, I proposed the creation of a preliminary short-form application, from which grants officers could select promising projects and work with applicants to produce successful full proposals. I wanted the council to provide outreach assistance with funding applications, perhaps one-to-one coaching, and I also suggested that grant officers should work closely with successful applicants in the initial stages of final budgeting, work-plan design and setting up their projects. I've found that too many projects fail to get started properly and quickly due to lack of guidance. The council should also help groups with renewal applications or finding alternate sources of funding, long before the council's funding comes to an end. Too many excellent community services suffer lapses and closure due to the short-term nature of funding.

The timing was right. The council was willing to look at my concerns because it now had a balanced budget: it was finally in a position to put more money aside for the voluntary sector and provide more support to applicants. Some positive steps have been taken, but it has been a rough transition. Firstly, they outsourced the administration of the funding process to the Association of London Governments (ALG), which turned out to be a good idea in the long run, despite having been a mess in the beginning. There were delays in transferring the system, partly because of funding restrictions, and partly due to some political squabbling between the Tories and the Labour Party on the process. Then Hackney and ALG had trouble working together, so it took a while to work out some glitches in the system.

Then there was the fight between two umbrella groups competing to act as the link between the London Borough of Hackney and the voluntary sector. The two umbrella groups were consortia that had a powerful influence in the sector. Previously, Hackney Community and Voluntary Sector (HCVS) had this contract but it failed to get its application in by the deadline, so Hackney Council chose Hackney Agency for Volunteering (HAVE) instead. Common sense would suggest that an agency that couldn't get an application in on time should not be in a position to offer support and advice to other charities in Hackney on how to fundraise. HCVS however made some challenges during the handover process, and the legal wrangling delayed the process, leaving many charities without much needed support.

It therefore took about a year after the election for the council to get things sufficiently in order for improvements to be felt and recognised across the sector. Training schemes were delivered, and workshops were held. The budget for the voluntary sector increased, and a small grants programme was introduced, which awarded £5,000 for the first year to new or small, community based groups. Half of the organisations awarded this grant were minority community groups. The council worked with often excluded communities such as the Somali and other African communities, Travellers, and more Turkish and Kurdish advice services.

But there was still more to be done. Another way in which I tried to help voluntary organisations was by pushing the council to help them to gain access to office space, and this again comes from my experience with the Vietnamese community. We struggled for ten years, and it was far from easy to find a space we could afford for an office. Eventually I was able to find my current space on Englefield Road, but we had been lucky. The council at that time knew it had this vacant space and agreed that, with some help to refurbish the building, the unused building could again serve the community. Subsequently the Planning Department was not so helpful to groups who call asking for assistance with office space. It was also inconsistent in how it decided which groups could have office space and which couldn't, who had an official lease and who didn't, or who paid rent at the market rate and who didn't. Then there were the continual complaints that council property was not being properly maintained.

Not only was this a missed opportunity for the council – rent from organisations would have been a helpful subsidy; tenant organisations might have invested in the property and increased its value. But the obstacles inhibiting voluntary organisations and others from occupying council property also made it more difficult for legitimate service providers in the borough to afford office space. Lack of office space hinders everything from accessibility for clients, to being taken seriously by funders. The fact that the council sold off a lot of properties that were being used by the voluntary sector did not help the problem.

After the election, a group of us pushed for the council to regulate the policy on occupation of council owned properties by voluntary sector groups. But this met with some resistance, which was hardly surprising – many was frustrated by the ad-hoc manner in which the council made arrangements, while others benefited. It wasn't an easy process. Some groups were allowed to use buildings for years without a lease or licence. A few properties had umbrella groups acting as the landlord, sometimes for the better and sometimes for the worse. Others were paying a reduced rent and were suddenly expected to pay the market rate. For those who were in council property paying little rent, the simultaneous drop in funding and lack of ability to buy the property left them with few options for finding premises for their services.

But regardless of all this, a standardised policy was needed so that there would be a more stable environment for voluntary groups who already had to work in an insecure setting. We needed to become more transparent and fair, but several noted that this sudden push for regularised lease arrangements and charging rent at the market rate was less about protecting the voluntary sector, and more about bringing in extra money for a borough in the midst of a financial crisis.

Eventually, a policy was written that reflected good practice recommended by the Royal Institution of Chartered Surveyors for letting policies, and a pilot programme was introduced to 'test' the future vision of housing voluntary sector organisations in 'hubs' – premises that would house multiple voluntary bodies. The participating voluntary organisations would benefit from sharing a reception area and facilities such as meeting rooms.

I believe that successful voluntary bodies, when allowed the time, funding and creativity, can benefit the borough on so many levels. The voluntary sector is saving the council millions by providing services that the council should be delivering. And by supporting the smaller charities who work daily with those in need in simple, sustainable ways, everyone in the community benefits. I felt that the council was finally moving in the right direction, and I wanted other charities and community groups to have the luck that I had.

Reconciliation

After a period, Chiền began making trouble again. He again accused me of trying to kill him during the war, he threw things at me and tried to damage An Việt's property. I spoke to a friend of mine about it. A few weeks later he gave me a number of someone to call – someone who knew Chiền in the refugee camp in Hong Kong.

I was eager to learn as much as possible about why Chiền was targeting me, so I made the call and I spoke to this man at length. I learned that apparently Chiền was found reading a book on mental illness and suddenly he began acting strangely. I was confused, I wasn't sure I understood what this man was telling me. I asked for more details and learned that Chiền never had a mental illness but one day decided to behave as if he did. He had no idea why someone would do such a thing, but we guessed that he must have felt he'd receive more money in the camp if he had a mental illness, or perhaps he wanted to stay in the camp and not be resettled in the UK and thought his behaviour would influence the decision.

Since reading the book about mental illness, Chiền began taking the ash from his cigarettes and injecting it in his veins so his eyes would go really red and his heart would race in order to make himself look like he had a mental illness. He was prescribed medication but he never took it.

We assumed that Chiền continued with his acting once he arrived in the UK when he learned that he would be eligible for disability payments if he had a mental illness.

So not long ago, when I ran into Chiền again and he began making more trouble, I wrote him a letter. I stated plainly that if he continued to harass me I would ask for a court order and tell the government that I believe he is being fraudulent and recommend that they assess him again for mental illness. I reminded him that if they learn he doesn't actually have a mental illness, they would cut his benefits. Since then, I haven't had any more trouble with Chiến.

Return

It wasn't long before this that Tâm went to visit Vietnam. There was no way I could ever go back: I was still in danger. I still hear stories of men like me, who continue to be active in protesting against the Communist regime, who are captured, or mysteriously killed, when they return to Vietnam. For instance, Father Điềm, the priest from Đà Lạt who was my friend. When he arrived from the camp in Singapore in 1980, he became a priest of the Archdiocese of Birmingham. About a decade later he was awarded the title Monsignor and continued to help Vietnamese refugees in his diocese. In 2003, Mgr Điềm left for his first visit to Vietnam after twenty-three years living in the UK. He traveled in North and South Vietnam to visit family and friends. He also went on pilgrimage to some sacred sites, including one in Huế. He died in his hotel room very mysteriously. No one knows really how he died but many of us suspect he was murdered.

There was no way I could go to Vietnam, it still wasn't safe.

That was why I missed my father's funeral. It was a few years after the fall of Saigon before my father was able to travel south to see me and the rest of the family, but by then I had already fled the country. He met my wife and children. At first, we couldn't correspond for many years because the Communists blocked any letters I sent. But then in the mid-1980s our letters got through. He would write telling me to pray every day and to continue believing in God.

Over the years, some family and friends have travelled back to Vietnam and visited my father for me, and I have some photographs that they sent so I could see him. I also sent him money, but of course he did not spend it. He saved some gold for his funeral and gave the rest of it to the church. This is very typical of old Vietnamese Catholics. He died in 1995 – he was ninety-seven years old. I organised a Mass here in London to commemorate his death.

Tâm wanted to go to North Vietnam to see my family. She had met more of my family than Linh as a child, since she had stayed in Vietnam with my wife and son when Linh and I had fled. But she had never been in the North. Before flying, Tâm went to an English fortune-teller. This clairvoyant told her that she had a special guide that looked after her: a guardian. She went further to say that this guardian was a member of her family: a girl who had died when only thirteen years old, and who looked just like Tâm. Tâm thought the entire reading was very strange, and had never heard anyone in her family mention someone dying at the age of thirteen, so she forgot all about it until she went to Vietnam. She went to visit my youngest sister in the North, and saw a fortune-teller in Vietnam who said the same thing as the English fortune-teller. She thought this was very odd, and wasn't sure what to think. She still did not know about any family member who could meet the description of her guardian.

Tâm later described to me all the details of my childhood village and it sometimes sounded like nothing had changed. The community spirit, the simplicity of life, the generous nature of the villagers all seemed untouched by time, and knowing that makes me happy. I knew my family struggled and suffered from great poverty through the war and afterwards, but by the time Tâm went to visit, the money sent over by family members now living in the West had helped return the vitality of the village. People had repaired their houses and there was an abundance of food at the feasts. The most noticeable change was the massive new Cathedral being built in the sister village. Both our villages always had two churches and three priests - ours was dedicated to the seven martyrs while theirs was the parish church. But this new church would rival any cathedral here in the UK. From the photos I can tell it will be glorious. The three priests in the village today, including the two monks, are all relatives of mine.

Tâm seemed to really enjoy spending time with my family. During this visit, my sister told Tâm about how difficult it was for her when she had had to bring all the family bones back together. In Vietnam, we have a custom that three years after someone dies, we should dig up the grave and place the bones in the family tomb. At that time, the Communists wanted to get rid of all the tombs, and they destroyed them without inviting family members to identify the remains. All of the bones of the village had therefore been piled together, and my sister was worried about identifying our ancestors. She heard from a woman in the market that you could test by pricking your finger and dropping some of your blood on the bones. If the blood stayed in place, then it was a member of your family. If the blood moved around or dripped off, then it was not. So my sister went to the pile of bones and identified a small skull that belonged to someone who was around thirteen years old. My sister told Tâm about Chuộng (our sister who died in 1945, aged thirteen). Tâm instantly felt very scared, her body covered in gooseflesh, and she knew then that what that fortune-teller had said was true.

I wasn't surprised by the news. Tâm always seemed protected and always found it easy to succeed. The Vietnamese have a proverb that children born with the birth sack still intact are very lucky. So, when my wife's water did not break before Tâm emerged, we knew she would be very lucky and successful. And she survived the dengue fever. Today, Tâm is a millionaire. She was appointed as the Director of Development of a housing group in Maidenhead when she was only twenty-five years old. People always seem surprised to see this young, small Vietnamese woman deliver such effective and impressive work.

Immigration

Greyhound

I sat beside a Hmong man–shorter than me!
This guy drank milk the whole trip.
You might have thought he was a loser
hoping for a second growth spurt.
But I know why he guzzled so much milk:
his stomach hurt.
I, too, suffered from gastritis once.
The result of years of starvation
and bitterness from growing up in a piss-poor nation.

Excerpt of poem by **Phan Nhiên Hạo** (Translated from the Vietnamese by Hai-Dang Phan), 1992 (Published online in Intranslation; Brooklynrail.org: http://intranslation.brooklynrail.org/vietnamese/poems-by-phan-nhien-hạo)

I was outraged in 1992 when the UK government began repatriating refugees in Hong Kong back to Vietnam. The international community, including the USA, France and the UK claimed that the Boat People in refugee camps in the late 1980s were actually economic migrants and not refugees. I was one of many Vietnamese around the world who protested and campaigned against their return. We knew that the Vietnamese in Hong Kong would be subject to severe punishment if returned to Vietnam. The reason Vietnamese left Vietnam after 1975, and continued to leave throughout the 1980s, was because they could not live safely under an oppressive, ruthless and inhumane regime. This self-imposed exile was not simply a pursuit for a more prosperous life, but a flight from persecution to safety. I was incensed at the levels of misinformation and prejudice, as well as ulterior motives, behind the government's push to repatriate Hong Kong refugees to Vietnam.

The Foreign and Commonwealth Office actually compared Vietnamese refugees in Hong Kong at that time to illegal immigrants from Mexico in the United States. Mexico's governance was not perfect, but they in no way oppressed its citizens the way the Communist government in Vietnam treated its people. The Foreign and Commonwealth Office also made placating assurances that the Vietnamese government had promised not to punish those who left Vietnam and that the international community was monitoring the situation. It also claimed that those who were being repatriated were people who had gone through the entire screening process involved in applying for asylum, including appeals, but had been then found not to be refugees. The international community believed that most of the new arrivals in Hong Kong were from North Vietnam seeking a better life overseas instead of people who had connections with the old South Vietnamese regime or who had a well-founded fear of persecution.

But these people would have been persecuted if returned to Vietnam at that time, and we had concrete examples of the dismal fate that befell Vietnamese returning to Vietnam of their own accord. The case of the crew and passengers of the *Việt Nam Thương Tín* is still vivid in the memories of a great many Vietnamese. This ship arrived in Guam in 1975 with fifteen hundred passengers. Not long after, homesickness led them to ask for repatriation. On their return to Vietnam, instead of an expected welcome, all of them were immediately sent to various re-education camps where they remained for more than fourteen years. This precedent concerning voluntary repatriation made me shudder to think what would happen to those who were forced to return. Of course the authorities in Hanoi would promise to treat returnees fairly but no organisation, not even the UNHCR, would have had enough staff and resources to monitor whether they kept their promise or not. I couldn't believe that the countries in the West that were pushing for repatriation, would believe the Vietnamese authorities – these same western countries should know all too well that Hanoi rarely keeps a promise. The western governments also seemed to overlook the fact that articles 85, 88 and 89 stipulate that it is illegal to leave Vietnam clandestinely and the offence is punishable by severe prison sentences of at least twenty years. So, despite Hanoi's promises, this real danger was like a sword of Damocles hanging over their heads, ready to strike at any moment.

Despite this awareness, the UK, in negotiations with China over Hong Kong, agreed to pay each Vietnamese £1,000 to repatriate back to Vietnam. I heard the Vietnamese government profited from this agreement.

To this day, I stand by my decision to fight the repatriation of Boat People in Hong Kong, because they were refugees fleeing persecution. Today however the situation has changed. Those leaving Vietnam today are often business people, students or economic migrants.

In 2015 we celebrated the fortieth anniversary of the fall of Saigon, and we have also celebrated thirty-five years of Vietnamese in Hackney. It astounds me to see how the mentality of the Vietnamese who have lived outside Vietnam for thirty years, and the mentality of those who lived under the Communist regime for thirty years, is totally different. The way of life is very different as well. This isn't just something I noticed in Great Britain. Everywhere – Poland, Australia, the US – no matter where they resettled after the Fall of Saigon, these Vietnamese refugees have more in common with each other than with the Vietnamese migrating West in the past few years.

I think the Vietnamese who lived under Communism changed because life was very difficult and people had to struggle to survive. Confucian philosophy has long recognised that it is the leader who influences the followers. If a leader is immoral then the people will be immoral. The Communist regime has continually lied to the people every day – lies about the health of the economy, lies about targets, lies about national heroes, even lies about Hồ Chí Minh himself. So I guess it should not be surprising that most people who grew up under communism have changed.

Life must have been difficult for everyone in communist Vietnam. The character of the entire nation has changed after Vietnam was united, and this seems to be especially true of people from North Vietnam. The North remained very poor over the years, even after *Đổi Mới*, when the government rebuilt the country through large industrial zones. Today, they are building everywhere, and Vietnam is no longer as poor as it once was. The gap between the poor and the rich is growing, however, which means that even after all the economic reforms many are still suffering.

This might be why there is a frightening rise in people smuggling and trafficking of children in Vietnam, and it is easy for gangs to get away with it because of all the corruption in the country. The smugglers and traffickers have powerful links with Vietnamese authorities, just as in China. The smugglers use the fact that many are desperate in Vietnam. They spread the news that it is easy to make a lot of money in the West and promise at least £300 or £400 per week in catering work. Then they assure desperate people that it is easy to get a job and to feel secure for life. People who once had no hope are now excited and optimistic about their future. They borrow money and sell everything they own to pay around £10- £15,000 to come to a country like the UK.

What many new immigrants are finding, however, is that the promises made by the smugglers are not true. Those who make it through immigration find it is not easy to get a job, and few make enough money to get rich. However, many don't make it through the immigration checks and are detained and sent back. I feel sorry for these people who have been lied to – they will be destitute when they return.

Sadly, one of the ways the younger Vietnamese in London are making money is through drugs. There are some gangs who are now growing really strong cannabis in their houses. The gangs are often the same gangs who are trafficking people into the country. The gang members are making millions.

The violence between the Vietnamese gangs worries me. For example, a few years ago the media uncovered a case of a Vietnamese man who was beaten to death. He was dumped at the hospital by two other Vietnamese men but it was too late, he died of his injuries. With the help of the hospital's CCTV the two men who dumped him were caught. When they were questioned by the police, it transpired that they had beaten the man to get him to pay them money. They claim they never meant to kill him. The two thugs were deported and sent back to Vietnam which has now agreed to take convicted criminals in the UK and keep them in prison in Vietnam.

What the media didn't really find out was that the man who was beaten was told to watch over the cannabis plants. He would have been paid half of a promised salary for this job, with the rest of the payment when the crop is sold. It is now common for rival gangs to go in and steal the plants and to ask the one watching them for all their money – these gangs usually know how much the watcher has been paid. Sadly, these men would have sent most of the money back to Vietnam and so they are then forced to call their family to ask for the money to be returned. Many of these men are so desperate to earn more money after it is stolen that they would often stay on and keep working for the new gang in order to try and earn the money back. A modern form of slavery.

The same thing happened to a man who worked for me in the canteen. He used to work for a gang that sold drugs. A Vietnamese gang beat him up and demanded £20,000 from him. If he didn't find the money, they'd beat him up more. He tried to break out of the drug scene and earn honest money but when he worked for me he was always distracted and nervous. He left the restaurant and is now back with a gang trying to earn all his money back.

Most of these gang members are not just dealing in drugs, they are trafficking vulnerable people. I find this very disturbing. They are bringing great shame to the Vietnamese community who are honest and have worked hard to start a home and contribute to this country.

CHAPTER FIFTEEN

Optimistic

As mentioned earlier, I still want to try to buy our building on Englefield Road. I want to continue to host An Việt Foundation's offices here, continue with the employment and training work, the English classes, the programme for the elderly in the community, and a restaurant. There is still so much potential for the space – perhaps a crèche facility run like our restaurant where we could train Vietnamese in childcare and they would work here to gain experience and then in time they could move on to their own centre if they wished. I have a good feeling it may happen.

In Hackney, the system has improved a lot over the years, and not just related to property. In 2012 the Labour Party could boast that they had made enough changes to earn the London Borough of Hackney a place in the Audit Commission's top ten most improved councils in the country. It is impressive, considering how much of a mess we inherited, that we went from being ranked as one of the worst boroughs in the country to a borough with a ranking of 'poor'. I laugh when I think that I never expected to be so proud to have a 'poor' ranking.

I think the success is due to a combination of factors: the committed councillors who work well together; improved frontline staff, and the Mayor, Jules Pipe. Improving the financial situation became his top priority and, under his leadership, Hackney Council now has a balanced budget without a reduction of services. I think people can already see a difference: crime is down, Social Services are no longer the worst in the country, more students are doing well in their GCSEs, even recycling is up. I mentioned this to a friend, but he is cynical and said: "the only improvements have been achieved by the government pumping millions into Hackney." When I replied that was a good thing, what the council needed, he countered: "Perhaps, but will the improvements be sustained when the government funding stops?" I'm optimistic, but only time will tell.

For the 2015 election, my goal was to encourage the young generation of Vietnamese to stand for election. I want more Vietnamese to join mainstream society. Compared to the Vietnamese community in France and America, here in the UK we are not very politically active. I translated the voter registration form into Vietnamese to make it easier for them to complete, and I sent out 500 letters over three years to encourage Vietnamese to register to vote. In 2002 a group of us set up an organisation called Chinese for Labour; our main goal was to rally support for the Labour Party, but first we focused on encouraging Chinese and Vietnamese to register to vote. We then encouraged people to become more involved in the community, invited them to get involved in politics in any way that suited them – volunteering, raising awareness or even standing for election. After all that work, six Vietnamese expressed an interest in joining the Labour Party and standing for election. Out of those six, two actually submitted the paperwork: one in Hackney and one in Tower Hamlets. The one from Tower Hamlets was successful.

Councillors have the power to enforce change. Councillors can intervene on an individual's behalf, and can ask council officers to do something for the people. When I was a councillor, I was one of the direct links between the people and the government. In the UK, people are allowed to publicly raise concerns and make demands of the government, but with the help of their representatives, their voice can be louder. I'm very proud that I have been able to contribute something to improve Hackney. And I hope to continue working to give back to Hackney.

Retirement

Jen, in the Analects, expresses the Confucian ideal of cultivating human relations, developing human faculties, sublimating one's personality, and upholding human rights.... Thus it is defined as "perfect virtue", which transcends the barriers of race, creed, and time.

The Sacred Books of Confucius, and other Confucian classics, edited and translated by Ch'u Chai and Winberg Chai, page 1

In 2006, I was awarded an MBE – Member of the Order of the British Empire – for my 'valuable service' to the community. Meeting the Queen was an honour of a lifetime, and an occasion I'll never forget.

I've always said I'd work until I die, and I still mean that, but the cancer has slowed me down a bit. After I stepped down as councillor for Hackney in May 2006, I focused my attention back on the day-to-day running of An Việt Foundation, but I found I was often too tired and felt weak, although I usually wouldn't let this keep me from the office. When I found I was too sick to work, I went to the doctor. First they assumed it was gout, then they assumed it was something wrong with my stomach, then my bowel. But no tests could find anything. No one could figure out what was wrong. Then I had a full body scan – I had to lay inside a small cylinder for what seemed like hours. I did not like that at all, but it was worth it because that is when they discovered a 7cm tumour on my kidney.

I had the tumour removed and am feeling better now, but I'm still tired and don't have the energy I used to. My family keep telling me to slow down, so now I allow myself to rest more, spend time working in my garden and spend time with my grandchildren.

I'm over 70 now and until 2015 continued mixing recipes in

the kitchen at 7:00am for the restaurant. The kitchen staff used to shake their heads saying "Mr Vũ, how are you still so strong? When I am your age, I won't be able to do this." They don't understand. I never stay in bed, not even for a day. If I'm in bed, that means I'll die soon.

I'm not done serving my community or country yet. I can't stop dreaming: it is in my nature. My main goal still remains to try to encourage Vietnamese around the world to keep traditional Vietnamese culture alive and at the same time to interact with their new society. I want the Vietnamese to engage more with mainstream society, which is important for all immigrant groups, but especially for the Vietnamese. We're called the silent group, because the Vietnamese never demand anything; they just get on with life.

That is one of the reasons why I want to set up a research centre at An Việt. The young generation, from the beginning, worked hard for their studies and after that, they worked hard to be successful with their careers. But when they interact with the host society, as they live and work with the wider community, they may come to realise they have lost some of their identity. Some have tried so hard to assimilate – even dying their hair to change their appearance – but they can't change who they are. People may ask them about their history or their background, and over time, they may realise they are not totally part of the white community. One day soon, some Vietnamese who grew up in the UK may wish to return to the community to find out more about their origin, their history. I hope the research centre will give the young generation of Vietnamese a place to study and learn more about their culture, about their ancestors, about the relationship between the Vietnamese and Chinese. The research centre is devoted to the study of *Vietology*, the study of traditional Vietnamese life that has overturned conventional theories about our ancestry and heritage. In fact, some scholars like Stephen Oppenheimer have been able to prove Vietnamese ancestors were the first to cultivate rice and establish a highly civilised way of life preceding the civilisation of the Han people of China. We have a lot to be proud of. I want to encourage the next generation and wider community to do a Masters or PhD on Vietnamese culture.

If I am able to purchase the building, I intend to expand the library and research centre, and I hope to convert some of the space in the back into small studios or one bedroom flats. I hope to rent out these flats to students who wish to do research at the centre for 1-2 months. The rent will be cheap so students can afford it. I have saved up enough money for the deposit so I can purchase the building and start the building work from income generated by the restaurant.

This research centre is very important to me. I want An Việt to exist after my generation is gone. In the future, Vietnamese in the community won't need specialist advice that is provided by An Việt Foundation anymore. I want a place where the next generation can meet, as they themselves grow old. I want a focus point, a gathering place, for the Vietnamese community of the future. I hope the research centre will maintain the link, and maintain a connection between the young and the old generations of Vietnamese in the UK.

It is my hope that the Vietnamese will always have a way to pass on the gifts of our ancestry and culture to future generations. This is the gift that I wanted to share with everyone in the Vietnamese community: *To acquire the means to stand on their own two feet, to be independent and thus able to thrive.*

To my mind, the greatest gift I can give my children is the wisdom of my culture and the freedom needed to get the best out of life.

My grandson and granddaughter are half English and half Vietnamese. They physically embody in their genes what I have struggled to achieve in my heart - a balance of East and West. I want my grandchildren to know as much about their Vietnamese culture and ancestry as they will learn about their British heritage.

That couldn't happen in Vietnam, but it can happen here in the UK.

Appendix

Toi Lay Tho

Toi lay Tho thua con di hoc
Buoi gap nhau dau Tho da biet toi yeu
Tho cua toi hoi dy dep nhu Kieu
Long lay nhu Tan Cung nu!
Nhung co Ly, co Hinh, co Su
Toi quen, toi qua yeu roi
Tho thuong buon, Tho cung nhu toi
Chi co ban la Mo va Mong
Tho lay toi vi toi khong the song
Khong Tho an ui ben minh.
Dam cuoi chung toi, mot dam cuoi tinh
Chi co Mong, Mo phu dau, phu re.

Tho gio da tay bong tay be
Tu lao day doa, xanh gay
Tho don nha ra khoi cung may
Tu buoi mong, mo hoa thanh ngu xuan!
Doi che Tho nhieu buon dau, hon gian
Khong chiu boi hong, trat phan
Ban minh cho Dang nuoi than
Can bo cung toi, Tho kho vo ngan
Chia se bao sau, bao han
Tho chiu am tham chung thuy tan khi nao?
-   Tan khi nao
Anh noi voi Tho loi doi tra!

Nguyễn Chí Thiện (1963)

I Married Poetry

I married Poetry since my student days
From our very first encounter, she knew I was in love
My verses at the time were beautiful like those from the Tale of Kieu
And magnificent like the imperial concubines from the Qin palace!
I was so in love that I soon forgot all my earlier paramours
Miss Phys, Miss Geo and Miss Hist
She would be rather sad, like me, Poetry
For she had as friends only Dream and Vision
And she agreed to marry me simply because I could not live
Without her by my side, to console me.
Our wedding was truly one made in heaven
Since our best man was Dream, and Vision our bridesmaid.
With all our offsprings Poetry now has her hands full
She has grown pale with all these years of imprisonment
And having moved out of the palace among the clouds
She has grown from dream and vision days into a kind of dumb stupor!
So they blame her for being too sad and angry
Refusing as she does to put on rouge and makeup
So that she can sell her body to the Party for a living
By sticking with me, she knows nothing but tragedy and suffering
Sharing o so many sad stories that boil us up
Darling, until when will you silently carry on your faith?
- Until such day
As you tell me your first lie!

Nguyễn Chí Thiện (1963)

For centuries, poetry has been considered one of the highest art forms in Vietnam. Poetry is also the primary means of expressing oneself regardless of class or education. In Vietnam, and in the diaspora, poetry is a way to communicate your romantic feelings for another, to honour your love of your family or community, or to express your love of nature. Poetry has also long been a way to voice political dissent, anger, cynicism or irony at societal norms or to highlight injustice.

For those of us reading Vietnamese poetry that has been translated into English, much of the meaning and beauty is lost on us. Vietnamese is a tonal language, which means that the same combination of letters pronounced with different inflections, tones or rhythm mean very different things.

John Balaban, a well-respected specialist in Vietnamese poetry gives an example in his article "Translating Vietnamese Poetry":

> *Là*, with a falling tone, is the verb "to be." *Lá*, with a high, rising tone, means "leaf." *La*, with a low, constricted tone, means "strange."

Thus, Vietnamese poetry becomes a musical expression invoking humorous word plays, clever innuendos or poignant insights due to the poet's ability to puzzle together surprising combinations of words, melodies and imagery just with a change of tone or accent.

Because of the importance of poetry in Vietnamese culture, Mr Vũ has included some relevant poems throughout this book. As you read through the memoir, we hope that you will begin to feel how intertwined the poetry is with the lived experiences of the author.

In addition to traditional and modern poetry, we have also included some ancient wisdom and old Vietnamese proverbs, often quotes from wise men and women who have influenced Mr

Vũ's view of the world.

He also enjoyed including a few *vè*, a simple short verse by an anonymous author. These are prolific throughout Vietnam, too numerous to recount. They are passed by word of mouth, with variations and twists added at each telling. They often highlight the complaints of the common man in Vietnam. But the fun in retelling the *vè* is in the clever word play. Sadly, these multiple levels of meaning are lost in translation. Most of the verse will sound only sad and angry to English speakers while the Vietnamese reading them will laugh at the clever and humorous use of the Vietnamese language.

To learn more, we highly recommend you read:

John Balaban. "Translating Vietnamese Poetry". *Manoa* 11:2. University of Hawaii Press, 1999.

Sources of poetry in this book:

1. **Nguyễn Ngọc Phách.** *Life in Vietnam: Through a Looking Glass Darkly* Publisher: Tổ Hợp Xuất Bản Miền Đông Hoa Kỳ; 1st edition (2005)

2. **Nguyễn Chí Thiện.** *The Flowers of Hell (Hoa Địa Ngục)*: a bilingual edition of poems selected and translated from the Vietnamese. 1996 Publisher: Tổ Hợp Xuất Bản Miền Đông Hoa Kỳ. Translator/editor: Nguyễn Ngọc Bình

3. **Nguyễn Ngọc Bích**, editor. *War and Exile: a Vietnamese Anthology.* Springfield, VA: Vietnamese PEN Abroad, East Coast USA, 1989.

Poems from the above sources were printed with the permisson of the publishing company and the translator/editor Professor Nguyễn Ngọc Bích. (Prof Bích is also a dear friend of Vũ Thành)

4. **Self-published Vietnamese poets.** Many individuals have penned some poems and placed them on their websites for everyone to enjoy. The weblinks have been included with the text of each poem.

Poet my friend

Poet, my friend,
You must know how to keep your soul always unsullied
Like that proverbial pink lotus that spreads fragrance even
in the midst of slime
Like a lone star shining in the pristine night sky
Twinkling far, far away, and glistening with dew…
You must also know, friend,

How to live in this world as if you were deathless
Despite all its misery and cold, dangers and tragedies
And though your body may be ravaged by illnesses and
shrinking by the day
Your spirit must still be stronger than rock or steel
Standing firm in the midst of destructive time.
Only then can you let your poetic mind roam free
Flying high and wide even in an iron trap.
As for dying or getting out of here
That's heaven's decision, not one that is up to you!

    Nguyễn Chí Thiện. 1988

References

Air Force Association – magazine online (www.afa.org); April 2000 Vol. 83, No. 4

Vietnam Revisited - BBC online 16 November 2000

Bruce Grant. *The Boat People: An 'Age' Investigation*. Penguin books, England. 1979

John Balaban. "Translating Vietnamese Poetry". *Manoa* 11:2. University of Hawaii Press, 1999.

Photos from North Vietnam

I did not have any photos from my life in Vietnam when we fled. The photos on this page were sent to me by family and friends

Above: Vũ extended family at a wedding circa 1980 - my father in the top left corner and my younger sister Chi is standing behind the bride (her daughter)

Upper right: The path to my family home (alongside the side of the church

Above: The Catholic church in my village which house the tombs of four martyrs killed by King Tự Đức

Left: My father Triệu (estimated age 90 – he lived to be over 100 years old)

Above: My father at one of the Vũ family burial plots (North Vietnam)

Below: My older brother, Hán and his family circa 1950 – I'm the boy on the left, about aged 9, Hán and his wife Thùy, with their children Ngân (toddler) and Hạnh (baby). Taken in South Vietnam

South Vietnam

Above: Grand Seminary
Back row from left – me, Nghiêm, Châu,
Front row, Hán, Lý and Trị (Of this group, only Trị is still a priest)

Below: Family Photo Back row from left - Me, my older brother Hán, my brother-in-law Ngật, Hán's wife Thủy, my younger sister Yến,
Front row: Their children, my nieces and nephews

Resettlement centres in the UK

Above: Sopley Resettlement Centre

Right: With Linh (we think this was taken at Sopley Centre)

Above: Thorney Island Reception Centre – main building

Above: Guarding the entrance (and exit) to Thorney Island

Below and left: Excursion to London from Thorney Island

Above: Linh in front of staff housing in Thorney Island, aged 9

Family

Above: Reunified family in a London park – in clockwise order: me, Điệp, Tâm, Toàn, and Linh

Left: Photo of the family together at Christmas – photo taken in our old flat in the Manor Park area (the flat has since been demolished)

Above: An Việt Foundation (upstairs) with the restaurant in the front section of the ground floor and the elderly centre in the back (*photo right*)

Left: Protesters outside An Việt Foundation

Celebrations at An Việt

Above: Hackney Mayor Jules Pipe; Vietnamese New Year's celebration – 1992

Above: Dragon puppet for the celebration

Above and left: Linh and I make speeches at the New Year's celebration - 1992

Above: Dinner with with Tony Blair when I was a local councillor, 2002

Above: Awarded MBE - 2006

Today

Above: Family photo 2015

Back row from left– Me, Điệp, Tâm, Linh with her daughter Mai, Toàn; Front row – Tam's son Alex

Right: with my beloved grandchildren, Alex and Mai

ABOUT CHRISTINA PURYEAR

Tina Puryear is a writer, researcher and trainer who has worked with refugee communities since 1991. She began her career managing refugee integration projects within the Vietnamese community in North Carolina then managed several refugee youth programmes and community development projects in Atlanta, Georgia. Tina's passion for oral history, life stories and cultural diversity led her to get a Masters degree in Social Anthropology. She met Vũ Thành when she moved to London, UK and began as a volunteer for the An Việt Foundation before collaborating with him to write his life story. Tina now works with not-for-profit / charity organisations as a writer, facilitator, and trainer raising awareness about the rights of refugees, asylum seekers and migrant groups.

.

Printed in Great Britain
by Amazon